Banjo

PAUL TERRY

ALLEN&UNWIN
SYDNEY·MELBOURNE·AUCKLAND·LONDON

First published in 2014

Copyright © Paul Terry 2014

Permission to reproduce material from Banjo Paterson's *Illalong Children* courtesy of the copyright owner Retusa P/L.

Allen & Unwin
83 Alexander Street
Crows Nest NSW 2065
Australia
Phone: (61 2) 8425 0100
Email: info@allenandunwin.com
Web: www.allenandunwin.com

Cataloguing-in-Publication details are available
from the National Library of Australia
www.trove.nla.gov.au

ISBN 978 1 74331 797 6

Set in 12/17 pt Bembo by Bookhouse, Sydney
Printed and bound in Australia by Griffin Press

10 9 8 7 6 5 4 3

MIX
Paper from
responsible sources
FSC® C009448
www.fsc.org

The paper in this book is FSC® certified.
FSC® promotes environmentally responsible,
socially beneficial and economically viable
management of the world's forests.

Banjo

Banjo Paterson, 1935. Painting by John Longstaff (Australia, b. 1862, d. 1941), oil on canvas, 90.5 × 84.3 cm. Art Gallery of New South Wales. Gift of Mr J.H. Curle, 1935.

CONTENTS

PROLOGUE

The artist was in a state of almost constant motion. One moment he was studying his subject from the corner of the long studio, the next he was painting feverishly at the easel. After a burst of brushstrokes he dashed back to the corner for another view of the subject before resuming his attack on the canvas. Sometimes he made a false start and had to scurry back to where he began, apparently fixing a detail in his mind, before starting all over again. He kept up this pace for two hours without once sitting down, each dash at the easel adding a little more detail to the image appearing on the canvas.

The subject of the painting, a poet of note, was cool and slightly amused by the footrace unfolding before him. Conservatively dressed in a three-piece suit, with a handkerchief in his breast pocket and a watch chain across his stomach, he sat with his left leg crossed over his right. His right arm, curiously shortened, rested on the arm of a chair, an unlit pipe loosely held in the hand. His hair and moustache were greying, but he sat alert and upright, a lively intelligence in his dark eyes. He looked every inch the refined city gentleman that he was.

Except for a weathered countenance, there was little in the steadily appearing portrait to show that the subject was a legend of the bush, a man famous for celebrating the lives of the drover, the swagman, the bullocky and the brumby catcher. Appearances can be deceiving. The man in the painting had done more than any other to immortalise Australian icons that were already being consigned to history.

The artist was Sir John Longstaff, one of Australia's most celebrated painters, and the subject was the seventy-one-year-old Andrew Barton Paterson—'Barty' to a select few who knew him well, and 'Banjo' to millions who never met him but had thrilled to the people and places he had created. The year was 1935 and A.B. Paterson was nearing the end of an eventful life that had made him a household name from Darwin to Hobart.

Paterson had lived through some of the most defining events in Australian history. Born four years before the last of the convicts landed in Australia, he grew up in the dying days of bushranging and was starting to make his own way in the world when Ned Kelly's famous last words closed a chapter in history. As a young man, Paterson observed a country convulsed by labour strikes that helped to form the national political landscape, and when a disparate bunch of colonies squabbled over whether they should put aside their differences and unite under one flag, 'Banjo' Paterson saw the funny side of it.

When Australia went to war for the first time, Paterson was in the thick of it, and when Australians were called to arms for an even greater conflict, he was among the thousands who wore the khaki for his country. A consummate horseman and a champion of the bush, he was quick to join the revolution when the horse began to give way to the motor car. His contemporaries included the tortured Henry Lawson, the devilish 'Breaker' Morant and the far-sighted founder of *The Bulletin*, Jules Francois Archibald. Paterson was a member of the squatter class. He met great men—among them Winston Churchill and Rudyard Kipling—but the heroes he created were ordinary folk. The adventures of horsemen, drovers and swagmen leapt from his pen. They were as Australian as a gum tree and they were equally loved in the halls of power as they were in shearing sheds or by flickering camp fires.

By the time his portrait was painted in 1935, Paterson could look back on a life that saw him rise from a bush boyhood to national fame. He had matured with Australia, chronicling its growing pains and celebrating its triumphs and tragedies. The words he wrote became part of the national psyche. Today, his image is close to us all; a profile of a young Banjo is printed on our ten dollar note, accompanied by lines from one of his greatest poems.

Paterson's is the story of an Australia that no longer exists, yet it still resonates in a society that was built on the legend of the bushman. He left us with 'The Man From Snowy River', 'Clancy of the Overflow', and, of course, 'Waltzing Matilda'. His tale of the swagman who drowned in a billabong rather than face the squatter and the troopers is, for many Australians, an alternative national anthem. Thanks to Paterson, free-spirited drovers still ride the endless, sun-drenched plains in Australian imaginations and the deeds of legendary horsemen are still remembered around camp fires under starry skies.

Paterson thought his 'ruined rhymes' would not stand the test of time, but he was wrong. Partly because of him, Australia's almost-lost bush heritage lives on, and the words he wrote mean as much today as they did when swagmen waltzed their matildas on dusty roads through drought and fire and flood. Humble, humorous and reserved, Paterson was close to few but loved by many. Andrew Barton Paterson was the bard of the bush and his legacy helps to define us today.

1

BUCKINBAH

In the summer of 1863–64, a young woman called Rose Paterson crested the last hill on a taxing journey and looked down on the broad and busy valley of Narrambla Station, near the town of Orange in New South Wales. In the centre of the valley stood a three-storey tower of convict-made bricks flanked by a tall, circular chimney. A rhythmic thumping could be heard coming from inside the tower as a heavy steam engine ground rich local grain into flour. Further down the shallow slope, the sound of clashing metal rang out from a busy wheelwright's shop. Sheep grazed serenely on yellow hills that folded gently up from a tree-lined creek, and the distinctive odour of cheese rose from a small factory.

Overlooking it all was the homestead—a modest timber building of eight rooms shaded by a wide verandah. Bright English flowers bloomed in carefully tended gardens around the house and fruit hung ready to be picked from trees in a large orchard. It was a welcome sight to Rose, who had come here to have her first child.

Narrambla was the home of the Templer family—Rose's aunt and uncle. Rose had travelled there—probably with her husband Andrew—from their home 100 hilly kilometres away to the north-west. The road they had followed was rutted and narrow, rising steadily as it cut its way through an unfenced semi-wilderness of sheep, emus and kangaroos. A hard-driven horse and sulky could make the journey in one day, but it would be a long and sweaty day that took its toll on both horse and passengers. Rose and Andrew had probably broken their journey by stopping on the way at the home of close friends at a station near the town of Molong. Now, as the sulky jostled its way down the final hill, the parents-to-be looked forward to a warm welcome at Narrambla.

They had married in April 1863 at Rose's childhood home of Boree Nyrang Station near Molong. Rose was just nineteen and still under-age when she wed thirty-year-old Andrew, but her father had given his blessing to their union. Andrew was a gentle man, invariably good-natured and slow to anger. He knew the value of hard work—indeed his dedication to his work was one of his few faults as it meant he was often away from home.

The marriage of Rose and Andrew had completed a neat family link; Andrew's brother John had married Rose's sister Emily in 1861 and the brothers had gone into partnership running three properties—Buckinbah in the district of Obley, Illalong near Yass, and Stainbourne Downs in Queensland. John and Emily lived at Illalong while Rose and Andrew began their married life at Buckinbah. Their home in a small stone cottage at the edge of a creek was isolated and a long way from medical help. For this reason, they had chosen to come to Narrambla to begin Rose's confinement.

Rose Paterson was a young woman of excellent breeding. Refined and educated, she would raise her child to be a gentleman or a lady and to be successful. And while Rose and her husband were not wealthy, the child would be given every chance to make its mark on the world. But as the journey to Narrambla came to a welcome end, Rose could not begin to dream that the baby she carried would earn lasting fame by capturing the essence of a nation that was still going through growing pains of its own.

*

The only surviving home from Narrambla's glory days is a ramshackle house of weatherboard and tin that once stood near the main homestead. A fancy building for its time, it was brought to Narrambla as a kit home from America in the late 1840s or early 1850s. At an unknown date, the house was moved to the top of a hill in the centre of the Narrambla run, where it commanded sweeping views over the hills to the east, while the back door opened on to an impressive sight of the deceptively high Mt Canobolas to the south-west. There is no way to be sure, but some believe the little timber cottage that once stood near the Templer family's historic mill was the place where Rose Paterson delivered her first child on 17 February 1864.

Eight days after the birth, somebody—perhaps the proud father—rode the 3 kilometres into Orange where the new arrival was registered as 'Baby Paterson'. On 11 March, the Anglican minister H.H. Mayne baptised the baby at Narrambla homestead. The parents christened him Andrew Barton Paterson. He was always known within the family as 'Barty', but for generations to come, the rest of Australia would know him as 'Banjo'.

After three months of recuperation, Rose took little Barty back to Buckinbah, where he would spend the next six years. As an adult, his memories of Buckinbah were limited but years later, when he was an old man, he wrote down his childhood memories after persistent questioning from his four-year-old granddaughter. The result was

Illalong Children, a wonderful, evocative account of a bush boyhood written for his grandchildren, Rosamund Campbell and Philippa Harvie, and published in 1983 by the two women in *Singer of the Bush*—one of two large volumes celebrating the 'complete Paterson'.

Illalong Children was a rose-coloured reminiscence that overlooked the hard times for people on the land, the tribulations of having a father often absent from the home, and the grinding reality of genteel poverty for a family with good breeding but little money. Yet it also delightfully brings to life the people and animals that shaped young Barty's life. It begins with 'First Impressions', a brief account of a little boy's early memories at Buckinbah. It tells of emus wandering without fear up to the house, mobs of wild horses galloping through the gum trees and long days when 'a motionless sun brooded over a motionless forest till one could almost hear the leaves whispering to each other'.

Home was a solid stone cottage of five rooms overlooking a creek of clear water that curved its way around a broad flat. A second stone building incorporated a storeroom and a tool house with a loft on the top floor. Nearby were a kitchen and servants' quarters as well as stables and a storehouse, also with a loft. Vegetable gardens dotted the creek banks and fruit grew in a small orchard near the main house.

Andrew Paterson ran sheep and cattle on the mostly unfenced property, but the demands of the family's other property, Stainbourne Downs in Queensland, meant he was often away. Because of Andrew's absences, young Barty spent much of his time with the men who worked at Buckinbah. He did not attend school in those early days but he gained an invaluable education from the shepherds and station hands. One, 'Jerry the Rhymer', gave the boy an early introduction to verse, and, although Jerry's rhymes were of no literary merit, they sounded wonderful to Barty's young ears. In

Illalong Children, he recalled a rhyme about two dogs that Jerry created for his son Jimmy:

> Baldie and Nigger gets bigger and bigger,
> with eating their muttons like so many gluttons,
> and if we don't stop 'em,
> your Pa'll have to whop 'em.

Tall and bearded, Jerry was something of a local celebrity who had been sent from the 'old country' for a minor offence he had supposedly not committed, but he had 'done very much worse things which had never been found out'. Jerry was a man of extraordinary skills. As well as being able to rhyme, he could plait stockwhips, was a dab hand at smoking bees from their nests and knew how to brew honey beer that 'would make a native bear dance a jig'. He was a man for a small boy to admire.

There were few children in the area and Barty grew up playing with his sisters, Rose Florence (Flo), who was born in 1866, and Emily Jessie (Jessie), who arrived two years later. It was a kind household where corporal punishment of the children was rare. Laid-back Andrew was particularly lax in this regard. As Rose later wrote, her husband 'was so good tempered that it would be a hard matter to offend or quarrel with him'.

Barty and his younger sisters played along the reed-lined creek that enclosed the house's home paddock. Sometimes the creek was almost dry, but when heavy rain fell, a wave of brown water roared between the banks. At these times, the children would recall the story of a family friend who had been cast away in the wreck of a small schooner on the Great Barrier Reef. A party that included the children's uncle had sailed on the brig *Maria* to rescue the castaways. If the children saw a log carrying a snake surge past in the rushing water of the creek, they would name the log *Maria*, and if the snake clung to the log without it rolling over, the real *Maria* would safely return with the rescued sailors.

Like many stations, Buckinbah had a roadside store that sold to travellers everything from mohair coats to mouse traps. A passing parade of swagmen stopped at the store, but other children were rarely seen. The only other young person at the station was Jerry the Rhymer's son, Jimmy—a boy aged about twelve. Jimmy was a person of substance in Barty's eyes because he could ride a horse, boil a billy and track sheep across the plains.

To his delight, Barty was put to work with Jimmy as a trainee shepherd, but their careers suffered a setback—a terminal one for Barty and a painful one for Jimmy—when they carelessly allowed two mobs of sheep to become mixed. At the time, Jimmy was climbing a tree and his father – who was supposed to be supervising the boys - was absent, possibly asleep. As a result, the mobs became so mixed that 'separating them would have been like unscrambling scrambled eggs'. It cost a day's work to redraft the sheep and Barty was sacked as a shepherd. Jimmy got a beating from his father, and a passing swagman with a dog was put in charge of the sheep. For their part, according to Paterson's memories in *Illalong Children*, the sheep took it all in their stride:

> Not a word was heard as we marched the two mobs back to the homestead . . . The sheep put up with it with their usual lack of interest in life. I suppose they thought the sorrow was divided about fifty-fifty between them and their owners, and when a sheep comes out anywhere near square with anybody, he thinks he is doing rather well. They don't expect much.

*

These were the sun-drenched memories of a child, written for children. They were carefree, school-less days for Barty and his sisters, but in the world of adults, the reality was far harder. Despite Andrew's hard work, the family continued to struggle financially. The price of wool began to fall late in the 1860s and a long dry spell had left little feed for the station's sheep and cattle. The Paterson brothers had overstretched in their investments and the downturn meant that Andrew was increasingly away tending to the property in Queensland, leaving Rose at home alone to raise the children and maintain the house.

When Barty was a baby, Rose had to deal with a terrible situation. One of the workers at the station was trying to extinguish a fire in a chimney when he fell on to a paling fence and was horribly impaled. The *Bathurst Free Press* reported the man was taken to the hospital at Wellington where 'human skill and kindness were unavailing' and he died a few days later. He had been working at Buckinbah for only a few weeks and left a wife and children in Scotland.

All sorts of characters drifted in and out of station life. Some were not savoury. In one case, a shepherd named Howard was implicated in a highway robbery in which a traveller was robbed of gold on a nearby road. A trooper arrived at the homestead one night, seeking a warrant from Andrew Paterson, who was a police magistrate, to arrest the shepherd. But Andrew had just left for Queensland and Rose was unsure what to do. Old Jerry's advice was sought. Jerry said that Howard 'had more names than the King of England' and he was sure to clear out. Sure enough, Howard had already vanished and the robbery presumably remained unsolved.

Throngs of swagmen regularly made their way along the road looking for work or a feed. Most were well-behaved but some might commit theft, or worse. Rose, who had been taught music, classical languages and painting as a girl, now had to learn to use a gun. Her son never forgot the evening Rose handled an old muzzle-loader in the house after a particularly 'villainous-looking' stranger arrived:

> Putting the hammer down, she let it slip and the gun went off with a frightful bang, bringing down a shower of whitewash from the calico ceiling and scaring the life out of a family of possums who lived up among the beams and were just preparing to go out for the night. I suppose the stranger must have heard the shot down in the travellers' hut, for he was very civil when he came along in the morning to draw his meat, tea and sugar: 'And if you could spare a bit of bread, lady, I'd be glad of it. I ain't much hand at makin' damper.'

When Barty was about three, he had an accident that affected him for the rest of his life. He had a fall—possibly as a result of being dropped by his Aboriginal nurse, Fanny—and broke his right arm. The accident was never reported to his parents and they did not realise the bone had been broken. But as the days passed, the boy's distress grew, so Rose took him to a doctor in the town of Wellington, about 45 kilometres away to the north-east.

The doctor thought Barty was suffering from 'inflammation of the brain' caused by teething, and three times a day for three weeks, the little boy's head was blistered and his gums lanced. Of course, this did nothing for the broken arm and it was only two years later, after Barty fell from a horse and hurt the arm again, that Rose learned it had been broken in infancy. Paterson's arm was shortened for life, and while it must have caused him discomfort, it did not prevent him from becoming an accomplished athlete and a master horseman.

Moments of drama aside, life at Buckinbah was often lonely for Rose. It did not help that Andrew had to travel to Sydney in May

1866 to give evidence in the trial of a man who forged a cheque for £10 in the names of Andrew and his brother John. Far more serious was the worsening drought. As the 1860s drew to a close, farmers across a vast swathe of the western country looked in vain to the skies for a sign of rain. Day after day they were disappointed. Creeks stopped flowing, the earth cracked open and pastures wilted. Over-extended and battling to meet repayments, the brothers were soon in trouble.

Paterson later recalled that, in desperation, Andrew drove a flock of sheep from the Queensland property to Buckinbah. But disaster struck when the ever-cruel weather changed again. This time the land of drought delivered flooding rains and Andrew and his sheep were trapped on a sand hill that became an island surrounded by rushing brown water. The sheep had to be sheared on the hill and the wool was lost. It was the final straw. Their properties would have to be sold.

In May 1869, Buckinbah, Illalong and Stainbourne Downs were offered for sale with a combined total of almost 23,000 sheep in what stock and station agents in Sydney said was a buyer's market. The drought and falling wool prices were stifling interest in sheep stations—unless sold at a bargain price—and investors were looking at the safer option of cattle properties.

The Patersons' properties were passed in at auction, but the auctioneers later received interest from private buyers. Illalong remained in family hands—but Buckinbah and Stainbourne Downs were sold at a loss in 1870. Andrew and Rose packed up their children, horses and whatever goods remained, and headed south-east to Illalong. For the parents it was a humiliating blow, but for their son it was the beginning of a wonderful new adventure that left him with cherished memories. It was also a farewell to the western country, a place that left a small but indelible imprint on his memory:

> Across the landscape moved mobs of kangaroos and flocks of emus, quaint uncanny creatures moving silently through that grey light like the creatures of a dream. If ever a great Australian play is written, the scene will be cast, not in the hills which never change, but in the flat country which can stage anything from the desolation of a drought to a sea of waving grasses, with a march of strange animals and a dance of queer, self-conscious birds.

These were the memories that remained. Not the hard scrabble of a bush family struggling to stay afloat, but a place where opal and pearl colours glowed in the false dawn way beyond the Divide, a place populated by strange animals where a boy could see forever under a silver sky.

2
A BUSH BOYHOOD

Andrew and Rose Paterson arrived at Illalong with Barty and his two younger sisters in the winter of 1870. It had undoubtedly been a gloomy journey from failed Buckinbah. The loss of their properties had been humiliating and Rose, in particular, worried about their finances and the children's futures. No one would go hungry at Illalong, but the children needed, among other things, good educations. Six-year-old Barty had already shown himself to be a bright, active boy—if a little accident-prone—and it was important that he learned all he could to become a gentleman. At four and two, there was more time to think about the future of the girls, but they too would have expensive needs. As well as a standard education, they would have to acquire an appreciation of music, art and books. A daughter of Rose Paterson might be poor but she would still learn to be a lady. All of this would have to be paid for.

But Illalong now had to support two families. John's family would remain in the main homestead—a rather grand description for what was a rickety and weather-beaten bush construction of slab and bark—and Andrew, Rose and their three children would move into an even smaller and more dilapidated house nearby. Their old home at Buckinbah must have seemed a palace compared to the new one.

On the plus side, Rose was enjoying a hiatus from pregnancy and childbirth. Two-year-old Jessie had been the last baby and it would be a further three years before Rose fell again for what she called the 'common cause'. There was much to do and it was a good time *not* to be pregnant. It helped that the Paterson name was respected in the district. John Paterson was a country gentleman. He had been a member of the New South Wales Parliament and, like his brother, he supplemented his income as a magistrate, hearing minor cases in a small courtroom at the nearby town of Binalong.

The town itself was another positive. It had only been thirty years or so since the area was such a wilderness that the government had declared it off limits to European expansion. A plough line had been dug at Mt Bowning, half way to Yass. This furrow in the earth delineated the end of civilisation and the beginning of savagery. No white men were to cross this line until the government was ready to let them. This, naturally, did not impress the squatters and settlers who wanted the land past the plough line. Ignoring the government's decree they crossed the line and began to 'civilise' the wilderness. Others followed and soon Binalong was an established Cobb & Co stopover on the long road between Sydney and Melbourne. Less than an hour's ride from Illalong Station, by 1870 the town boasted a post office, a police station, at least two hotels and, most importantly, a school. It was there—in that single room with its sole teacher—that Rose's children and their cousins would get the beginnings of the education they needed.

Such was the situation facing the young Paterson family as they ended their old life in the rolling lands to the west and started again in the hill country to the south. For Rose and Andrew it was an unsettling time, where the only certainties were hard work, worry and limited reward. For six-year-old Barty, though, it was the beginning of an adventure that would create a lifelong love for the wondrous bush, its remarkable people and its strange, beautiful animals.

*

Whatever hopes the families had for Illalong were shattered a little over a year later. On the morning of 15 August 1871, John Paterson left the station for a day's business in town. He returned home that evening in good health but a few hours after retiring to bed he was convulsed by agonising cramps across the chest. A station hand was sent on an urgent dash to fetch the doctor at Yass, 30 hilly kilometres away to the south-east. But it was already too late. Moments after the messenger galloped over the nearest hill, John died in his bedroom. When the doctor arrived the next day, all he could do was to diagnose an 'effusion of blood on the chest' as the cause of death.

The news quickly spread around the district and the following day's *Goulburn Herald and Chronicle* remembered John Paterson as a 'most esteemed neighbour and . . . a painstaking magistrate'. In a brief obituary, the paper told the story of a man who had been active and respected in his community. He had been elected unopposed to parliament in 1858 but found the practice of politics distasteful and was glad to have resigned. He had recently delivered an interesting lecture on 'Scottish Eccentricities' at the Yass Mechanic's Institute and he had penned many 'communications of great merit' that were published in that very paper. The report finished by drily recording that 'the deceased' was survived by a wife and young family.

The loss of a husband, father and brother was a shattering emotional blow—and it was also a financial catastrophe. Without his brother's help, and bending at the knees under a mountain of debt, Andrew could not meet the repayments on their mortgage. Inevitably, the bank foreclosed and Illalong had to be sold. There can hardly have been a bleaker time for both families. Already bereaved, they now faced losing their homes and their livelihoods.

But it was then that they received a stroke of luck. The new owner of Illalong was a neighbour, a man named Henry Brown, who owned five runs nearby. He took over Illalong's debt, adding it to his estate, and hired Andrew as the manager of all six properties. It meant that Andrew had gone from property owner to hired hand, but the good news was that the family could stay at Illalong and Andrew would earn the useful sum of £200 a year. Although they would not be wealthy, Andrew and Rose at least had a stable home for the children.

Rose's sister Emily, however, now faced life as a widow and there was nothing to keep her at Illalong. Taking her youngest children, she left for Sydney, where she moved into her mother's house at Gladesville. Emily's oldest child, ten-year-old Jack, stayed behind on the farm. The permanent inclusion of Jack in the household was a delight to Barty. Just two years older, Jack would become Barty's constant companion for the rest of their childhood.

Rose's family now moved into the main homestead. It had suffered through years of extreme weather and a lack of funds meant it had been rather neglected. Draughts whistled through gaps in the slabs in winter and in summer the same gaps admitted squadrons of buzzing, stinging insects. But Barty either did not notice these shortcomings, or as an old man he chose to overlook them when he remembered the house in *Illalong Children* as 'an old-fashioned cottage, built of slabs covered with plaster, whitewashed till it shone in the sun'. The roof was made of bark (later replaced with tin) that regularly needed to be replaced with new strips peeled from the trunks of eucalypts. A verandah provided some shade at the front, and, inside, sheets of calico made a ceiling that acted as a thorough-fare for possums seeking a shortcut from the house to the garden.

For Barty and Jack, the house was just a place to eat and sleep, and *Illalong Children* makes little more mention of the homestead. Instead, these childhood memoirs run free outdoors, taking a wide-eyed delight in the wonders of the bush. There was a caste of furry and feathered characters. Magpies lined up on a fence to be handfed, curlews wailed in sorrow and little blue-cap wrens hopped cheerfully up to the kitchen door for scraps. Fleeing kangaroo rats provided endless and usually fruitless fun for pursuing boys and dogs, and the creek behind the house was a natural wonderland where a wild black duck took her troop of fuzzy ducklings for their first swim and a platypus drifted downstream as 'silently as a brown streak of waterweed'.

Some of the characters were semi-permanent. Others came and went in a flash. The parakeets screeched their greetings as they dashed past in blazes of colour, an owl shrieked like a banshee at night and soldier birds, 'fierce-eyed little grey ruffians', inflicted a reign of terror over crows, snakes and hawks. The permanent residents included 'Oily Gammon', the water rat—'quite a dandy with his black satin coat'. Oily Gammon defied all efforts to catch him; a snare made of a bent sapling trapped him once but he escaped by biting through the rope and he lived to create oily descendants that live in the creek today.

Then there was 'Uncle', a tame cockatoo who had learned to call the farm dogs. The dogs 'regarded him as a superior intellect' and never dared to trouble him. Uncle took delight in removing the pegs from the clothes line with his beak so that the clothes fell to the ground, but to his disgust the wild cockatoos would have nothing to do with him. Any flight into the paddocks would end in Uncle's screeching retreat to the house.

A stern-looking eaglehawk who lived atop a hill was nicknamed 'The MacPherson' because his hooked beak and fierce eyes reminded the children of a Scottish chieftain in a book. When a younger eaglehawk—MacPherson Junior—was found injured in the bush, he was brought to the house to convalesce. 'Mr Wattles', the Muscovy duck, made the mistake of waddling too close to the tethered eaglehawk. Suddenly, a talon shot out. Mr Wattles was instantly quite dead and Macpherson Junior had a tasty lunch of fresh duck. Luckily, Mr Wattles was not popular in the farmyard and his demise caused little distress to anyone.

The swallows were a nuisance. Year after year, resisting stiff opposition, they built their nests under the verandah roof and left their calling cards in the form of droppings that coated the verandah floor like oily white paint. Continually smashing the nests seemed cruel and so a compromise was reached. Planks were hung beneath the nests to catch the droppings and everyone was happy, especially the swallows.

There were plenty of human visitors to the house, too. The road past the homestead carried a stream of swagmen, bullock drivers and horsemen travelling to and from the nearby towns or mountains. The girls, Flo and Jessie, sometimes worked at the station store, a slab-and-bark building that smelt of leather. They sold provisions to these passing travellers, although many only wanted tobacco. Meat, flour and sugar were sold to those who could afford it and given to those who could not. The signals of the road—perhaps a blaze on a tree or a cairn of stones on a fence post—told the swagmen they would get a friendly welcome at Illalong. A free feed was repaid with a little labour around the farm. But for Barty, the best payment came in the form of yarns told by the rugged bushmen. With wide-open eyes he devoured the stories told by bullockies, swagmen and stockmen and each tale added its own little layer to the store of knowledge he would one day parlay into some of Australia's greatest bush poems.

Barty's parents tried to discourage him from contact with the bullockies—they were thought to be 'up to stratagems and spoils, especially in the way of stealing horses'—but he sought them out nonetheless. The young Paterson was pleased to discover that the tough bullock drivers did not deserve their bad reputation. They often travelled with their families, sometimes with dogs and chickens walking alongside their drays, and, as Paterson later recalled in *The Sydney Morning Herald*, the men treated their bullocks with kindness:

> One of them [a bullocky] gave me a demonstration with a bullock whip, cutting great furrows in the bark of a white gum tree. When I said it was no wonder that the bullocks pulled, he remarked feelingly 'Sonny, if I done that to them bullocks I'd want shooting, every bullock knows his name, and when I speak to him he's in the yoke. I'd look well knockin' 'em about with a hundred miles to go and them not gettin' a full feed once a week.'

At about this time, Paterson got his first introduction to what became a lifelong passion—the 'sport of kings'. One New Year's Day, a station rouseabout took the boy to the picnic races at Bogolong (now the hamlet of Bookham), about halfway between Yass and Jugiong on the Sydney–Melbourne road. It was an instructive experience for young Barty. Bogolong was notable for its two pubs, 'half a mile apart and nothing in between'. The rouseabout, a man of the world at eighteen, explained to his eight-year-old companion that there was 'one pub to catch the coves coming from Yass and the other is to catch the coves from Jugiong'.

The racetrack was similarly unrefined. It had no grandstand and the track itself ran through box and stringybark scrub. But it was the characters he met there that really impressed the boy. As he recalled later in *The Sydney Morning Herald,* the racehorses were ridden by 'wild men from the Murrumbidgee Mountains'—men who did much to develop Barty's fascination with the rugged horsemen of the high country. Among the racegoers were 'a sprinkling of more civilised sportsmen from Yass and Jugiong, blackfellows . . . and a few out-and-outers who had ridden down from Lobbs Hole, a place so steep that . . . the horses wore all their hair off their tails sliding down the mountains'.

An event that took place that day probably inspired Paterson to write one of his better-known poems 'Old Pardon, the Son of Reprieve'. He had learned to ride and had travelled to the races on a pony with a lightweight child's saddle. One of the mountain men took the saddle from Barty's horse and placed it on his own. The mountain man, 'about seven feet high', said he wanted the saddle for his racehorse, Pardon. The boy was promised a ginger beer when Pardon won his heat. The horse won not one but two heats and Barty got his reward:

> I had the ginger beer—bitter luke-warm stuff with hops in it—but what did I care? My new friend assured me that Pardon could not have won without my saddle. It had made all the difference. Years afterwards, I worked the incident into a sort of a ballad called 'Old Pardon, the Son of Reprieve'—the story of a champion racehorse who won his owners pockets full of money.

In the poem, Pardon was taken to Menindee to race in the President's Cup where 'villains' nobbled him with green barley:

> He munched it all night, and we found him
> Next morning as full as a hog—
> The girths wouldn't nearly meet round him;
> He looked like an overfed frog.
> We saw we were done like a dinner—
> The odds were a thousand to one
> Against Pardon turning up winner,
> 'Twas cruel to ask him to run.

But Pardon recovered to win, ensuring his name would go down in racing folklore. Confusingly, Paterson also claimed later that the ballad was inspired by a completely different event. In this account, he said the poem had its foundations in a family tale about a horse, also called Pardon, who stuffed his belly with barley and still managed to win a race. Regardless of the poem's source, it typified Paterson's lifelong love of horses and racing. They were themes that underpinned some of his greatest works, and, whether or not Pardon ran at the Bogolong races on that New Year's Day, the experiences that Paterson had there helped to shape his future writing.

The boy was comfortable on horseback from an early age. When he was about seven, he and his cousin Jack were sent to school at Binalong, and the only way to get there was to walk or ride. Each morning, the boys would catch their horses in a paddock near the house and trot off to learn what they could from the schoolmaster.

Paterson later recalled that Binalong's claim to fame was the fact that the bushranger Johnny Gilbert was buried in the town's police paddock after having been shot dead by police in 1865. Gilbert had committed many armed robberies—first with the infamous bushranger Frank Gardiner and later with Ben Hall. Gilbert was no

Robin Hood. In 1864, he shot dead a policeman during a robbery on a mail coach near Jugiong. Less than a year later, Gilbert's violent career came to an end after he and John Dunn robbed a woolshed at nearby Murrumburrah. The police cornered the bushrangers at the home of Dunn's grandfather at Binalong. Gilbert died in the ensuing shootout. John Dunn escaped from the police that day, only to be caught and hanged a year later.

Bushrangers had already captured the young Paterson's imagination. In *Illalong Children*, he remembered hoping that the gold escort from the diggings at Lambing Flat (now Young) would be held up on the road past the station 'so that I might see something worthwhile'. Sadly for young Barty, no bandit ever dared to take on the heavily guarded gold escort and the closest he came to meeting a bushranger was sharing a schoolroom with some of Dunn's nieces and nephews.

As an adult, Paterson never held much regard for bushrangers. When he was sixteen, the most infamous bushranger of all—Ned Kelly—fought his Last Stand at Glenrowan and was subsequently hanged. At the time it was the biggest news story of a generation, but years later, when he looked back at his life, Paterson never publicly referred to Kelly—even after the armour-clad bushranger evolved from true-crime figure into something more mythical. Paterson was not one to glorify criminals, but, in 1894, he made an exception for the violent John Gilbert. Like many bushrangers, Gilbert lived by the gun and died the same way. Paterson painted his death in flattering colours in a ballad that told of the bushranger's demise, 'How Gilbert Died':

> But Gilbert walked from the open door
> In a confident style and rash
> He heard at his side the rifles roar,
> And he heard the bullets crash.

But he laughed as lifted his pistol-hand,
And he fired at the rifle flash.

Gilbert and Dunn were the last of the bushrangers to trouble the Binalong district, but the area was not new to violent crime. A particularly bloody mass murder at nearby Conroy's Gap might have given Paterson the title for a jaunty little poem by the same name. The poem told of Ryan, a celebrated sheep thief who made the mistake of drinking too much one night at 'Shadow of Death Hotel'. This dark place was a den of the 'roughest crowd that ever drew breath' and it was there that a trooper found Ryan drunk and with his guard down. But Ryan had the love of Kitty Carew, a girl who worked at the pub. She helped the thief escape on the back of a legendary horse called The Swagman. The horse was the only hero of the story; Ryan, 'the slinking hound', escaped to Queensland and sold The Swagman, never returning to the love-struck girl at Conroy's Gap.

The real story of Conroy's Gap was much darker. In March 1868, *The Yass Courier* reported on the 'most atrocious and bloodthirsty murders it has ever been our lot to record' when an ex-convict, William Mundy, savagely killed five people with an axe. Mundy was on a ticket of leave after serving fifteen years for a murder he had committed at Maitland. In 1868, he was working as shepherd for a farmer named John Conroy at Conroy's Gap, about halfway between Yass and Jugiong. Mundy shared a four-roomed hut with Conroy and several shearers. It was there that Mundy ran amok with his axe on the night of Tuesday 17 March.

Mundy rose from his bed and, without warning, swung the axe and killed a man who was sleeping in the room. The horrifying noise of the axe splattering through flesh and bone awoke a man in an adjoining room. He ran into the bedroom, where Mundy stabbed him in the stomach with sheep shears before battering him several times with the axe. Then Conroy—who had been asleep in a skillion room at the rear of the hut—rushed into the bedroom in his shirt and nightcap, and he, too, was stabbed and hacked to death. The next victim was Conroy's wife. She was awoken by the screams and ran into Mundy's blood-soaked bedroom, where she was also stabbed and then struck in the face with the axe. The final victim was another shepherd named White. He, too, was hacked to death. Mundy topped off the carnage by trying to burn all five bodies.

The only reason that Mundy gave for his horrific crime was that he was badly treated and poorly paid by his employer. The *Courier* noted that the killer did not 'appear to be at all concerned at the horrible tragedy in which he had been the principal actor' when he appeared in court. In due course, the 'inhuman monster' was sentenced to death. As the sentence was handed down, Mundy showed the same indifference to his own fate as he did to that of his victims, and a few days later he was hanged in Sydney.

This bloody event was the worst single crime to have ever been committed in the district, and to young Barty Paterson and his schoolmates the very name Conroy's Gap surely carried a black reputation. But the poem by the same name was a humorous, rollicking piece with no connection to Mundy's dastardly murders. If Paterson drew inspiration for the grim Shadow of Death Hotel at Conroy's Gap then he never said so. But the murders at Conroy's Gap are a reminder that life in the quiet country community was not always as idyllic as Paterson remembered it.

*

For Rose and Andrew Paterson, life on the land was challenging. As always, Andrew worked very hard and was often away. Rose filled in many lonely evenings by writing letters. A favourite correspondent was her younger sister, Nora, who lived in Queensland. Over the years, they exchanged dozens of letters filled with family news and gossip. Some of the letters that Rose sent to Nora have survived. Spanning fifteen years between 1873 and 1888, the letters provide a remarkable insight into the life and times of the Paterson family at Illalong.

On 9 April 1873, Rose wrote to Nora, who was pregnant with her first child. The pregnancy had made Nora ill and Rose commiserated with her sister as she suffered through the 'common cause'. Although Rose hated being pregnant, her children brought her great joy. Her latest, Mary Edith (Edie) had been born a year earlier and was now 'a nice fat little brown-headed brown-eyed cherub'. Rose also had news of Barty and his cousin Jack, who were both growing to be clever boys. Rose told Nora how the boys went out at daybreak each morning to catch and saddle their ponies to ride to school, returning home each evening at about six o'clock. She was impressed with the education they were getting:

The present schoolmaster seems to be a very painstaking man [which] I think is better for a schoolmaster than being brilliant & I think he is giving the boys a better foundation in English and arithmetic than they would be likely to get in a more fashionable school.

On 14 December, Rose wrote again to her sister. The previous year, Nora had married an aristocratic widower named Thomas Lodge Murray-Prior, who had twelve grown-up children of his own. Aware of Rose's constant battle with the family finances, the pregnant Nora had sought help from her new husband, who was a well-to-do property owner and, at that time, the Postmaster-General with the Queensland government. Murray-Prior offered to find Andrew Paterson a job at a post office on a salary of £50 a year—only a quarter of the wage he earned as the manager of Illalong and its adjoining properties. Rose politely declined.

Rose was troubled by her relationship with Mrs Brown, the wife of the station owner. She felt spied upon by the Browns and noted they not only listened at keyholes to hear what people said about them, but they also questioned 'servants and people of the lowest character to find out what we, & others, say and do'. Rose hastened to add that any hard feeling was between her and Mrs Brown. Andrew and Mr Brown got along very well. In the same letter, however, Rose also noted that she was concerned for Andrew's health. He was regularly laid low with an unspecified illness, and that summer he was afflicted by what Rose described as influenza.

Rose's next letter introduced Andrew's accident-prone cousin 'Blenty' Paterson. Short-sighted Blenty was fond of a drink and had a habit of getting into trouble. One hot night in February 1875, he was riding across a decaying wooden bridge on the road to Yass when his horse fell through rotted timber, throwing Blenty to the ground. The newspapers reported the incident, leading many readers to believe it was Rose's husband Andrew who had been involved in the accident. But those who knew Blenty would not have been surprised that he was the hapless horseman. This was his third serious accident within just a few months.

The relentless repetition of Blenty's misfortunes did little to induce him to take more care on his nocturnal outings. As Rose ruefully wrote to Nora, the first accident had happened when Blenty fell from his horse at a canter. It left Blenty unconscious at the side of the road with two broken ribs. No sooner had he recovered than he took a buggy trip with Ned Dunn (the brother of the bushranger John Dunn) that went very wrong. A harness broke and the horses ran out of control. As Rose recounted the story to Nora, Blenty leaped for safety but poor Dunn rather foolishly tried to stop the runaway buggy by sticking a leg through the spokes of a wheel:

> Of course the bone was shattered & he [Dunn] was thrown on the roadside while the horses made off with the £40 buggy, banging against trees & leaving wheels here, spokes there & harness everywhere . . . Blenty (always a philosopher) walked to a shepherd's hut & *got his dinner* [Rose's italics] & then made arrangements for sending Dunn home to his friends and getting a Dr for him.

Rose thought Blenty something of a clown and wrote about his misadventures in a tone of amused resignation. She was far harder on herself in relation to her son's misfortunes. The arm that had been broken in the fall at Buckinbah continued to cause problems and Rose feared that Barty would have to go to Sydney to get the bone broken and re-set. In a letter to Nora, Rose said she and the Wellington doctor who first examined Barty were 'a pair of thoroughbred donkeys' for not realising the arm had been broken at the time. She worried that the damaged arm would leave Barty with a deformity but noted that he was a clever boy who 'ought to have a profession which will need more head than hands'.

Barty's misadventures were generally less spectacular than Blenty's, but infinitely more worrying for his mother. In the most sensational incident, the boy suffered the rare indignity of being speared by an Aborigine. There was only one family of Aborigines in the district—a 'source of sorrow' for the Paterson children—but this family of three fascinated the youngsters. The head of the family was Billy Budgeree, who wore a brass plate around his neck declaring him to be 'King of the Lachlan'. Billy's wife was Sally. Barty's sisters thought Sally should also have a brass plate identifying her as queen, but Sally was far too practical to be bothered with such nonsense. Their only child was Nora, a six-year-old who could 'swim like a duck'.

The family lived in the traditional way. Their home was three saplings covered with bark, and a 'blackfellow's fire which never got any bigger or smaller' constantly burned at the door. Sally and Nora carried the family's food and other possessions in bags made of twisted grass and Billy wielded a spear and woomera. In a concession to modern times, he also had a tomahawk that he used to shape boomerangs from pieces of timber. As well, Billy owned a piece of limestone, which could conjure rain in return for a reward of alcohol or tobacco. Paterson noted in his memoirs that the laws governing the supply of alcohol to Aboriginal people were not stringently enforced at that time. On at least one occasion, Andrew Paterson declined to reward Billy with alcohol for his own good, and instead gave him tobacco, flour and sugar.

Billy would sometimes give a demonstration of spear-throwing in return for gifts, but one day he refused. His wife Sally took it as an excuse to prove her own abilities with the spear and woomera. She launched the spear with unerring accuracy at a tree, where the spear stuck 'quivering, in the bark'. It was a one-off performance that Sally refused to repeat. As Paterson later remembered in *Illalong Children*, the child Nora then stepped in to fill the breach, with rather less impressive results:

> We could hardly believe that she could handle a spear at all; and, wishing to see better, I ran across the line of flight just as she let the spear go on its journey. Her throw was in no way comparable to that of her mother, for the spear began to drop when it had travelled ten yards; and it was just too bad that it landed fair on the calf of my leg. Aided no doubt by the momentum of its fall, it stuck about a quarter of an inch

into the flesh. With the spear still trailing from my leg, I ran crying to my mother and the show broke up in confusion.

This drama caused little comment in the district, but Paterson later heard it was briefly discussed by two station hands on a nearby property. One of the station workers was not surprised by the spearing. He felt that somebody was remiss by allowing a female to throw a spear when children were about. After all, it could have done some real damage. It might have hit a horse.

*

In 1873, when Barty was nine, a great change came to the district when the Sydney-to-Melbourne rail line was built right through the middle of Binalong. Although this huge leap forward would soon bring Illalong closer to the rest of the world, the noisy, clanging construction project alarmed Rose. It was a huge job that involved the work of dozens of navvies—rough, brawling men whose awesome drinking bouts were sometimes so intense that they ended in 'the horrors'. With Andrew away so much, Rose worried that some of these uncouth strangers would invade the house at night. For her son, however, the navvies were a source of amusement.

Barty trained his pony to jump over prostrate navvies as they lay drunk and unconscious on the ground, but gave no thought to what might happen if the comatose man happened to wake with the horse in mid-air above him. It was one celebrated navvy, 'Big Kerrigan', however, who left the greatest impression on the boy. One Monday afternoon, the local policeman called at the schoolhouse seeking the help of the teacher, George Moore, to arrest Big Kerrigan who was down by the creek wielding an axe and in an advanced state of delirium tremens. He thought somebody was after him and was at risk of running amok.

Against his better judgement, the teacher reluctantly set off with the policeman to help arrest the angry giant. With much more enthusiasm, Moore's students followed 'like a small pack of hounds after their master' to witness the excitement. As Paterson recalled, it could have ended in bloodshed, but the brave trooper and his teacher sidekick talked Big Kerrigan into surrendering his axe. A nip of brandy at the police station was enough to render the drunken Irishman insensible and the drama was over. This incident had two lasting impacts on the nine-year-old Barty. Big Kerrigan's terrible state of alcohol-induced madness established in Paterson a detestation of anyone who would sell liquor to a drunken man, and it cemented his view that his teacher, Mr Moore, was a hero:

> Thus did my teacher justify his claim to be considered my first great man. True, he had first shrunk back when adventure called, but look how he behaved afterwards! It was my fate, in later years, to meet many great men—Lord Roberts, Lord French, Lord Kitchener, Rudyard Kipling and Winston Churchill. Would any of them have done any better?

*

As the years went by, the family outgrew the old homestead and two skillion rooms were added to the back. Soon even more space was needed and a house was brought in on a bullock dray from another property and tacked on to the homestead. The boys, however, stayed outdoors as much as possible and the creek behind the house remained a playground. Catching crawfish, or yabbies, was a favoured pastime. Using the same method that country children use today, the Paterson children tied a piece of raw meat to a length of twine and cast it into the water. When the twine began to draw away, the children knew a yabby had taken the bait. The line was then gently retrieved and the 'whiskers and goggling eyes of old Mr Crawfish appeared on the surface'. A net or tin dipper could be used to scoop him on to dry ground but the children thought this would spoil the fun and preferred to do it with their hands.

Barty and Jack were fascinated by the bird and animal life that surrounded their home. Jack was particularly puzzled by the actions of a crow, which was seen tapping at the door of a parakeets' nest. Barty had no explanation for this behaviour as crows 'have more brains than most other birds, and they do not waste their time tapping on dead timber'. The puzzle was solved with the arrival of Mr Masson, the Government Surveyor. Masson 'who had been a small boy himself and was still a small boy at heart' had an encyclopaedic knowledge of birds and animals. He revealed that the crow was knocking at the parakeets' door in the hope of enticing the young birds to answer, whereupon they would become a snack. Masson then amazed the boys by luring two crows to an abandoned picnic and promptly shooting them both:

> So died two detestable villains, who had taken just one chance too many; and the parakeets were free to fly headlong through the trees and gather food for their young in the almost certain hope of finding them alive on their return.

The story of the crows concluded *Illalong Children*. The bush boyhood of young Barty was about to come to an end. He was now ten and his parents decided that he had learned all he could from the bush school at Binalong. With his cousin in tow, the young Paterson would be sent to Sydney to be educated at the city's Grammar School. He would live at 'Rockend' cottage in Gladesville, the home of his grandmother, Emily Barton. In the refined atmosphere of Rockend, Barty would complete his transformation into a young gentleman.

3
GROWING UP

Emily Barton, *née* Darvall, was well educated with an appreciation of the classics. In a childhood that saw her raised in the United Kingdom and on the Continent, she became fluent in Latin and French, and developed a lifelong love of art, music and poetry. At the end of her long and productive life, she was remembered as cultivated, kind and gentle. These were qualities that helped to make her the much-loved matriarch of a broadly scattered but loving family.

The Darvalls were a family with excellent connections. Wealthy and cultivated, the men were prominent in business and the military, and the women were accomplished in the arts, music and languages. Their dynasty, however, was not without a whiff of scandal: Emily's father, Major Edward Darvall, had sensationally eloped with sixteen-year-old Emily Johnson in 1805. Pursued by the runaway bride's outraged brothers, the young lovers had later married at London's fashionable St Martin in the Field and everyone was happy. Emily—their first daughter—was born twelve years later.

Major Darvall had served in India and in 1822 he had moved his young family to Brussels. In their sixteen years on the Continent, they divided their time between their fine home in the Belgian capital and a chateau near Boulogne, France. The Darvalls had everything an upper-class European family could want, but with his wife's health failing, the major decided to move to a warmer climate. In 1839, the family packed their many bags for a passage to the colony of New South Wales on the other side of the world.

Major and Mrs Darvall sailed with their four youngest children on the *Alfred* in mid-1839, and arrived in Sydney in January the following year. During the long journey, their eldest daughter Emily Mary—a writer and poet—helped to produce a shipboard newspaper. Her contributions to the paper caught the eye of Robert Barton, a fellow passenger and an officer with the East India Company. As befitting a family of their status, the Darvalls were regulars at the captain's table on the *Alfred*'s voyage to Sydney. A space was left at the table for Barton but he was suffering from lumbago and was absent from many evening meals.

Emily Mary made a note of Barton's illness and absence from the table in her diary on 15 October. A week later, she wrote that Barton had recovered enough to make an appearance on deck but 'not having spoken to me I cannot give anything like a good description of him'. A few days after that, they had a chance to converse when a cry of 'Man overboard!' rang out across the ship. Fearing a child had fallen into the sea, the passengers rushed to the poop deck to see the rescue attempt.

Emily was relieved when 'Mr Barton kindly stopped me to say that it was a sailor' who had fallen into the water. The sailor, who was very drunk, was rescued and spent the rest of that day in irons as his penance. It was a day of mixed fortunes for the drunken sailor but a good one for Emily and Robert. They began a friendship that blossomed into romance as the voyage continued. It was a relationship that led the refined and cultured Emily into a life that she surely had not imagined—as the mistress of a sprawling station in sunburnt western New South Wales.

Barton had gone to sea as a midshipman, or a trainee officer, with the East India Company at the age of fifteen. He made three voyages to China and India and worked his way up through the ranks to become a captain. He returned to London from his final voyage for the company in October 1830. Now aged twenty-one, he was eligible to receive £2500 his father had left him in his will. He spent the next few years in Berlin and, in 1839, sailed on the *Alfred* with the aim of making his fortune in the Australian wool industry. Bolstered by a parting gift of £3000 from his mother, Barton bought a half share in Boree Nyrang. Soon after inspecting his new purchase, he returned to Sydney, where he renewed his romance with Emily Darvall. They were married in July 1840 and soon left for Molong where they made their home in a bark hut on the edge of their 66,000 acre (26,709 hectare) property.

What a shock this must have been to the young bride! Although the bark hut would soon be replaced by a proper homestead with a beautiful garden, the wild country and primitive conditions at Boree Nyrang were a far cry from the genteel drawing rooms and parlours she had known in Europe. But refinement was no barrier to toughness, and Emily—assisted by servants—equalled the role played by other, less cultivated pioneering women. Boree Nyrang would be her home for the next twenty-five years.

The first of Emily's nine children, Emily Susannah, was born in June 1841. A little boy, Robert, was born in 1843 and Rose Isabella—the future mother of Barty—arrived in December 1844. There were more babies at regular intervals over the next few years. The children had a governess and were given an education at home.

The governess was not able to teach Latin to the children, so at these times their mother took the lessons herself. As the children got older, they were encouraged to recite French and Latin verbs at the kitchen table.

The homestead was an oasis of refinement. Visitors could be sure of a warm welcome and fine hospitality. John Hood, a gentleman from England, who toured the area in 1841 and 1842, wrote warmly of the 'delicious sauterne and excellent porter' he enjoyed with Robert Barton at the homestead. Hood also wrote of his pleasure at meeting local Aboriginal people and his enjoyment at witnessing a corroboree.

The local Aborigines were peaceful, but drama came to Boree Nyrang in December 1849 when a group of young men from a neighbouring tribe in the Yass district invaded. The Boree Aborigines—mostly older men—fled to the homestead but were cornered in the garden. The men from Yass were younger and more aggressive than the defenders from the Lachlan, and some of the older Lachlan men were killed. A number of young Aboriginal women were carried off. Sensationally, the *Bathurst Free Press* reported:

> Shocking to relate, the savages skinned the body of one of their victims, an old man, and took a portion with them . . . The Boree [Lachlan] blacks are a remarkably quiet tribe.

Emily's husband Robert was away so she took refuge in the house with the children and some servants. The raiders tried to break in but were driven away by station hands with guns. The next morning, a worker discovered what appeared to a bundle of animal skins rolled up under a bush near the stables. The skins turned out to be a possum cloak. Huddled inside were an Aboriginal woman and her baby. The brave woman had literally played possum all night so that she and the little one could avoid abduction.

The episode was one of the most alarming in the Bartons' time at Boree Nyrang, but his grandmother's bravery in a crisis served as a model for bush heroines in some of Paterson's future works. The station itself is thought to have inspired one of his best poems, 'On Kiley's Run'. Published in *The Bulletin* in December 1890, it is a melancholy reflection on the end of 'the good old station life'. In the verses, an old man remembers the bright days of his youth when he rode side by side with Kiley, the kindly station owner, on a run that lay nestled between a sleepy river and the mountain ranges in the hazy distance. The ballad tells an idyll of the bush life, a place of 'roving breezes' where the air was rich with perfume, swagmen were never turned away hungry and neighbours visited for days full of sport and laughter:

> We kept a racehorse now and then
> On Kiley's Run.
> And neighb'ring stations brought their men
> To meetings where the sport was free,
> And dainty ladies came to see
> Their champions ride; with laugh and song
> The old house rang the whole night long
> On Kiley's Run

But the run was scorched by drought and crippled by losses. Kiley toiled in hope by day and dreamed of overdrafts by night. His loyal workers stuck with him until the end but eventually the bank possessed his cattle and the stockmen who had served him for so many years were sent away. The run was taken over by a man who lived in England. The new owner cared nothing for the run, except for what it could earn. He gave the property a new name—an English name—and moved an overseer into the beloved old homestead. The stockmen were replaced by sour-faced boundary riders and the cattle with sheep. The gardens died, wages were cut and swagmen and drovers were turned away. Poor Kiley died of a broken heart.

The theme of loss on the land is a recurring one for Paterson. It reflects the experiences of his own family, partly those of his parents but more particularly, those of his grandparents. The Bartons had weathered drought, illness and falling wool prices, but the death of Robert Barton in October 1863—less than six months after Rose's marriage—was a shattering blow that brought a traumatic end to the 'good old station life' at Boree Nyrang, just as drought did to Kiley's Run.

Robert had travelled to Sydney, partly for business but also to see a doctor about a persistent cough. On 1 October, the doctor sent Robert to his bed at the Australian Club. He was found dead in his room three days later. His death devastated Emily. Unable to accept that her husband was gone, she plunged into a melancholy so deep that many months passed before she was able to resume normal life. In the meantime, Boree Nyrang would have to be sold.

According to newspaper notices advertising the probate of Robert's will, Emily might have lived for a time with Andrew and Rose at Buckinbah during her convalescence. In 1866, however, she was well enough to begin a new life in Sydney. As complicated sales proceedings for Boree Nyrang dragged on, she moved to lightly settled Gladesville on the Parramatta River, west of Sydney. The home that Emily Barton—'Mama'—made there provided a nucleus for her large family over the next forty-three years.

Originally known as Tarban Creek, the waterside areas of Gladesville had been developed on rocky land that edged the broad expanse of the river. In the 1830s, two significant developments paved the way for the riverside settlement to eventually become a well-to-do suburb of Sydney. In 1832, a punt was opened at the end of a rough road that descended a gentle hill to end at the river's edge. The punt created a crossing over some 200 metres of river between Bedlam Point and Abbotsford, providing easier access to the city. Soon after that, an elevated bluff on the new Punt Road was chosen as the site for an asylum to house Sydney's growing populations of 'lunatics'. The patients began arriving from November 1838. The ferry and asylum provided the catalyst for further development and the land around the river was soon subdivided into a residential estate, named Gladesville after John Glade, a local property owner.

In 1852, a builder named John Crotty bought Lot 47—one of the best blocks in the estate. Facing the asylum, the elevated block overlooked the punt landing and boasted spectacular views of Looking Glass Bay. Crotty built a fine cottage of stone on his prestigious block. The house boasted seven rooms with a kitchen and attic, while a verandah along the Punt Road frontage provided shelter from sun and rain. Built in a three-sided square, the cottage had its own well driven deep into the sandstone bedrock and at the river's edge was a fine bathing house. When Emily Barton bought the cottage, she gave it the name it carries today—'Rockend'. Barty Paterson's years there helped to define the rest of his life.

*

Barty had to briefly attend a preparatory school before he could begin his education at Sydney Grammar. These new surroundings were a far cry from the one-roomed schoolhouse at Binalong. He traded his moleskin pants and hobnailed boots for fine city clothes and, to his disgust, even 'had to learn dancing' in order to be polished into the young gentleman that his mother expected him to be. The transformation required little work, however, and soon Barty was ready to begin his education at 'Grammar'.

The journey to school each morning was markedly different to his experiences at Binalong. Rather than catching and saddling a horse on frosty mornings, the young Paterson and his cousin Jack caught a steam ferry to the King Street Wharf in the city, where they alighted for the short walk through the crowded city centre to the school in College Street.

As an adult, Paterson was as modest about his educational achievements as he was about his writing, but in fact he was a good student who did well in the five years he spent learning alongside other young men of good breeding. One year, he shared the Junior Knox Prize—essentially a competition to be dux of the junior school—with a fellow student, George Rich, who grew up to become Justice Rich of the High Court. Years later, in *The Sydney Morning Herald,* Paterson said: 'If I had paid as much attention to my lessons as to fish and rabbits, I, too, might have been a Judge of the High Court. There is a lot of luck in these things!'

The young gentlemen at Sydney Grammar were not required to wear uniforms but were expected to wear a jacket and tie. Sober dress, however, did not necessarily preclude rough behaviour. The schoolboy Paterson—who later said his first published work was 'an account of a glove fight'—witnessed a fight between two doctors' sons that started one lunchtime, continued that afternoon after school and resumed the next morning. It only ended when one of the boys' hands gave way in the third round. The 'account of a glove fight' has never been found but perhaps it had its genesis in that bloody schoolyard conflict between two well-bred boys. It also helped Paterson to form a view that boys should be given boxing gloves and encouraged to use them. In this way, schoolboy fisticuffs would be controlled and harm minimised. He perhaps had this thought in mind when he penned a poem, 'Old School Days', which was published in the school's magazine, *The Sydneian,* in 1903:

But on wet days the fray was genuine,
When small boys pushed each other in the mud
And fought in silence till thin streams of blood
Their dirty faces would incarnadine.

Rough and tumble behaviour was not unusual at Grammar. Paterson recalled the robust practice of 'wallerooing', in which groups of lads roamed the schoolgrounds, looking for an unsuspecting victim. With a cry of 'Walleroo him!' the pack would jump on the victim, force him to the ground and stuff grass into his mouth. The boy's hat would then be squashed flat and his boots thrown away. Whatever other knowledge the victim acquired at Grammar, he soon learned to show a clean pair of heels when a 'wallerooing' loomed.

But Paterson also had many positive memories of the school, and of its alumni. In more recollections penned for *The Sydneian*, he said Grammar offered a fair field for all, with no favours to anyone, regardless of class and creed. It was only after he left that he realised the benefits of attending the school. Wherever he went in Sydney as an adult, old classmates popped up working in government offices, tailors' shops and law offices. Sydney Grammar, he said, was a place where 'if a boy liked to work he "got on", and if he didn't, he got a certain amount of information forced into his head whether he liked it or no'.

In the same article, he fondly remembered schoolboy pranks. A favourite pastime was to catch a large fly and tie scarlet thread to its feet, 'creating a very fair apology for a wasp'. This delighted the boys, especially as the 'wasp' deeply frightened one of the teachers. A former student, whom Paterson declined to name, strewed vile-smelling wattle beans over the floor, and another successfully set a Grecian wastepaper basket on the top of a door as a booby trap.

But perhaps the best-remembered former classmate was a lad who became a hero by fleeing a caning to 'live a bandit life in boilers and empty cases on the wharves for several days'. That boy later became a solicitor.

Sydney was undergoing a growth spurt during Paterson's time at Grammar. In recent years, it had lagged behind Melbourne, where the gold rush had caused a population explosion twenty years earlier, but now the harbour city was catching up. Like a teenager outgrowing her clothing, Sydney was bursting free of her inner-city confines. Houses, factories and hotels spread as new suburbs sprang up and soon the suburban population outnumbered that of the old city. The former convict town was growing up.

The streets clattered with the sounds of horse-drawn omnibuses that would soon be replaced with noisy, hissing steam trams. On the water, whistles blew and ferries and steamers jostled for right of way and, at night, gas lamps lit the streets where larrikins and hustlers gathered on corners, eyeing off finer folk promenading until late in the evenings. The young Paterson sometimes caught the ferry into the city on Saturday nights, where these sights and sounds exploded around him. Although this experience must have enthralled the wide-eyed country boy, the hustle and bustle of the city had little influence on his later writings and it was always the bush that truly inspired him.

There were plenty of opportunities to reconnect with nature. Holidays were spent at Illalong, and at other times he camped with friends in the high country of the upper Murrumbidgee. But it was in Sydney that his lifelong affection for agricultural shows started. His uncle Frank Barton, who shared their home at Gladesville, took the boy to several Royal Agricultural Society shows at Prince Alfred Park where the best of the bush came to town. The show was a place where the smells and sounds of the farmyard competed with the calls of carnival barkers; where freaks and fighters caused jaws to drop in sideshow alley and well-dressed city toffs rubbed shoulders with country yokels.

In April 1875—the first year of Barty's schooling at Sydney Grammar—Rose Paterson, who was pregnant with her fifth child, came to stay at Rockend. In a letter she wrote to Nora one Sunday evening in April, Rose revealed that she was in Sydney to find a governess to begin the education of her oldest daughters Flo, now aged nine, and Jessie, seven. Rose had the perfect employee in mind—a 'perfect gem of a governess, cheap, cheerful, [and] clever at housekeeping'. The governess would need one other quality—she should be elderly enough 'not to set the Browns whispering in their usual fashion'.

Rose also imparted the news to Nora that the ne'er-do-well Blenty Paterson had finally married his sweetheart, Mary Wilson. Marriage had done little to mend Blenty's ways, but at least his new wife had met with Rose's approval because while Rose was in Sydney Mary was entrusted with the care of Rose's youngest children back at Illalong. Rose's letter also included a hopeful note. Her husband's wealthy uncle Hamilton Howison had died in Scotland and, as luck would have it, his fortune was left intact. Rather waspishly, Rose hoped that 'Providence [had] put a touch of natural feeling into old Hammy's heart at the last' and that he had remembered his Australian relatives in his will. If so, it would provide some much-needed relief to the stretched family budget back at Illalong.

The late Uncle Hamilton did indeed come through with the financial goods. In Rose's next letter to Nora, on 14 May, she revealed that the old man had left £3000 in trust to his relatives. The Illalong Patersons could expect to receive a little over £100 a year from the bequest—quite a substantial sum given that Andrew earned

£200 a year working for the Browns. When her baby was born four months later, Rose and Andrew named him Hamilton Howison in honour of Uncle Hammy. In the meantime, Rose felt the windfall might solve the problem she had with her husband's employers:

> . . . I hope a time may come when Andrew may see the advisability of either striking out for himself again or getting some more genial employment in [which] I shall feel happier than I do under the smothering influence of the low-bred, whispering, slandering suspicious snobs who have poisoned the whole atmosphere of our formerly friendly simple-minded neighbourhood . . .

Barty and Jack, of course, were barely interested in these adult troubles. Gladesville—in particular, the river—offered them an entirely new playground, vastly different to rural Illalong but equally fascinating in its scope and diversity. They had obtained a little timber boat which they rowed into the shallows to fish for flathead and bream. It mattered little that the boat, 'mostly held together by tar', took on an alarming amount of water—it simply meant that the catch of the day could be kept fresh as it swam in the salty ballast that sloshed around inside the wooden hull.

Rockend provided spectacular views of the river and the water teemed with sail boats carrying fruit and timber from the hinterland into Sydney Harbour. Sometimes the doldrums struck and the boats petered to a halt. Barty envied the happy-go-lucky sailors whose fortunes depended on the winds. As he remembered later in *The Sydney Morning Herald*, the failure of those winds did little to faze the stoic crews:

> If the wind died away and they were left in the doldrums— well, they didn't worry. They anchored and caught themselves

feeds of fish which they cooked on their little galley fires, the scent of frying red bream mixing not unhappily with the aroma of guavas, grapes, and the big hautboy strawberries which now seem to have gone out of fashion . . .

The Sydney Rowing Club lay just across the water at Abbotsford, and the boys had grandstand seats for watching professional rowers as they sculled the broad waters of the river. It was a time when rowing provided as much interest to the sporting public as cricket and football. The rowers were heroes to their young fans and the boys 'knew every man of them'. There was the legendary Ned Trickett, the quarryman who had defeated the English champion on London's famous Thames course no less; and 'the greatest of them all', Henry Searle, who had learned his art as a boy by rowing his siblings 5 kilometres across the Clarence River to school every morning and home again in the afternoons. When these men, and others like them, strolled through the quiet streets of Gladesville it was as if gods had descended among the townsfolk and, although the rowers could not walk on water, their prowess in their narrow boats was the next best thing.

Emulating his broad-shouldered and brawny-armed heroes, the teenaged Paterson spent hours sculling the broad waters outside his grandmother's windows. His damaged right arm did not impede his progress on the water, although it continued to cause problems. At around this time, Barty broke the arm again, in the same place as before. The cause is unknown but it might have happened during a school holiday at Illalong. The arm was placed in splints, which, according to Rose, 'ruined his holiday'. But as soon as the splints were removed, Barty returned to his usual active self and was less troubled by the arm than his mother was.

Back at school, he played cricket for his school team. There are

9

few records of his prowess at this sport, but it was not his forte. In one of his final games, he batted for the Second XI and was caught for a duck. His affection for the game was strong enough, however, to attract him to first-class matches in the city. He paid a shilling to spend many Saturday afternoons at the Sydney Cricket Ground where he could see his heroes in action. As it happened, he was there for one of the most infamous events in Australian sporting history.

In February 1879, New South Wales took on a visiting England XI at the cricket ground. As was normal practice for the time, both sides picked an umpire for the match. England, led by Lord Harris, had appointed a Victorian footballer and rising cricketer, David Coulthard. The New South Wales side chose Edmund Barton, a relative of Paterson's who would go on to become the first prime minister of Australia. Coulthard, the Victorian, was at the centre of the trouble that was about to erupt. The stands were full of bookmakers, and punters' money was flowing for the home side. *The Sydney Morning Herald* noted reprovingly that 'the printed placards notifying that betting was prohibited were ignored'.

On the second day of the match, Saturday 8 February, the fifteen-year-old Barty Paterson was among a crowd of about 10,000 people watching New South Wales trying to chase down England's first innings score of 267. It was a tense afternoon as the local side collapsed to be all out, ninety runs shy of England's total. For New South Wales, only the wicketkeeper and opening batsman, Billy Murdoch, provided any hope. Murdoch was unbeaten at the end of New South Wales' first innings and that afternoon he returned to the crease when England's captain Lord Harris ordered the colonials to bat again.

Murdoch had put on a handful of runs in his second innings when the Victorian umpire Coulthard gave him out on a controversial run-out call. The crowd was incensed that their man had been dismissed by an umpire appointed by the English. Cries of, 'Not out!' and 'Go back to the playing field, Murdoch!' rang out across the ground. Coulthard bore the brunt of the crowd's ire. The punters had heavily backed New South Wales to win and, what is more, Coulthard was a Victorian—an inter-colonial rival. Some in the crowd even believed he had placed a large bet on England to win.

Suddenly a wave of larrikins surged on to the ground. Coulthard was jostled and shoved in the ensuing melee and the English skipper, Lord Harris, was struck with a stick. England's opening batsman, Albert Hornby—a keen amateur boxer—rushed to his skipper's defence and triumphantly dragged the stick-wielder off to the pavilion. Hornby's shirt was torn from his back as he wrestled his way through the crowd. Two other English cricketers pulled stumps from the pitch to use as weapons and escorted their captain to safety. Chaos reigned as angry spectators milled around the ground and there were fears that thousands more still on the sidelines would join the invasion. It was only after play was abandoned for the day that order returned.

It was, said the *Herald*, a national humiliation:

> It is a good thing that we should be able to boast of our cricket but it is a good thing also that we should be in a position to boast of our manners. The latter consolation is presently denied us, and an apology is certainly due to our guests for our breach of hospitality.

Barty Paterson was among the mob that invaded the ground that day, but he later downplayed the seriousness of it. The well-brought-up Paterson was no larrikin. He might, in fact, have agreed with Lord Harris, who, in an open letter to the newspapers, later described the Australian larrikin as being like 'the most exuberant Californian hoodlum . . . [with] the local enthusiasm of the English yokel'. But more than fifty years later, Paterson remembered the scandal with typical humour:

> When we got to the wicket, we didn't know what to do. Everybody was hooting and shouting and arguing and the people from the members' stand were crowding in to help the English. Nobody really interfered with the English players— we just hooted them off the ground, and then it struck us that if we didn't go back to our seats we wouldn't see any more play. So back we all went and that was the end of the great Lord Harris riot which gave Australia a bad name for years.

After a long delay, England won the match by an innings and those punters who had so heavily backed New South Wales lost their money.

*

In March the following year, Barty came home to Illalong for a short holiday. He travelled by train—much faster than a coach and still a novelty—but his journey was anything but refreshing. The train was so crowded that he could only find standing room in the guard's van. The van was stored with salt fish, which did not smell very pleasant in the early autumn warmth. He alighted at Binalong station and walked the 4 miles to the homestead. It was the morning of Good Friday and he was dismayed to discover that there was only fish for breakfast.

He had recently turned sixteen and, while not yet a man, he was no longer strictly a boy. His mother noted in a letter to Nora that he had grown a lot over the past six months and 'is on the turn for improving his looks'. Dark-haired with an aquiline nose, he was growing into an attractive young man who, according to his mother, had 'brought his brain into better subjection than before'.

Although he was a mature and considered young fellow, he was not immune to the waywardness of teenagers and later that year he earned Rose's wrath for some unspecified act of rudeness. In a letter to Nora—who was holidaying at Rockend at the time—Rose asked her sister 'to tell Barty from me that I don't like little boys to be pert to their elders, more particularly to their mothers'. Rose enclosed two shillings and sixpence in stamps for Barty to buy a book about a good boy so that he could improve his mind. She did not specify which book Barty must read, but firmly stipulated it should not be one of Mark Twain's. Rose was clearly offended by her son's ungentlemanly behaviour and, in a rare criticism of her easy-going husband, Rose said that Andrew was too indulgent in 'allowing smartness & not rebuking rudeness and sauciness'.

Saucy or not, Barty was no longer 'a little boy' and in fact his school days were almost over. His parents encouraged him to pursue a career in law, and it was hoped that he could win a scholarship to Sydney University or could become articled to a solicitor. Rose was optimistic. As she wrote to Nora, her son had 'plenty of good sense & I think no desire for fast ways and fast companions. So I think we may fairly hope for a good fortune for him'. These bright thoughts were encouraging, but what Rose could not have known was that an unexpected death would soon threaten to turn her family's life upside down.

4

A HORSE CALLED BANJO

Barty was in more trouble with his mother in October 1880. Cousin Jack had contracted typhoid fever and Rockend was placed in quarantine. Barty had been sent to stay with a neighbour, Mrs Blaxland, who strictly forbade him from going within 50 yards (45 metres) of Rockend until the quarantine order was lifted. But the cousins soon 'got yarning' over the back fence, in clear defiance of the order. Rose worried about what Mrs Blaxland would think of the Patersons' code of honour and resolved to write to Barty to give him 'a good blowing up'.

The boy was at something of a loose end. He was meant to sit exams at school that month, but the typhoid outbreak had disrupted his lessons and he had little to do while he waited for Rockend to get the all-clear. His inactivity was a source of concern to his mother but, on a brighter note, an uncle had provided £50 to pay for Barty to return to school the next year, where he would either sit the matriculation exam or try for a scholarship to university.

In the meantime, as the desultory end to Barty's penultimate year at school petered out, it was almost time for him to return to his beloved Illalong for summer holidays. Rose was looking forward to his return because Andrew had been made returning officer for the electorate of Burrowa, which meant he was away from home even more than usual. Andrew's health also continued to be a concern. In a letter to her mother, Rose said her husband was recovering from his annual 'spring attack', an unspecified illness that was as debilitating as it was mysterious.

But Barty's holiday had barely started when an upheaval threatened the family's future. On New Year's Day, 1881, Henry Brown, the owner of the Bendenine estate, the conglomerate of properties that included Illalong, died suddenly from complications arising from bronchitis. Brown's death left Andrew without an employer and, more importantly, Brown's will threatened to leave the Paterson family without a home. The will, written twelve years earlier, stated that all of Brown's property should be sold and divided between his wife and other parties. It left Rose—who always held an inflated opinion of her husband's abilities—clinging to forlorn hopes that Andrew would get a permanent and well-paid job as a police magistrate. At night, her thoughts also turned to buying the increasingly dilapidated Illalong homestead and a few surrounding paddocks, and 'keeping a few sheep & horses & heaps of poultry and living by selling eggs and fat turkeys'.

Unfortunately, there was no job offer for Andrew and even less hope of buying any of Illalong. The family's future would depend on the sale of Brown's properties as one big lot. A Melbourne-based stock and station agent advertised the entire estate in newspapers around the country. The property totalled more than 66,000 acres (26,709 hectares) of 'excellent pastoral and agricultural land'. The advertisement noted that the main homestead at Bendenine was a comfortable building of ten rooms with a detached kitchen, a servants' room, a coach-house, a vineyard, orchards and flower gardens. Almost as an afterthought, the advertisement revealed a house on the Illalong portion of the property was also for sale. This, of course, was the cottage that the Paterson family called home. The entire estate would be offered at auction on 4 November.

In February, Andrew and Barty set off for Sydney. The purpose of the trip was two-fold. Andrew was to meet with the executors of Brown's will to discuss his future and, at the same time, seek to place Barty with a solicitor as an articled clerk. During their absence, Rose wrote to Nora expressing her fears that the cost of finding an appointment for the boy would be prohibitive:

> Should the Sydney solicitors all be so stony-hearted as to charge the full premium for admittance, £250, there is a more moderate man in Goulburn, a Mr Davidson, whose premium is only £50, with whom we may place him. He is a gentleman & a rising lawyer & promises to look after his clerks himself, which is something in his favour.

But another setback occurred in April when Barty came down with a severe case of typhoid fever that left him confined to bed for more than a month. It meant that he could not take his matriculation exam on 7 June as scheduled, and in order to qualify to become an articled clerk he would either have to sit the Senior Public Exam in November or wait until the next matriculation test in June the following year.

He had tried for university entry and later said that he 'missed it by about a mile and a half'. In fact, he performed quite well, scoring a high pass in English and Latin. It was a good effort but not quite good enough, and his prospects seemed to have dimmed. But then there was a stroke of luck when Rose's cousins Henry and Ned

Kater visited Illalong with a view to buying the estate. Successful businessmen, the brothers decided not to buy the property but they did pull some strings and got Barty articled to a lawyer at the Sydney firm of Spain & Salwey. In July, the boy had been at home recovering from his fever and preparing to return to school. Three weeks later, thanks to the intervention of the Katers, he began his career as a lawyer and his schooldays were over.

Although the practice of law never filled him with delight, it did teach him something of the world. One of his first jobs was to help in the defence of a ship's captain accused of failing to show a riding light on the stern of his vessel. The captain lost and was fined £5. It was a valuable lesson for Paterson, the young lawyer-in-training, who later recalled:

> [It was] an unnerving experience, but it taught me that a case at law is like a battle. If you listen to the accounts of the two sides you can never believe that they are talking about the same fight.

Meanwhile, at Illalong, Rose was now largely free of worries for her oldest son but she had plenty of other things to keep her awake at night. In March or April she had fallen pregnant with her seventh child and was finding this pregnancy just as troublesome as the previous six. She was suffering from rheumatism, no doubt made worse by the draughts and chills that sneaked through the gaps at the old homestead, while Andrew had added lumbago to his other ailments. Their situation was left in limbo when the Bendenine estate was withdrawn from sale on the day of the auction, but throughout that cold and blustery spring the optimistic Andrew was confident he would remain as manager after the sale eventually proceeded. The pregnant Rose, however, had her doubts.

Portrait of A.B. Paterson. *Photograph courtesy National Library of Australia.*

She found consolation for this uncertainty in the joy of her children. The baby, a little girl named Gwendoline, arrived safely after a breech birth on Christmas Eve. In a letter to Nora in January, Rose described Gwendoline as a *'queenly* child' who 'has not cried for half an hour since she has been born'. Tempering the joy of Gwendoline's arrival, however, was the fact that the nurse engaged to oversee the baby's care was 'a dejected whining woman, always talking of her own ailments'. Rose had travelled to Yass to have the baby and was staying at an inn where the Chinese cook refused to prepare any of the simple dishes that Rose requested, and so she made do with porridge. Andrew, meanwhile, was busy preparing a long report for the trustees of the Bendenine estate.

In the stiflingly hot summer of 1882, the estate was broken up and part of it sold to two brothers named Friend, with Henry Brown's widow retaining one third. Rose liked the brothers, who had supplied materials to renovate the decaying homestead, but she had a very low opinion of their wives and thought even less of the widow Brown. Naturally, Andrew got on well with all parties and was in negotiations to manage the property for the new owners, supposedly for the healthy salary of £500 a year.

Barty continued to live at Gladesville and enjoyed the company of his friends, including his cousin Jack who had left school to become a clerk with the New South Wales Railways. Although they were well-behaved young men, they might have indulged in high-spirited behaviour typical of lads their age. In one account of their youth, the daughter of Paterson's uncle Frank remembered the cousins sharing a shack at the edge of the river. They had bought a battered horse-drawn buggy that hurtled around the streets, much like today's young men 'hooning' in ageing but fast cars.

At around this time, the young Paterson gained his certificate to practise as a solicitor and he became the managing clerk with a large firm that acted for three banks. Later, he went into partnership with the Sydney lawyer, John Street. In the meantime, the troubles of the poor helped to instil in Paterson a certain cynicism for his chosen profession and, with the idealism of the young he began to think that 'it was up to me to set the world right'.

In his spare time, he studied history and economics, and, driven by a desire for reform, he produced his first literary effort—a political pamphlet called 'Australia for the Australians'. Although this work—which was published in 1889—later caused him much embarrassment ('I blush every time that I think of it!'), it was a heartfelt treatise that showed that Paterson in his twenties was fired with youthful idealism.

'Australia for the Australians' was nationalistic, protectionist and humanist. It contrasted the high life enjoyed by property owners in Sydney with the struggles of inland settlers who had little hope of reward for their toil. At the heart of the treatise was a call for land reform, and a demand for the abolition of granting large tracts of lands in 'fee simple'—an ancient rule that gave almost unlimited rights to property owners. Ominously, it warned that Australia could become like Ireland—a land of poor and dissatisfied tenant farmers.

Paterson's treatise also urged its readers to walk in the shoes of the poor. Leading by example, Paterson wrote that he had resolved to live for a time in a low-class Sydney lodging house to see how the poor lived. He was used to roughing it in the bush and was no shrinking violet when it came to hardship—but he lasted just one night in the lodging house:

> To the frightful discomfort was added the serious danger of disease from the filthy surroundings and unhealthy atmosphere. I fled. And yet what I, a strong man, dared not undertake for a week, women and children have to go through from year's end to year's end . . . Do you, reader, believe that it is an inevitable law that in a wealthy country like this we must have so much poverty?

The treatise revealed Paterson to be an angry young man, fired with a need to 'put things right'. But 'Australia for the Australians' caused almost no stir at all. As an older, far more conservative man, he noted that it 'fell as flat as the great inland desert', but even as he aged, he did not lose empathy with the poor, especially those of the bush. It was not the last time he dabbled in politics but, by his own admission, it was the failure of the treatise that pushed him further from politics and closer to poetry.

*

Paterson the lawyer worked hard to get the best for his clients in troubled times, but his thoughts were rarely far from the bush and he took every chance he could to escape the city for the clean air of the hills and plains. Sports also remained a passion. He rowed for Balmain and regularly played tennis but racing was his favourite pastime. He won several steeplechase races and rode as an amateur jockey at Randwick and Rosehill. In more refined outings, he joined red-coated gentlefolk in pursuit of foxes with the Sydney Hunt Club. Paterson loved the thrill of the sport and he was at ease in the company of Sydney's social elite.

For the first few years, his work as a lawyer was demanding, if a little tedious, but he found time to produce verses that were published anonymously in a radical new paper called *The Bulletin*. Paterson was vague about these early efforts; the first, he said, was the 'account of a glove fight' that has never been identified. It was followed by 'some sentimental verses' which, to his surprise, were also published. Paterson later said he decided not to use his real name with these early works because he feared the editor would associate him with 'Australia for the Australians'. This might have been true, but it is also possible that as a rising man about town and a respected young lawyer Paterson was reluctant to see his real name linked to the provocative and outspoken *Bulletin*.

One of his early poems, 'El Mahdi to the Australian Troops', was inspired by a military campaign on the other side of the world. In 1881, rebels had revolted against a British-backed Egyptian government in the Sudan. Led by Muhammad Ahmad—or El Mahdi—the rebels won a decisive victory and trapped the Egyptian army. The British sent the revered general Charles Gordon to extricate the trapped Egyptians while a force of troops and artillery was mustered in New South Wales to join the campaign. To the dismay of the Empire, Gordon was killed before the New South Wales contingent set sail and the Mahdi rebellion was ultimately successful. But the colony's readiness to rush Australians off to this useless mission irked Paterson, so he 'strung together four flamboyant verses' in opposition to the venture.

It was a cynical work that, seen through the eyes of the rebel leader El Mahdi, spoke of the Australian soldiers striking 'a blow for tyranny and wrong'. It would have been frowned upon by some in the establishment in Australia, which was surely why *The Bulletin* decided to publish it in 1885. Just five years old, *The Bulletin* was nationalistic, avowedly republican and sometimes just plain contrary. Although his flamboyant opposition to the Mahdi expedition was not his best work, it did strike a chord with the freethinkers at the radical new paper and, to Paterson's delight, the poem was published on 28 February.

In 1886, history was made when Paterson thought up a lasting pseudonym for his work. He had dabbled with several pen names, including the simple 'B', and 'Cincinnatus"—a nod to the colourful American poet Cincinnatus Miller—but when Paterson chose to call himself 'The Banjo', it stuck for life. It had nothing to do with music—Paterson had never even held a banjo, far less played one. Instead, it came from his passion for horses. When he pondered potential pen-names, an image of one horse sprung to mind. It was a 'so-called racehorse'—no more special than any other—that had been on the family property when Paterson was a boy. That horse's name was Banjo and it seemed to the aspiring writer that 'Banjo' was as good a name as any for a poet. It was a decision that gave the obscure horse its own little place in history and Andrew 'Banjo' Paterson an identity that would help to shape modern Australia.

In June, *The Bulletin* published 'The Bushfire, An Allegory'—the first poem to appear under the Banjo pseudonym. It caused little commentary although, like 'Australia for the Australians', it is noteworthy for its youthful idealism. It linked a deliberately lit fire on a tinder dry property in Australia to Ireland's demand for Home Rule from England. In the poem, Billy Gladstone (British Prime Minister William Gladstone) fights the fire with a blue-gum bough (Gladstone's Home Rule Bill) but a 'cornstalk kid' (a colonial) tells Billy that there is no use in fighting the fire unless he catches the people who lit it. The point was that Britain should not fight the Irish cause unless it understood the anger that underpinned it. In the poem, Billy refuses to listen to the cornstalk kid and, while he is rejecting the advice, the bushfire flares up anew.

In August, the twenty-two-year-old Paterson received a short letter from Jules Francois Archibald, *The Bulletin*'s charismatic editor. Baptised John Feltham Archibald, he changed his given names to sound French during the Bohemian days of his youth. In 1880, at the age of twenty-four, he co-founded *The Bulletin* with the aim of promoting radical, humanist ideas and a promise to deliver only 'the interesting half of the news'. From its first edition—which featured extensive coverage of the execution of Captain Moonlite, 'the Wantabadgery Bushranger'—*The Bulletin* had grown to become known as 'The Bushman's Bible'. It was amusing, highly national-istic, and fought for the underdog against cold-hearted banks and absentee landlords. It was also a nursery for emerging artistic and literary talent. Archibald had a gift for discovering such talent and his letter to Barty Paterson in 1886 offered the young poet a chance to make his name:

Will you drop in and see me at your earliest convenience, as I'd like a long talk with you about a lot of things. I shall be glad to have from you any topical Australian verses which may come into your head and you would do me a great favour by trying your hand at writing for us weekly some short sharp snappy paragraphs—two, three or four lines each, no more—suitable for production under any one of our headings. As you no doubt see, *The Bulletin* aims at being an Australasian rather than a mere Sydney or N.S.W. publication so we endeavour to get matter, which while acceptable to the reader in this city will also suit his brother at Cape York and the other fellow down at Cape Otway or Perth. The remaining chief items in our policy are to 'howl for the undermost dog'—all of the rest of the press are generally engaged in sooling on the pup that's got the grip—and to print all the awkward things procurable.

*

It was with a sense of trepidation that Paterson approached *The Bulletin* office in Sydney. Pitt Street was alive with humanity in a rush. Tram bells rang, hoofs clattered on the road, iron-rimmed carriage wheels rumbled across the neatly sealed roads and children shouted and squabbled while their parents went about their business. But the noise and the crowds and the smoke from factory chimneys were a world away from Paterson's thoughts, for these were turned to the meeting he was about to have with Archibald.

Paterson nervously climbed a dingy flight of stairs to a dusty first-floor office where he found himself standing before a closed door marked, 'Mr Archibald, Editor'. Paterson noticed that a 'spirited drawing' was pinned to the door. It showed the body of a man lying 'quite loose on the strand with a dagger through him'. Accompanying the stabbed man was a message: 'Archie, this is what will happen to you if you don't use my drawing about the policeman!' Clearly, the creator of the policeman drawing had no fear of the editor's wrath. It was an enormous relief to the nervous Paterson who immediately thought *The Bulletin* must be 'a free and easy place'. Feeling a little more confident, he knocked at the door and was admitted for an interview that changed his life.

His discussion with Archibald lasted just ten minutes. The editor said he would like the young writer to try his hand at more verse. Did he know anything about the bush? He did? He was born and raised there? It was perfect. 'All right,' said the bearded and bespectacled editor, 'have a go at the bush. Have a go at anything that strikes you. Don't write anything like . . . other people if you can help it. Let's see what you can do.'

As it turned out, what Andrew Barton Paterson, alias The Banjo, could do was rather remarkable.

*

The Bulletin published 'A Dream of the Melbourne Cup' in October. Paterson subtitled the poem 'A Long Way After Gordon' as a way of stating his belief that the work was inferior to the poetry of Adam Lindsay Gordon, the poet, politician and horseman. His next effort was the ballad 'The Mylora Elopement'. Encouraged now, he soon produced more verses including 'Only a Jockey', a sad account of the death of a fourteen-year-old jockey in a race fall in Melbourne, and then 'Old Pardon, The Son of Reprieve'—one of his better works that might have been inspired by that trip to the Bogolong Races years earlier. This effort was followed by other works dealing with subjects as diverse as politics, circuses and minstrel shows.

But writing provided only pocket money. Each published poem netted a standard sum of thirteen shillings and sixpence. Accordingly, the practice of law had to be his priority. Ironically, though, it was his work as a lawyer that introduced Paterson to another young man who would define the Australian landscape with words. That man's name was Henry Lawson. He was a painter by trade, but his true talents lay in his pen and he came to see Paterson at his office for legal advice on dealing with publishers. Their meeting began an association that would see both men remembered as the 'Twin Deities of *The Bulletin*'.

Unlike the confident Paterson, Lawson was introverted, thanks in part to a serious hearing impairment and a history of social awkwardness as a child. Lawson was a fervent republican with a deep concern for those suffering poverty or injustice. He had appeared on the literary scene as a result of the 'Republican Riots' of 1887—a series of heated and disorderly meetings in Sydney to discuss public celebrations of Queen Victoria's Golden Jubilee. It was a time when republicanism was a potent political force in Australia. At the first meeting in June, the monarchists, led by the New South Wales Premier, Sir Henry Parkes, proposed a grand fete for Sydney's Sunday school students to celebrate the Jubilee. But militant republicans stacked the meeting and voted down the proposal as 'unwise and calculated to injure the democratic spirit of the country'. The meeting ended in turmoil and another was scheduled for the following week. This time, admittance would be by official invitation to keep out the troublemakers.

The republicans, however, forged their entry tickets and occupied the town hall in huge numbers. The loyalists tried to maintain control by erecting physical barriers against the militants but the barriers were shoved aside and mayhem ensued. In a wild stoush, a motion to honour the Queen was howled down before it could even be put to the floor. *The Bulletin* tore strips from the loyalists, saying 'they violently assaulted the speakers selected by the people, and roughly ejected them from the chamber!' But *The Sydney Morning Herald* railed against the rebellious republicans, who it said, turned 'the proceedings into an absolute chaos of uproar, confusion, faction-fighting and ruffianism . . .'

Both papers probably got it at least partly right, but Lawson was so infuriated by the *Herald*'s words that he penned some of his own. Angrily, he wrote 'Sons of the South', a stirring call to arms for Australian radicals to 'Awake! Arise!' On 1 October, *The Bulletin*'s Archibald published the poem, which he retitled 'A Song of the Republic', and Lawson's brilliant, tragic career as a writer began to take flight. Soon, he wrote the indignant 'Faces in the Street'—a bitter denunciation of the urban poverty he had seen in the crowded streets of Sydney—and then 'The Army of the Rear', which railed against the huge disparity between rich and poor.

Henry Lawson had been born—by his own account—in a tent on the goldfields at Grenfell in New South Wales on the dark and stormy night of 17 June 1867. His father was a Norwegian sailor named Neils Larsen (anglicised to Lawson) and his mother was Louisa Albury, a bright young lady with a talent for literature and music. It was a marriage characterised by conflict and hardship. Hoping for a change of luck, Neils looked for gold, but when this met with little success, the family returned to the land. For a short time, they lived in a two-roomed hut on a rather poor selection at Eurunderee, near Mudgee, but farming proved to be just as unproductive as prospecting.

Henry's hearing began to fail when he was about nine and was almost completely lost five years later. His disability made it hard for him to socialise with other children and he did poorly at school, except in English composition where he showed significant ability.

When he was about fourteen, he left school and travelled with his father, who was now working as a builder. There was little to keep Lars and Louisa together and, in 1883, she moved to Sydney. Henry soon joined her there and was apprenticed to a coach painter.

Free from her husband, Louisa became involved in the tumultuous world of revolutionary politics in Sydney. She became the founder and publisher of *The Dawn*, a newspaper described in the mainstream papers as being 'essentially for ladies, in which to vent their wrongs, to proclaim their victories over heartless men and to give advice'. *Dawn* was in fact more than a ladies' journal. It was published from Louisa's home in Phillip Street—an address that was said to be a hotbed of radicalism where such controversies as women's rights were passionately discussed. Louisa—who was always referred to in the papers as the mother of Henry Lawson—later said in a letter that she hoped one day to 'be strong enough to look the public in the face as Louisa Lawson, and not as the mother of a man. A man writes me up, a man takes my photograph and I appear as the mother of a man'.

It was hardly surprising that her son—partially deaf, socially withdrawn and afflicted with a drinking problem that would worsen as he aged—burned with genuine social outrage and a desire for change. Barty Paterson shared Lawson's empathy with the people of the bush but, unlike Lawson, Paterson was a son of the squattocracy, with no driving force towards radicalism. Nonetheless, each recognised admirable qualities in the other and, although never close friends, they hit it off when they met as lawyer and client.

In one conversation, perhaps as an antidote to the boredom of processing Lawson's publishing contracts, Paterson asked his fellow poet how he got his ideas. Lawson replied: 'I can catch ideas anywhere, but I can't always make 'em go into harness. Simple stuff is the best. One day I picked up a pair of pants and found they had a hole in the stern and I wrote, "You've got to face your troubles 'When Your Pants Begin to Go'."

It was advice that Paterson could have given himself. He often found his own inspiration in the small things he saw and heard around him. The thought of an overweight racehorse, the ordered explosion of colour in a glorious English garden at a country station or the wind-baggery of a talentless politician might be enough to spark verses tender in nostalgia or lacerating in political satire. These 'small things' continued to set off little lights in Paterson's mind, but little things grow to become big things and by the end of the decade, the anonymous poet 'Banjo' created a landmark ballad, grown from one tiny seed of an idea. It helped to establish him as one of the greats, and, more personally, it came at a time when good news was even more than usually welcome.

*

Some time in 1888, not later than October, Paterson became engaged to Sarah Riley, a cousin of his business partner, John Street. At twenty-six, Sarah was a young lady of wealth and class. She was a good catch for Barty and it seemed the course of his life was set—marriage, children and steady progression in a career as a city lawyer. Raised in Geelong, Sarah had attended Oberwyl, a prestigious finishing school in Melbourne. There she learned, among other things, an appreciation of music and art, and how to conduct conversation. The engagement met with the approval of Barty's grandmother, who in a letter on 18 October, 1888, revealed that she thought Sarah a good match for her grandson:

> Barty's fiancée, Sarah Riley, has been staying with us, and does credit to his taste; she is an exceptionally nice girl, well connected and educated. I sometimes wonder that she should

not have look'd higher, but his talent goes a long way, and also makes his worldly prospects pretty secure.

Perhaps marriage was indeed what Paterson planned in the hopeful spring of 1888. But any intentions he might have had for an early wedding were derailed by a family tragedy in the following winter, and as time passed it became clear that his heart was not in the practice of law and nor was it in his engagement to Sarah Riley.

*

In March 1889, Paterson again dabbled in politics, and this time the target was, inexplicably, one of his relatives. For some reason Paterson was incensed to read in the papers that his mother's cousin Henry Kater, the same man who had helped Barty begin his career in law, had been appointed a life member of the New South Wales Legislative Council. The stinging 'Who is Kater Anyhow?' attacked Kater's appointment and claimed he only got the job because he had married well. The verses were published not under the pseudonym 'Banjo', or even 'B' but 'J.W.'—the initials of Paterson's law partner, John William Street. It was a rather cowardly assault on Kater, who had done little to deserve it and Paterson's motivations are unknown. In any case, Archibald was pleased to publish it.

Less than three months after the publication of 'Who is Kater Anyhow?' the Paterson family was rocked by an unexpected tragedy. On the morning of 30 May 1889, Barty's father, Andrew Bogle Paterson, bid farewell to his wife Rose and left Illalong for a day's business at Binalong. Andrew's health was no worse than usual when he left, but soon after he got home that night he was taken ill and retired to bed. Expecting him to improve as always, Rose did not call a doctor. Instead, Andrew was given sedatives and cared for at home. But he did not improve. On the night of 6 June, he collapsed and quickly became unconscious. He died the next morning in his bed. A life of toil for little reward had come to an end. He was fifty-six.

An inquest was told Andrew's heart had suffered from fatty degeneration and was 'very much enfeebled'. A coroner's report might have shed light on Andrew's long history of illness and the treatment he received for it, when 'an overdose of opium . . . and continued heavy drinking' were found to be the causes of death.

Dozens of people attended Andrew's funeral at the little cemetery at Binalong. Later, Rose erected a headstone on the grave. It is inscribed with a line from Psalm 127: 'He giveth his beloved sleep.' Observers noted later that the psalm also includes a message well suited to Andrew Paterson, the father of seven who worked himself to death: 'It is vain for you to rise up early, to sit up late, to eat the bread of sorrows.'

Without Andrew, Rose could no longer remain at Illalong and she soon followed the widow's tradition set by her mother and sister, retreating to the refuge of Rockend in Gladesville, with the youngest children, Hamilton, Grace, Edie and Gwen. Rose and her mother would care for the children but, as head of the family, it was now Barty's responsibility to support them financially. It was a significant demand on a young man still trying to secure his own fortune and it might have been enough to hold him back from marrying. Sarah Riley, a patient young woman, had to be content to wait.

In the meantime, Paterson the poet returned to his familiar metier of bush verses. In September, the *Bulletin* published 'Tar and Feathers' and 'How M'Ginnis Went Missing'. November's issue was equally productive for Paterson, with the publication of the sketch 'Hughey's Dog', and the romping doggerel of 'Mulligan's Mare'. 'The Banjo' was showing that he could indeed tackle this writing caper, and in his straitened circumstances, the handful of shillings earned for these works were warmly received. But it was December's *Bulletin* that really made 'Banjo' a name to notice. The last of four poems he wrote for that month's edition was one of his greatest. Engaging, evocative and dreamy, it sings the glories of the bush, celebrating its beauties and freedom. It is the story of a humble drover, a simple man, whose greatness lies not within himself but in the landscape around him. The drover's story is an Australian classic which, for all its importance, had its genesis in an event just as mundane as the hole in Henry Lawson's pants.

At some unspecified time, Paterson's firm sent a 'business letter' to a man named Clancy somewhere in rural New South Wales. Clancy owed some money and the letter demanded he pay up. Soon, a note arrived in reply. Written by a friend of Clancy's, it said that Clancy had 'gone to Queensland droving and we don't where he are'. The fractured grammar caught Paterson's imagination but, more than that, he was enthralled by the thought that Clancy had escaped to the bush, free of the boss and the balance sheet. It seemed to Paterson that Clancy's carefree life with only his sheep and cattle to worry about was in stark contrast to his own. Where Clancy travelled the long paddock with fresh air and starlight as his companions, Paterson was enslaved to a musty office in a choked and crowded city. Clancy, whoever he was, had a freedom worth singing about, and soon Paterson soon came up with the song—an eight-stanza ballad he called 'Clancy of the Overflow'. It began:

I had written him a letter which I had, for want of better
Knowledge, sent to where I met him down the Lachlan,
  years ago.
He was shearing when I knew him, so I sent the letter
  to him,

Just 'on spec', addressed as follows: 'Clancy of the Overflow'.

And an answer came directed in a writing unexpected,
(And I think the same was written with a thumbnail dipped
    in tar)
'Twas his shearing mate who wrote it, and *verbatim* I will
    quote it:
'Clancy's gone to Queensland droving, and we don't know
    where he are.'

The ballad went on to speak of 'the vision splendid of the sunlit plains extended' as Clancy enjoyed 'pleasures that the townsfolk never know'. And in his 'dingy little office' in the 'foetid air and gritty of the dusty, dirty city' Paterson could only dream of the freedom of the bush and the pull of the plains and the mountains—a yearning that was summed up in the poem's wistful final lines:

And I somehow rather fancy that I'd like to change with
    Clancy,
Like to take a turn at droving where the seasons come and go,
While he faced the round eternal of the cash book and the
    journal—
But I doubt he'd suit the office, Clancy, of The Overflow.

As he worked long hours in the busy city office through the latter half of 1889, still grieving his father's death, Paterson's thoughts might often have strayed to Clancy, free in the bush with only his beasts to care for and a camp fire to sleep by at night. Contrasted to his own big city life, with its new responsibilities, the carefree existence of his creation Clancy must have seemed idyllic to the young lawyer-poet. Paterson could not 'change with Clancy', but he could seize upon any chance to escape the city, even if only for a short while, and a favourite destination was the southern mountains.

It was probably late in 1889 when that chance arrived, thanks to his acquaintance with wealthy high-country squatters Peter and Walter Mitchell, who invited him to visit their home at Bringenbrong Station near Corryong in Victoria's mountainous north-east.

Nestled under shady trees on the wide green flood plains of the cold and clear Murray River, the station looked over the grassy flats and up to the timbered peaks where cattlemen grazed their herds on pretty alpine meadows and brumbies ran wild through the snow gums. The air was clear and alive with birdsong. There were long trails where a man could ride from ferny gullies to windswept ridge tops and not see another soul. After a difficult year, it was just what Paterson needed and he accepted an invitation to visit the Mitchell brothers that summer with delight.

The way some see it today, that visit resulted in the creation of a character even greater than Clancy, one so powerful that it helped to define a nation's identity. Before long, 'The Man From Snowy River', the story of a courageous young horseman who performed a feat so spectacular and so dangerous that even grizzled veterans of the bush dared not attempt it, made 'Banjo' Paterson as a household name. In the years since, many came forward—or were thrust forward by others—to claim the honour of being the original Man from Snowy River. According to the Mitchell brothers, Banjo Paterson met that original man during his holiday in the mountains, and took from that meeting a story that has captured Australian imaginations ever since.

5

THE MAN FROM SNOWY RIVER

Paterson thought highly of the Mitchell brothers. Passionate about horses, they were successful at breeding bigger, faster and stronger racehorses, and Peter had a theory that the same could be done for people. During his stay at Bringenbrong, Paterson went on long rides with the brothers and Peter's theories about breeding struck a chord. Paterson remembered those ideas and, many years later, he said Peter Mitchell proved to be as good as his word when he left a huge sum of money in his will to provide prizes to those who could 'improve the physique of the human race':

> I know there was a prize of a thousand pounds each year for the woman with the best physique and the best disposition and able to swim and cook and ride a horse. There was also a thousand pounds for the best man, to be judged on physique and good temper and ability to do outdoor work, just the same way as they give prizes for speed, style and action at a show.

During his holiday in the summer of 1889–90, Paterson rode with the Mitchells from Bringenbrong to the stony summit of Mt Kosciuszko, 2228 metres high and often blanketed in snow from May to November. After two days in the saddle, they reached Tom Groggin Station, high in the shoulders of the alps. As darkness closed in that night, they camped at a small timber hut on the edge of a straw-coloured flat. This was the home of Jack Riley, the reclusive overseer of Tom Groggin Station.

Jack was not fond of visitors but he did enjoy a drink. Those visitors who brought along a bottle of whisky or gin were tolerated, if not welcomed, and when the grog ran out, so did any lukewarm welcome they might have received. Paterson and the Mitchells must have brought a bottle with them when they dropped in on Jack Riley because, according to the way Peter Mitchell remembered it, Jack accepted the intrusion and even spent that mild summer evening sharing a yarn or two with his visitors. But it was one yarn in particular that the brothers wanted Paterson to hear, and, as the firelight flickered in the still alpine night, they persuaded Jack to tell it, as he had many times before.

The next morning, Jack's visitors continued their journey to the top of Kosciuszko. After reaching the peak, they headed south along the top of the Great Divide to Mt Pilot and from there back to Tom Groggin. After a brief reunion at Jack's hut, they bid farewell to the old bushman and returned to Bringenbrong, Paterson taking with him the memories of his journey.

According to the way it is remembered in the upper Murray, the tall, long-nosed poet had listened closely to Jack's story, and, a few months later, he came up with a verse that captured something of the yarn that had made Jack a local legend. The way Jack had supposedly seen it, the poet got a lot of it wrong, but the old bushman had to admit the young bloke knew a thing or two about horses and for a city slicker he was a useful hand in the scrub. At the time, though, it was just another telling of his story and, after sharing it, Jack thought nothing more of it.

*

Born in County Cork, Ireland, in 1841, Jack Riley sailed to Sydney on the *Rodney*, arriving in March 1854. According to research by Corryong man, Richard Hubbard, the thirteen-year-old Jack joined his sister Ann who had come out to Australia about four years earlier. After a short time in Sydney, they made their way to the Omeo diggings high on the southern flanks of the Victorian Alps. The young Jack was said to have trained as a tailor but, after arriving at Omeo, like thousands of others he tried his luck on the goldfields. Also like thousands of others, he failed, and so he set up business as a tailor in the fledgling town. Ann had married Joseph Jones, an argumentative character who was charged with threatening to kill her in 1862. He was acquitted of that charge but was convicted of assault in 1873. In 1876, Jones was fined because he and Ann had failed to send their three children to school.

Jack was no angel either. Apparently unsatisfied with sewing clothes, he left Omeo in the summer of 1863 to try his luck in the windswept Snowy Mountains' gold town of Kiandra, New South Wales. He was not there long enough to learn the hard way that the gold was already almost gone because soon after his arrival he had to 'go away'—thanks to the 'misappropriation of certain stock'. He served two years in Parramatta Gaol and never spoke of his imprisonment. It was widely thought, however, that the horse theft for which he had been convicted was actually committed by his troublesome brother-in-law, and that Jack had taken the blame out of family loyalty. True or not, it earned Jack respect among the mountain cattlemen.

After his release, Jack returned to the mountains, this time to the Snowy River region in Victoria. For a while, he drove stock between the Monaro in New South Wales and the highlands of Victoria's Gippsland, and from 1876 he worked as stockman in charge of cattle runs on the border between the two colonies. So far, he had lived an unremarkable life, but a few years later, probably in the early 1880s, he was said to have performed a feat that he is still remembered for today.

It began when he joined a party of riders on a dramatic mission to recapture a stallion that had escaped from a station and joined a mob of brumbies on the steep sides of Mt Leatherhead. Catching the mob was a matter of pride to the rugged bushmen. They built a stockyard at the foot of the mountain, each hoping to be the first to drive the escapee through the bush and into the trap. But the stallion was too fast, too strong and too smart for his pursuers. After a long and fruitless chase, the men gathered on a ridge top, ready for a final effort to box the stallion in. But then, in a ripple of gleaming muscle, the mighty horse charged down a fearsome slope at breakneck speed.

The hillside was a jungle of towering trees under-laid with grasping webs of spiky wattle and tea-tree scrub. The ground was pitted with wombat holes, some big enough to hide a cow, and loose shale that littered the slopes slid away from the stallion's hoofs as he careened down the mountainside. It would be suicide to follow him. It seemed the stallion had made good his escape.

But then, with a whoop, Jack Riley leapt his sturdy mountain pony from the ridge top and hurtled down the slope in hot pursuit. According to the way the cattlemen told it later, sparks all but flew from the pony's iron shoes as horse and rider raced down the steep and rocky mountainside. They cleared the wombat holes and fallen logs in great bounds. In a thunder of hoof beats, rocks flew and branches whipped the faces of man and beast. Headlong they galloped, faster and faster. Clutching the reins with one hand and his hat with the other, Jack leaned so far back in the saddle that he all but lay along the horse's rump. Only the bottom of the mountain could halt their break-neck charge and any slip meant certain death. The men at the top of the ridge were lesser riders that day, and all they could do was watch in awe as Jack and his horse did what no others dared to try.

The horse's name is not recorded, but it deserves as much credit as its rider because together, in a lather of foam and blood, they drove that half-wild stallion down the mountainside and into the stockyard at the foot of the slope. Their sides heaving and gasping for air, man and pony had captured the mighty brumby and Jack Riley's name was spoken in awe around camp fires for years to come.

It was partly for this spectacular deed that Jack came to the attention of John Pearce, the owner of the isolated Tom Groggin Station high in the shoulders of the Snowy Mountains. The station lay on a broad and picturesque flat bounded by soaring peaks and the Murray River. It owed its name not to a cattleman or explorer, but rather to the native Yaitmathang people, who knew the area as *Tong-ger-rogan*—the place of countless water spiders that swarmed in the river during the spring and summer. In the early days, Tom Groggin was used as a summer station where cattle grazed on the broad flat or were driven into the hills to feed on the tough grasses and herbs that grew in clearings between the trees. In winter, however, the station was a wild and often snowbound place where only a handful of cattle roamed and few white men ventured.

In 1884, Pearce hired Jack Riley as the year-round overseer of the station and Jack made his home in a cabin of logs and split vertical slabs with a roof of shingles at the far end of the sprawling property. One of the few photos taken of Jack shows him standing stiffly to one side of his home in a grassy yard enclosed by split timber palings. With just one door and no windows in the wall facing the photographer, the hut seems to grow from the virgin bush under a backdrop of soaring peaks. Built in two sections of horizontal logs and traditional Australian vertical slabs, the cabin had only one concession to comfort—a single fireplace and chimney.

This humble dwelling at the edge of the mountain flat was home to Jack Riley for some thirty years. In that time, he came to know every tree and every trail in the surrounding bush. With contempt for compasses and maps, he could find his way through the wilderness like a homing pigeon, and more than any other white man he learned the little-known routes through dense forest and over stony-headed peaks to the top of Mt Kosciuszko.

It was a country for loners. In 1838, Robert Mason and his wife—whose name is not recorded—were among the first Europeans to settle the area. Mrs Mason was believed to be the region's first white woman. She was certainly the mother of the first white child to be born there, because Robert junior arrived in the couple's hut in 1839. We can only imagine how Mrs Mason felt when the time came to have her baby in this wilderness. Perhaps she had Aboriginal midwives to help because the baby arrived safely, only to die two years later. Mrs Mason delivered nine more children—testament, if any is needed, to the strength of the women who pioneered this hard land.

Strange old men lived in the bush too. Known as 'hatters' after the Mad Hatter in Lewis Carroll's classic novel *Alice in Wonderland*, these strange loners lived with only the trees and animals for company. Today, old locals can remember the wild man who lived in a dugout next to the Hermit Creek in the Depression years. Clothed in kangaroo skins, he was more animal than human. He ate what he could catch—unwary animals, snakes, lizards and insects—supplemented by vegetables grown in a patch of cleared bush next to his cave, and he never spoke a word to another person. Whatever drove him to such seclusion will never be known.

Jack Riley was a loner, too, but he did make infrequent visits to civilisation. Riding a mountain pony and leading a packhorse to carry his supplies, Jack occasionally ventured into Corryong or Khancoban to buy what he needed for the long weeks in his self-imposed exile. Sometimes he stopped to visit a friend and share a bottle of whisky on the way home, but more often than not the white-bearded bushman preferred to turn his horses' heads back to the highlands and the serenity of his alpine home.

But if Jack wanted to leave the world alone, he could not count on the world to return the favour. The mountains were opening up to stockmen, miners and even tourists. Parties of riders regularly passed his hut on their way to Kosciuszko. Jack reluctantly greeted them—especially if they had been wise enough to bring a bottle of whisky—but soon enough he was happy to send them on their way. Sometimes, however, he showed the tourists to the top of the mountain, perhaps earning a few shillings for his trouble. Those who shunned his help occasionally came to regret it.

In the midst of one wet and bitterly cold winter, a group of riders from the city passed through Tom Groggin en route to the mountain. Jack offered to guide them to the top because in this weather he knew they were risking life and limb. There was no need, they said. They had a good compass and they knew which way to go because they could clearly see their destination starkly silhouetted against the grey and gloomy sky. Soon they were on their way, but within hours a dense fog closed in and the temperature plummeted.

Two days later, soaked to the skin and exhausted, the city slickers returned to Jack's hut. The weather and the mountains had defeated them. Jack gave them tea and something to eat and kept his thoughts about the foolishness of ill-prepared mountain travellers to himself. Warmed up by Jack's fire and recharged by hot food, one of the tourists offered Jack five shillings as a reward but he quietly refused. Soon he took them to the track that led to civilisation and he returned alone to the refuge of his home.

*

Barty Paterson's summer visit to the high country ended all too soon, and it was time for him to return to work in the 'dusty, dirty city'. At around this time, words began to form in his mind. Soon he had the opening lines for a ballad he titled 'The Man From Snowy River'.

> There was movement at the station, for the word had
>   passed around
> That the colt from old Regret had got away,
> And had joined the wild bush horses—he was worth a
>   thousand pound

Reprising some of Paterson's earlier characters, including Pardon the horse and Clancy of the Overflow, the ballad told how the 'tried and noted riders from stations near and far' had gathered at a homestead to chase the valuable colt. One of the riders was 'a stripling on a small and graceful beast'. 'Graceful' was later replaced with 'weedy'. In the poem, the old hands doubted the young horseman, who 'hails from Snowy River, up by Kosciusko's [sic] side', could keep up with the rugged bushmen on his scrubby little pony. It soon proved to be a valid concern. The mob easily outpaced their pursuers and even the remarkable Clancy could not hold the brumbies as they charged to freedom down the frightful side of the mountain. It seemed the chase had failed.

But then the Man from Snowy River showed his mettle. He gave a wild cheer and put the spurs to his horse. They raced 'down the mountain like a torrent in its bed' and ran the brumbies until their 'sides were white with foam'. Single-handedly, the rider and his trusty horse captured the brumbies and, as the final stanza explained, he had earned his place in history.

And down by Kosciusko, where the pine-clad ridges raise
    Their torn and rugged battlements on high,
Where the air is clear as crystal, and the white stars
    fairly blaze
At midnight in the cold and frosty sky,
And where around the Overflow the reedbeds sweep
    and sway
To the breezes, and the rolling plains are wide,
The man from Snowy River is a household word today,
    And the stockmen tell the story of his ride.

The Bulletin published the ballad in April 1890, several months after Paterson returned from Corryong. It instantly struck a chord with readers who clamoured to know the identity of this exciting new writer, 'The Banjo'. *The Bulletin* editor, Archibald, would only say that he was 'a modest young man of Sydney'. After finishing 1889 on a high note with the publication of 'Clancy of the Overflow', Paterson's anonymity was now working to his benefit and the mystery over his identity only served to heighten public interest in his work. Fortune would always elude him, but thanks to 'The Man From Snowy River', fame was assured.

*

The rise of the poet Banjo Paterson meant little to Jack Riley. The years passed at Tom Groggin Station and Jack continued his lonely work looking after the stock and keeping the property in order. As he got older, some of the duties became too much for him but he refused to leave his home. His visits to civilisation became less frequent and, each time, the townsfolk noticed that the old man seemed to be fading. In 1911, word reached town that Jack was in a bad way and a party was sent to check on him.

Father Patrick Hartigan from Albury was among that group. Fearing Jack would need the last rites, the priest had whizzed up to Corryong in his new Renault motor car before joining a group of horsemen for the ride out to Jack's hut. When they arrived, they found Jack unwell but conscious and not particularly pleased to see this party of well-wishers in his home. Father Hartigan, who was himself a bush poet of note (he wrote 'Said Hanrahan' under the pen name John O'Brien) filled in an awkward silence by reciting the first few lines of 'The Man From Snowy River'. The priest later recalled that the ailing Jack Riley was unimpressed: 'We often used to do that sort of thing and had tougher "goes" than that,' Jack supposedly said. 'I was taking a party up to Kossy and was telling them about it, and one of them put it in a book; but he brings in the names of a lot of men who weren't there at all. There was nobody named Clancy . . .'

Jack did not need the last rites that night. But, in the winter of 1914, his time was finally up. His mates came for him in July. It was a two-day ride from Corryong to Jack's hut and the rescuers knew time was running out. It had been several weeks since he had been seen in town and even then he was looking poorly. There was little time to lose, but the going was hard and it was a journey that could not be rushed.

Portrait of J.F. Archibald and Henry Lawson, Sydney, 1918. *Photograph courtesy National Library of Australia.*

The four rescuers on their hardy mountain horses followed a bridle track that wound its way over waves of hills that rose to steep, tree-crowned ridges and fell to ferny gullies divided by half-hidden creeks. After each descent, the horses picked their way over the gullies and then climbed again—every peak conquered bringing the rescuers a little closer to their destination. The riders urged their horses on as the heavens opened and the mountains fell silent but for the slap of raindrops against leaves. If Jack was alive, the riders would bring him out. If he was not, they would bring him out anyway. He would not be left to the dingoes.

When the riders reached Jack's hut late on the second day, they saw they were almost too late. The old man's only hope was to see the doctor at the Cottage Hospital in Corryong. The rescuers camped that night at the hut, hoping the rain would ease. Inside, they lit the fire and made Jack as comfortable as they could as the rain hammered down on the shingled roof. The next morning—14 July—they set out in the downpour on Jack Riley's final journey.

The rescuers decided to take a different route back to town to avoid a number of river crossings on the main bridle track and, carrying Jack on a stretcher made of saplings and hessian, they followed an old mining trail that hugged the course of the Murray. When the river fell through a series of gorges, the rescuers had to climb Hermit Mountain—a steep ascent that was too much for the stretcher bearers. The rain turned to snow and hopes faded that Jack would reach hospital in time.

The mountain men would not be defeated by mere rain and snow and, as they struggled up the steep slope, Jack was taken from the stretcher and placed in a saddle, one of the rescuers sitting behind him to keep him upright. Late that afternoon, they had made their way back down the mountain and, as night fell they took shelter in an abandoned hut at an old tin mine. Jack complained of being cold and his mates bundled him up in front of the fire. Jack seemed to rally a little and exchanged a few words with his companions. But as the chilly air closed in and the snow piled up on the ground outside, he swayed in his seat and fell silent. Shortly afterwards, he took his last breath. Jack Riley's life in the mountains was over.

He was taken into town where his body was laid out on the billiard table at the Corryong Coffee Palace. The next day, he was buried in a quiet corner of the town's cemetery. Visitors to his grave could lift their eyes and see the hazy mountains merge into the horizon above them. Jack's rescuers had failed but their efforts did not go unnoticed. The *Corryong Courier* published some words to honour the men who rode to the rescue of a friend:

> The bush asks big things of its men and they never fail to respond. Sometimes—as in this case—the task proves impossible, and a Higher Power intervenes; but the credit of a gallant attempt is theirs—and there are many failures which are finer than many successes.

*

The Mitchell brothers never doubted that Jack Riley was the inspiration for Paterson's famous ballad—a view that is widely accepted in the Upper Murray today. There have been other candidates for the Man from Snowy River, including Charlie McKeahnie from Adaminaby, 'Hellfire' Jack Clarke of Jindabyne and Jim Spencer from the Snowy, just to name a few. They were men cut from the same cloth as Jack Riley and their collective deeds made an impression on Banjo Paterson. But, as tempting as it might be to find one Man from Snowy River, the truth is that he was not one man but a compilation of many.

In December 1938, Paterson revealed as much in an article for *The Sydney Mail* in which he said he wrote the poem to describe 'the cleaning up' of wild horses near his childhood home. That was a tough job, he said, although it was infinitely harder in the high country. To create the ballad he had had to invent a character who could ride better than anybody else and 'where would he come from except the Snowy?' And Paterson made it clear that his Man from Snowy River was the embodiment of countless bushmen who once rode the hills and plains:

> They have turned up from all the mountain districts—men who did exactly the same ride and could give you chapter and verse for every hill they descended and every creek they crossed. It was no small satisfaction to find that there had really been a Man from Snowy River—more than one of them.

'The Man From Snowy River' certainly reflected Paterson's boyhood memories of the horsemen he admired so much at quiet Illalong. It has even been said that Paterson, the consummate horseman, saw himself as that courageous mountain rider. It must also be said, however, that of all the candidates, Jack Riley was the only one known to have met Paterson and echoes of Jack's story could be clearly heard in Paterson's poem. While it is true that Jack was not the only Man from Snowy River, at least part of his story shines on in the famous ballad. And, true or not, many folk in the Upper Murray today have no doubt that their man was *the* Man from Snowy River, a belief that was set in stone in 1947 when Walter Mitchell's son Tom arranged a headstone for Jack Riley. It reads:

In Memory of
THE MAN FROM
SNOWY RIVER
JACK RILEY
BURIED HERE
16TH JULY 1914

Ironically for a man who preferred to keep his own company, Jack Riley's grave in Corryong has become a destination for tourists seeking to connect with an Australia that no longer exists. Jack would not have liked being the centre of attention but, perhaps, he and Charlie McKeahnie and the other Men from Snowy River would have been pleased to know that their exploits helped to ensure the legend of the mountain cattleman lives on.

6

TWIN DEITIES

The end of the great drought of the 1860s was followed by a rise in wool prices and by the seventies, the industry was booming again. Demand for land led to rapid pastoral expansion in largely undeveloped areas as investors and settlers sought runs and stations. Among the big investors were fabulously wealthy squatter kings from Victoria's rich Western District. Feeling the pinch of encroachment from small settlers, the weight of land taxes and the depredations of rabbits, some of the southern colony's most successful grazing families now set their sights on newly opened pastoral districts in western Queensland. There, a squatter could take up a run—up to 100 square miles (259 square kilometres)—and if he could prove he had stocked it to a quarter of capacity or more, he could be granted a fourteen-year lease. With luck and hard work, more runs could be added and the squatter could become a station owner.

By the 1880s, Australia's economy was booming. There was rapid growth in the cities, especially in 'Marvellous Melbourne' which had exploded during the gold rush and was now roaring in the land boom. The city's population had doubled to almost half a million, making it bigger than some European capitals. Grand buildings of up to twelve storeys sprang up in the city centre as banks, hotels and speculators made a fortune. Helping to fuel it all were the riches from the land. It seemed the good times would roll forever from the sheep's back and even when wool prices began to fall it did not seem to matter because Australia produced so much of it.

But the speculation had created a bubble in the economy. When it burst at the end of the decade, it provided the young lawyer Barty Paterson with proof of a truism—where there's a boom, there's inevitably a bust. When the economy came crashing down, Paterson the lawyer was assigned the distasteful task of trying to gather some of the scattered pieces: 'For months I did nothing but try to screw money out of people who had not got it.'

It was the workers in the bush—shearers, shepherds, station hands and others—who had laboured to generate the wealth during the boom, but they saw relatively little of it. Inequity had already led to unionisation in the cities where miners, dock workers and factory hands were becoming a political force. But the army of workers from shearing sheds and stations scattered over tens of millions of square kilometres remained largely disorganised until the pastoralists moved to cut shearers' pay rates in 1886. It led to the creation of an industrial system that defines the relationship between employer and worker today.

In June that year, the Australian Shearers Union was formed in Ballarat. Within four years it had branches across the country and claimed to have 20,000 members. The union offered solidarity, support during a time when social security did not exist, and a united voice at the negotiating table. Importantly, it was a force for collectivism, creating a common cause in the shearing shed. And for the bushman, there was something attractive about the ethos of the union. In a country where Jack dared to think he was as good as his master, workforce solidarity offered independence and equality. Even though he might own little more than a billy and a swag, the wandering shearer had a sense of his own place in the wide brown land.

But it was the cities that became the battle ground for Australia's first great industrial dispute. In 1890, hundreds of sailors and wharf workers walked off the job in a demand for better wages and conditions. When coal miners joined the protest, more than 28,000 workers in essential industries were on strike. Known as the Great Maritime Strike, it was the first in a series of sometimes savage battles between labour and capital in the 1890s.

On the land, pastoralists and workers were also forming up for battle. At its heart was a conflict between the union's desire to not only fix rates and conditions for all workers in the shed, but also to decide just who worked in that shed. Against that was the employers' wish to seek individual contracts with shearers and to hire whoever they liked to shear their sheep. The spark was struck in 1890, when pastoralists at Jondaryan Station in Queensland employed non-union labour, or 'scabs', on a lower rate. Enraged, the union blocked the station's wool from the ports in Brisbane. By 1891 it had developed into a bitter and sometimes violent stalemate.

Strike camps sprang up, most notably at Barcaldine in central Queensland. Columns of blue smoke grew from camp fires between canvas tents and lean-tos. Billies gently boiled and the scent of roasting meat wafted over the campgrounds. People from small towns nearby provided discounted goods and organised concerts and games. Morale among the unionists was high. But the government was firmly on the bosses' side and troops and police were sent in to protect non-union labour. More strike camps sprang up. The government ordered the campers to disperse and the strikers responded with raids on shearing sheds. There were scattered acts of arson and vandalism, and scabs arriving by train or on foot were confronted and intimidated.

Soon the strike spread to New South Wales and Victoria, where the newspapers declared that 'half a dozen blatant and irresponsible anarchists' were trying to destroy capitalism. The strikers destroyed shearing equipment and in at least one case, tried to sabotage a bridge to stop scabs from reaching shearing sheds. In Queensland, the government deployed hundreds of armed police and mounted infantry to the strike camps.

In March, strike leaders at Sandy Creek were arrested while armed police raided the union offices at Barcaldine, holding the unionists off at bayonet-point. On 1 May, hundreds of shearers marched at Barcaldine, the flag of the rebellious miners at Eureka held aloft. But the might of the establishment was taking a toll on the unionists. In June, the arrested strike leaders were gaoled for three years and the strike was nearing an end.

With a degree of satisfaction, the newspapers said union funds were drying up and some of the men at the camps were 'in a deplorable state with no money and very little clothes'. In August, the strikers' resolve was finally exhausted and the strike was broken. It was a victory to the squatters and the government—but if they thought the fight was over they were sadly mistaken. The unions had suffered a body blow but they were not defeated yet.

Early in 1891, Henry Lawson had gleefully accepted a job at the Brisbane *Boomerang* and wrote prolifically for that paper as well as the labour publication, *The Worker*. The crushing of the strike later that year infuriated Lawson, who penned an inflammatory political poem, 'Freedom on the Wallaby'—the 'wallaby' referring to bushmen carrying their swags. Lawson's fiery effort warned that the 'tyrants' would feel the workers' sting and that the workers should not be blamed 'If blood should stain the wattle'. It caused a furore. In July, a Queensland MP named Frederick Brentnall read part of the poem in the Queensland Parliament, accusing Lawson of sedition and calling for his arrest.

Undeterred, Lawson responded with a bitter attack on class division in verses he wrote for *The Worker*.

> You hate the Cause by instinct, the instinct of your class.
> And fear the reformation that shall surely come to pass;
> Your nest is feathered by the 'laws' which you of course
>   defend,
> Your daily bread is buttered on the upper crust, my friend.

In what could have been a case of mixed fortunes for Lawson, he lost his job at the financially troubled *Boomerang* in September. It meant he had to return to Sydney, and he therefore avoided conflict with Brentnall and his supporters. But the politician and the squatters would have done well to take heed of Lawson's words in 'Freedom on the Wallaby'. In the first stanza, he had warned that the shearers' strike of 1891 would 'boomerang' and three years later he was proved right when another strike hit woolsheds across the eastern states. Driven by union diehards it was not as widespread as the first strike, but it was just as bitter. The controversial death of one of those diehards at the climax of the strike is seen by some as the inspiration for 'Banjo' Paterson's most famous work, 'Waltzing Matilda'.

*

By 1892, Henry Lawson and 'The Banjo' were literary celebrities. They were avidly followed in *The Bulletin* and readers had chosen their favourite. Some saw Lawson as the real voice of the bushman, especially after his support of the striking shearers. He was a champion of the underdog, a class warrior armed with a sharp pen and a passion for change. Banjo, on the other hand, found heroism and humour in his bush characters and a joy in the landscape that surrounded them. Where Lawson saw the raw edge of hardship, Paterson saw camp fires burning and brumbies running in a rural Australia that many in the cities could not experience for themselves. This division among their readers added to the interest in both poets and was helping to generate good sales for *The Bulletin*. It was also a chance for the writers to cash in on their own popularity. The result went down in folklore.

According to Paterson, it was the perennially hard-up Lawson who came up with the idea of staging a mock battle in the paper—each man putting his side of the debate and reaping a handful of shillings as the reward. In need of cash himself, Paterson readily agreed, later acknowledging in his 1939 series in *The Sydney Morning Herald* that his rival came to the battle already carrying scars:

> Henry Lawson was a man of remarkable insight in some things and of extraordinary simplicity in others. We were both looking for the same reef, if you know what I mean; but I had done my prospecting on horseback with my meals cooked for me, while Lawson had done his prospecting on foot and had to cook for himself. Nobody realised this better than Lawson; and one day he suggested that we should write against each other, he putting the bush from his point of view and I putting it from mine.

The way Paterson remembered it, Lawson said: 'We ought to do pretty well out of it, we ought to be able to get three or four sets of verse before they stop us.' This was hotly rejected by Lawson's widow Bertha, who said in a letter to the editor that 'Henry felt the pain of the people and the suffering of the women and the children of the bush . . . too keenly to stage a mock battle in the Press for paltry gain.' There is no doubt that Lawson was deeply moved by suffering in the bush, but he was never averse to making money—especially from publishers—and Paterson's account rings true. In any case, the poets staged their battle and it ended, not when someone stopped them, but when they ran out of material.

Lawson fired the first shot on 9 July with 'Up the Country', a cynical poke at poets who romanticised the bush from the comfort of their city homes:

> I'm back from up the country—very sorry that I went,
> Seeking out the Southern poets' land, whereon to pitch
>   my tent;
> I have lost a lot of idols, which were broken on the track
> Burnt a lot of fancy verses, and I'm glad that I am back.
> Farther out may be the pleasant scenes, of which our
>   poets boast,
> But I think the country's rather more inviting round
>   the coast,
> Anyway, I'll stay at present at a boarding house in town,
> Drinking beer and lemon squashes, taking baths and
>   cooling down.

Lawson did not name Paterson but it was clear he was the target. When Paterson replied on 23 July with 'In Defence of the Bush', he made it personal:

> So you're back from up the country, Mister Lawson, where
>   you went,
> And you're cursing all the business in a bitter discontent;
> Well, we grieve to disappoint you, and it makes us sad to hear
> That it wasn't cool and shady—and there wasn't plenty beer,

And the loony bullock snorted when you first came
    into view,
Well, you know it's not so often that he sees a swell
    like you . . .

'Mr Lawson' was replaced with 'Mr Townsman' in later public-
ations of the verse, but its initial appearance got people talking.
This was a debate with spice. Paterson's final lines of 'In Defence
of the Bush' only served to add to the sense of animosity between
the two bards:

You had better stick with Sydney, and make merry with
    the 'push',
For the bush will never suit you, and you'll never suit
    the bush.

In August 1892, Lawson hit back with a clever send-up of one
of his rival's greatest works, a nine-stanza effort that Lawson titled,
'The Overflow of Clancy'. With the lovely rhyming couplets that
Paterson fans so greatly appreciated in the real 'Clancy', Lawson's
parody told of a fancy Sydney man about town enjoying drinks
and girls at bars while a bush traveller endures a wretched night
in the rain:

And the pub hath friends to meet him and between the acts
    they treat him
While he's swapping 'fairy twisters' with the 'girls behind
    their bars',
And he sees a vista splendid when the ballet is extended
And at night he's in his glory with the comic op'ra stars.

I am sitting very weary, on a log before a dreary
Little fire that's feebly hissing 'neath a heavy fall of rain,

And the wind is cold and nipping and I curse the ceaseless
  dripping
As I slosh around for wood to start the embers up again . . .

The literary stoush was a sensation. Other writers joined in,
all taking Lawson's side in painting the bush in bleak but realistic
colours. It was wonderful stuff and the readers loved it. In a contest
that was more good-natured than many thought, Paterson fought
a lone battle to defend the romance of the bush against his critics.
On 10 October, he had the final word with 'An Answer to Various
Bards', which poked fun at the gloom of Lawson and his supporters:

With their dreadful, dismal stories of the Overlander's camp
How his fire is always smoky, and his boots are always damp

Paterson's reply to the bards referred to Lawson as 'The sad and
soulful poet with a graveyard of his own'. It was a powerful
description of the talented, troubled Lawson but showing the rivalry
was a friendly affair, Paterson also offered an olive branch to his
fellow poet:

But that ends it, Mr Lawson, and it's time to say goodbye,
So we must agree to differ in all friendship, you and I.

When he reflected on the duel almost fifty years later, Paterson
declared it a draw: 'So that was that, I think Lawson put his case
better than I did, but I had the better case, so the honours (or
dishonours) were fairly equal. An undignified affair in the end, but
it was a case of "root hog or die".'

Meanwhile, Lawson continued his 'prospecting on foot' and
Paterson remained, literally, on horseback. He had met an English
cavalry officer who introduced him to polo and 'we took to the game
like ducks to the water'. Paterson loved the thrill of the sport and was

very good at it. He also appreciated the connections it brought in society. He kept several ponies and captained the Sydney Polo Club to memorable wins. The matches attracted a better class of spectator and the twenty-eight-year-old Paterson undoubtedly enjoyed the attention his prowess on the ground attracted from young women. In May 1892, the *Australian Star* reported that Paterson played a game at Sydney's Rosehill and 'amongst the onlookers were a great many ladies, and it is easily to be seen that polo will be a favourite game amongst the gentler sex'.

Sports remained his passion, and polo was his favourite game. This love of the game led to the creation of one of his most popular works, 'The Geebung Polo Club', which got its first public reading in the little Snowy Mountains town of Cooma in southern New South Wales after a team from Sydney was invited to Cooma to play the locals in 1893. Among the Sydney players was A.B. Paterson, who was mounted on a splendid grey pony, named Snowy. The *Goulburn Evening Penny Post* reported that the match, on Saturday 6 May, attracted plenty of interest and that Paterson 'played splendidly throughout'. The paper also had high praise for Paterson's horse: 'The way in which Snowy followed the ball and left his pursuers behind was a treat to witness.' The *Post* also cheerfully reported that A.B. Paterson and 'The Banjo' were one and the same, yet the news did not spread for a while and The Banjo remained largely anonymous.

With the help of Paterson and his trusty Snowy, the Sydney side won the match by two goals to one. That night, a banquet was held at Cooma's Prince of Wales Hotel and, after dinner, Paterson stood to recite a 'jingle' that he had written in Sydney just a few weeks earlier. The poem was called 'The Geebung Polo Club', and, with typical modesty, Paterson said years later that it had 'outlasted much better work'. As usual, he was too hard on himself.

'The Geebung Polo Club' was a rollicking, funny tale about a rough mob of polo players from the bush who took on a team of toffs from the city—the Cuff and Collar team. The match was a bloodbath. It was so fierce that one spectator broke his leg simply by watching on, and at the end of the game, the score was drawn and all of the players were dead. The poem finished by revealing that the players' ghosts continued the battle on moonlit evenings:

'Till the terrified spectator rides like blazes to the pub–
He's been haunted by the spectres of the Geebung Polo Club.

This jaunty little ditty went down a treat with the players from Cooma and Sydney as they toasted the success of their game that night at the Prince of Wales Hotel. It was with remarkable foresight that Paterson had created the 'long and wiry natives' of Geebung and the 'cultivated' Cuff and Collar team prior to the Cooma match, but no doubt the worthies of both teams in Cooma that night took great delight in hearing themselves brought to life (and death) in Paterson's breezy yarn. Cheers and applause surely rang out as the poet finished his recital. The players and supporters had been treated to something special—but perhaps nobody in the pub that night knew they were in the presence of one of Australia's greatest ever poets.

*

As the final shots were being fired in the 'battle of the bards', and while Barty Paterson was living it up on the polo field, Henry Lawson had rolled up his swag to experience the 'awful desolation' of the flatlands out the back of Bourke. For that, he had his drinking problem to thank. Henry had been drinking heavily in those exciting days of the early 1890s. Soon his friends, already used to seeing him self-destruct, knew that something had to be done before it was too late.

One of his new friends was the writer and labour man, Edwin Brady, editor of the *Australian Workman*. They met after Brady 'lifted' one of Lawson's poems without authorisation or payment. When Henry went to the *Workman* office to remonstrate with Brady, a lifelong friendship was formed. They discovered they shared interests in poetry and politics and soon repaired to a pub where they bonded over threepenny glasses of beer, broken biscuits and small squares of cheese. From then on, as Brady recalled, they would meet many times to drink and discuss poetry and politics in an Australia that 'starves its poets and erects statues to their memories'.

Meanwhile, Archibald of *The Bulletin* was becoming increasingly worried about Henry who was turning up at the office with the smell of stale beer on his breath and tobacco juice running down his jaw. Archibald knew something needed to be done and in August or September, he enlisted the help of Edwin Brady to save Henry from himself.

The answer lay in the bush. Although Lawson wrote with compassion and feeling about the country and its people, he had probably never been further west than Bathurst and certainly no further out than Dubbo. Archibald decided to send Lawson to the real outback to see if it would straighten him out. A change of environment might give him a chance to shrug off the demons that tormented him in the city, and, besides, Archibald knew that Lawson wrote best of what he knew. A stint in the bush might not only be the salvation of Lawson, it would also provide some great copy for the paper. Using Brady as an intermediary, Archibald presented Lawson with £5, a one-way train ticket to Bourke in far north-western New South Wales, and a directive to find some stories truly of the outback.

It was not an assignment that Lawson relished. He preferred to remain with his friends in the familiar surrounds of Sydney, especially the hotels around Lower George Street. But Archibald, who was a true writer's editor and a big-hearted humanist, would not take no for an answer. He was so determined Lawson should board the train to Bourke that he sent two *Bulletin* staffers to Redfern Station to see him off, on or about 20 September 1892. One of those staffers was the irascible editor of *The Bulletin*'s esteemed Red Pages, A.G. Stephens.

Perhaps more than anyone else, it was Alfred Stephens who really understood what it meant to send the befuddled and bedraggled Henry Lawson alone into the outback. As the train pulled away from the station in a clanking cloud of steam and smoke, Stephens saw it carrying a man into a world he was utterly unprepared for: 'Here was this unfortunate towny [*sic*],' he wrote, 'deaf and shy and brooding, sent with a railway ticket and a few spare shillings to carry his swag through the unknown where he knew nobody.'

Lawson was all of these things, and not least a 'towny'. Apart from an unhappy childhood on the western slopes of the Great Dividing Range, he had little first-hand experience of life outside the city. Crowded, boozy Sydney would always be home. Yet he had a visceral connection to the bush—a place he saw as hard and dry and weighed under by hardship and imminent failure—and he cared deeply for the people who lived there. He rejoiced in their mateship, the triumph of humanity forged in toil and deprivation. The workers of the bush were part of 'the cause'. With £5 in his pocket, he was going to meet them—and it would produce some of the best work of his life.

At first it was exciting to see the last of the suburbs give way to the countryside as Lawson's train chugged steadily west towards the mountains. But after the train crested the ranges and rolled into the emptiness, Lawson began to find the scenes that flashed by his window stultifying and slightly depressing. The west was blasted by yet another drought—one that would drag on until it became the worst ever recorded—and the endless landscape of tired eucalypts and parched yellow grasslands was broken only by a series of small rail-side towns, each seeming dusty, and tired and depressingly alike.

When the train passed Dubbo, the last of the foothills faded and the outback stretched out, endless and hard and flat. The soil was a rich, sandy red that glared back at the deep blue dome of the sky. The trees were smaller now and more hunched over, and the settlements were farther apart. Jotting down these scenes in a notebook, Lawson observed 'the least horrible spot in the bush—in a dry season—is where the bush isn't—where it has been cleared away and a crop is trying to grow'.

The train picked up and dropped off bushmen at each stop. Lawson, who always accorded the bushman a capital B, took the opportunity to chat with them. He thought most of them hated the bush. He met a braggart who claimed to have been everywhere and argued with a shearer about how many sheep a man could shear in a day. He came to the conclusion that 'Bushmen are the biggest liars that ever the Lord created'.

Lawson arrived in Bourke at about five o'clock on the afternoon of 21 September. He was pleasantly surprised to find a welcoming town, a place of wide streets lined with gracious buildings of brick with iron roofs that reflected the afternoon sun in a blinding flash. He got a room at the Great Western Hotel—a labour pub where he would find kindred spirits—and that night he wrote to his aunt, Emma Brooks, in Sydney. Bourke was nicer than he had expected, he said, but the bush that lay in between was 'horrible'. This gave him a chance to score a private point in his 'battle of the bards' with Paterson when he added: 'I was right and Banjo wrong.'

Henry Lawson spent the next nine months in and around Bourke. It was a time that brought him into the world of the swagman, the shearer, the bullocky and the drover more than ever before. It did not cure his alcoholism nor mend his depression but it did inspire great writing and gave him a friendship that lasted a lifetime. During this western exile, Lawson even met a squatter he liked and respected—but none of it changed his opinion of the harshness and hopelessness of the bush.

*

Bourke sprawled out in neatly planned squares radiating from a bend in the Darling River. A towering wharf of red gum hung over the crook of the bend, its cranes and cables tending to a fleet of riverboats that plied the green-brown waters far below. In town, bullock drays rolled slowly along the wide streets and on the horizon camel trains driven by 'Afghans'—men from the east with strange names and even stranger customs—shimmered like mirages from another world. A bustling place, Bourke gave an impression of solidity, even elegance, as if in defiance of the unforgiving lands that enclosed it. The Metropolis of the West, some called it, a place of promise in the middle of nowhere.

The town was not without its attractions. Importantly to Lawson, there were no less than nineteen pubs. There were also many large stores, several bakeries and butchers, a Cobb & Co depot, three churches, a billiard room and even a fish and oyster shop that somehow sold its salty delicacies brought in from the sea 800 hot and dry kilometres to the east.

Lawson, who had carried his paint brushes from Sydney, found work as a casual painter. He wasted little time in connecting with the town's powerful union men and he wrote some political poems for *The Western Herald*, one of two local papers. But his exile did nothing to stop his drinking. A week after his arrival, a couple of barmaids 'as cunning as the devil' sent him to bed very drunk. In a letter to his aunt, he blamed the barmaids for his inebriation and although he vowed it would not happen again, inevitably, it did. But while Bourke did not solve his problems, it did provide inspiration for his pen. One of his most powerful poems, simply entitled 'Bourke', showed him in all his brilliance and despair:

> No sign that green grass ever grew in scrubs that blazed
>   beneath the sun;
> The plains were dust in Ninety-two, that baked to bricks in
>   Ninety-one.
> On glaring iron roofs of Bourke, the scorching, blinding
>   sandstorms blew,
> And there was nothing beautiful in Ninety-one and
>   Ninety-two.

Few of the townsfolk knew that the lean young house painter with the large, drooping moustache and the sad eyes was Henry Lawson, the famous poet of *The Bulletin*. The union men knew though. They knew him as one of them, a fellow warrior for the Cause. They also knew that in the political struggle 'nothing hits like rhyme' and they were quick to utilise Lawson as a weapon. In September Lawson wrote the first of a series of political verses for the progressively minded *Herald*. The poems were potent tools for the union cause but they paid only pocket money to the author, and the painting work was sporadic. Soon Henry was broke again. The £5 given to him by Archibald had long since disappeared in the town's bars and while a man could live for the Cause, he could not live on it. It was time to fulfil his mission to go 'on the wallaby'.

His chance came after he met a young man named Jim Gordon in November. Like Lawson, the eighteen-year-old budding bush poet was in Bourke to gain experience of the back country. Their meeting on a Bourke street on that hot spring day began a lifelong friendship, one that was cemented by an adventure along the hot and dusty roads at the 'back 'o Bourke'. Henry and Jim were about to learn what it really meant to carry a swag to an outback shearing shed.

On 24 November, Lawson and Gordon rolled up their swags and set out on foot, following the winding Darling River downstream towards the big shearing shed at Toorale Station, 60 kilometres to the south-west. Toorale, on the junction of the Darling and Warrego rivers, was a sprawling T-shaped shed with fifty-six stands to strip the fleece from thousands of sheep to be dispatched downstream by riverboat to Adelaide. Their union mates had secured Lawson and his young companion jobs as rouseabouts, but neither really knew what to expect when they arrived. They would learn on the job.

Toorale was typical of the big sheds scattered across the western plains. Each was a major centre of industry during the busy shearing season, attracting men who walked or rode the dusty tracks from job to job. The sheds had their own rules and hierarchy. The day might start with the breakfast bell at half-past six—sometimes a quick shearing run was completed even before breakfast was eaten—and the men would work until dark five and a half days a week, bent over the sheep and clipping away the wool with hand-operated shears. At some advanced stations, such as Toorale, the recent installation of steam-powered shears and electric lighting made the job infinitely more efficient, but by any measure it was tough work.

A shearer could earn twenty shillings per hundred sheep. Rouseabouts and general hands like Henry and Jim might earn only that amount for a full week. Penalties applied to those who got the job wrong. Cutting a sheep would incur a fine at many sheds. At some, a shearer might even be penalised for putting a knee or foot on the sheep, and, in a few cases, a man could be instantly sacked for drinking alcohol. If this last strict rule applied at Toorale then it would have been a hardship for poor Henry, yet good for his health.

Saturday afternoons and Sundays were times of rest when men could lounge around in the shade of the shed or a tall tree while the sheep complained in their pens. Hawkers in covered wagons set up camps nearby, selling necessities and little luxuries to the shearers and shed hands. Tucker was prepared by the shed's cook—a sought-after position. The shed was a democratic place and the cook was elected by the men. He would prepare food for separate messes—one for the shearers and another for the rouseabouts and shedhands. The cook's job was well paid but he risked being blamed bitterly if the food did not come up to scratch. Thankfully, in most cases the food was abundant and sometimes quite palatable, especially if you liked mutton. Otherwise, little treats could be bought from the station—flour, sugar and tea were readily available but a hungry man might be lucky enough to buy apples or raisins or a plug of tobacco. Women were rare and unwelcome visitors to the sheds, their arrival heralded by the hot and sweaty shearers with the warning call, 'Ducks on the pond!'

Henry and Jim arrived at Toorale near the end of the season. They were immediately put to work 'picking up', or gathering the shorn fleeces and placing them on the classers' table. It was hot and tiring work for men not used to it. Lawson did not enjoy his first experience among the rough and tumble men of the shearing shed although it provided him with excellent material.

Isolated from the other men because of his partial deafness—and perhaps enduring enforced sobriety—Henry was moody and withdrawn during his time at Toorale. At night, as the other men chattered and argued in their huts, Henry lay awake in his bunk staring at the cobwebbed ceiling or writing or dreaming up verses until it was late enough to go to sleep. But while he was never truly one of the men, Henry did gain from them important insights into the sacred concept of mateship. It was a concept he held dear. Jim Gordon later said of his friend: 'He was a stalwart mate, generous and unselfish, and ever ready and willing to take more than his own share of the hardships—and God knows there were plenty.'

The season at Toorale was winding up in mid-December and Henry and Jim returned to Bourke for Christmas. But their travels together were not yet over. In searing heat, they set out a few days after Christmas for a three-week walk to the hard-bitten settlement of Hungerford on the Queensland border. To get there they would have to cross more than 200 kilometres of some of the hardest and driest country in the world.

That afternoon, they crossed the Darling River at North Bourke and set out across Wild Turkey Plain—a sun-baked expanse of red earth and hardy mulga scrub. Carrying their water bottles and swags and batting away flies, they tramped the weary miles with the sun blazing over their heads and the red earth burning beneath their worn boots. At night they lit fires of camel and horse dung to drive away the mosquitoes before unrolling their swags to sleep beneath a million brilliant stars in a coal-black sky. As the sun rose each morning they packed up their gear and trudged wearily on to the next waterhole or isolated wayside station.

Other lonely wayfarers shared the road—dusty swagmen trekking from station to station, or teamsters, cursing the heat and the flies as they drove their wool-laden drays along the rutted tracks. Occasionally a mail coach clattered by, horses snorting and sweating as they drew the wagons over the searing roads of red dirt. The drought had scoured the landscape of moisture and man and beast alike wilted under the relentless sun. It was every bit as fierce as Henry had imagined. In a letter to his aunt in Sydney, Henry summed up the hardships he saw with typical gloominess: 'You have no idea of the horrors of the country out here. Men tramp and live like dogs . . .'

There is something romantic, yet also sad and rather aimless about the wanderings of Henry and his young mate Jim Gordon through these parched lands. A.G. Stephens, who seemed to have a knack for summing up the hopelessness of Henry's predicaments, later described Lawson's trek as being 'like a journey of a damned soul trudging through Purgatory'. Yet this seemingly pointless journey gave Lawson the insight he needed into the country that he both loved and hated. When it was over, he vowed never to return to the outback, but at least he could write about it as one who had been there.

Their arrival at Hungerford in mid-January was announced in much the same way as Lawson's arrival in Bourke—by the fierce glare of the sun from bleached iron roofs shining through the mulga scrub. Lawson's first impressions of Hungerford were under-whelming. The town, if it could be called that, straddled the border. A so-called rabbit-proof fence neatly dissected the main street but nobody had told the rabbits of the boundary that was supposed to contain them and they cheerfully hopped around on both sides of the fence. In a sketch, Lawson later wrote that Hungerford consisted of two houses and a humpy in New South Wales and five houses in Queensland. There were two pubs—both in Queensland—and neither could provide him with the glass of English ale he craved. 'I believe Burke and Wills found Hungerford,' Lawson wrote, 'and it's a pity that they did.'

Henry and Jim camped only a day or two in Hungerford before rolling up their swags and retracing their dusty steps back towards Bourke. It was on the return trip that Lawson accepted help from a man who made him alter his views of the ruling class. William

'Baldy' Davis, owner of Kerribree Station, gladly gave the travellers as much food as they could carry and threw in a £1 note to help them on their way back to Bourke. The generosity of Davis, who wore a wig to cover scars caused in a childhood scalding, inspired Henry to later write 'squatters are not all bad'.

Lawson and his young friend arrived back in Bourke in February, bonded by the tribulations of the road. It was time, however, for a parting of the ways. Jim soon left town to work at a remote station, while Henry remained for a short time in Bourke, working as a painter and fulfilling his duty to Archibald by writing for *The Bulletin*.

In June his exile came to end. He boarded a train for Sydney, still broke and still a drunk but a man who had walked in the shoes of the bushmen he wrote about. He felt no less pity for them and the burdens they carried were still on his shoulders as well as theirs, but at least he now understood them. He had worked and walked and drank with the tough men of the bush and had gained experience that he could never have found in Sydney's pubs. As his fellow poet Banjo Paterson admitted, Henry Lawson had done his prospecting on foot—and the experience he gained during those hard months in the west took him beyond writing about the shearers and swagmen and drovers and made him one of them. J.F. Archibald had got his £5 worth for this alone.

7
WALTZING MATILDA

Since the death of her husband, Rose Paterson and her youngest children had been living at Rockend with her mother and sister. 'Mama' was growing old but remained sprightly and actively involved in music, art and writing. Sister Emily—known in the family as 'Madam', supposedly because of her haughty manner—had become a devout Christian Scientist and worked at the asylum across the road from Rockend. A place of refuge, the cottage was a very feminine household that served as a gathering place for far-flung family members. But for Rose, now plagued by ill health, these final years at Gladesville were troubled.

Rose was just forty-four when she took the youngest children to Rockend, but a lifetime of self-sacrifice and worry had worn her out. Her chronic renal problems were worsened by heart palpitations and fainting fits. A doctor was called to treat her several times but her condition steadily declined. The end was sudden. On 24 February 1893, at the age of forty-eight, she collapsed and died a few hours later. Barty arranged that his mother be buried with her people at St Anne's churchyard at Ryde.

Rose did not live long enough to see her eldest son marry, although the engagement was still on at the time of her death. Barty seems to have genuinely loved Sarah. In 1891 he declared that love in a touching poem, 'As Long as Your Eyes are Blue'. A notable departure from his usual stock of bush ballads and political commentary, it spoke of his lover's kindly heart seen in her 'sweet blue eyes':

> For the locks may bleach, and the cheeks of peach
> May be reft of their golden hue;
> But mine own sweetheart, I shall love you still,
> Just as long as your eyes are blue.

It was perhaps the financial burden of caring for his ailing mother and youngest siblings that delayed his plans to marry, at least in the early years. By the time of his mother's death he was sharing lodgings at Wharf Road in Gladesville while supporting his brother Hamilton Howison and sisters Grace and Gwendoline at nearby Rockend. At seventeen, Hamilton was about to make his own way in the world but the girls were still children. Barty was close to his sisters and they adored him in return. There was no question that he would not support them, but he was not a rich man and the cost of their care came as a burden for a man thinking of taking a wife.

On the other hand, he managed to maintain an expensive interest in polo and racing, and kept several quality horses. It has been said anecdotally that when a young lady's father challenged him about his intentions towards his daughter, Paterson replied that he could not afford to wed. The father is supposed to have indignantly replied that if Paterson could afford to keep polo ponies he could certainly afford a wife. Whether this is true or not the years drifted by and there was no sign of a wedding. The sweet promise of life-long devotion in 'As Long as Your Eyes Are Blue', no matter how truly meant, proved hollow.

It was only after a deeply embarrassing incident in 1895—some have called it a scandal—that Paterson's engagement to Sarah Riley finally ended. The bitter termination of the engagement also ended the relationship between Sarah and her close friend Christina Macpherson. It left all three with deep regrets that they never publicly discussed. But it also left Australia with words and music that would ring out in pubs, on farms, on battlefields and in schoolrooms across the nation and around the world. At the cost of a broken love affair, an old folk tune heard at a race meeting and some scribbled words on a piece of paper combined to create a song that helped to define the essence of being Australian for generations to come.

*

The year of 1894 had been a busy one for Paterson. Early in the year, he met with George Robertson from the publishing house Angus & Robertson to discuss a book deal. The result was the release in 1895 of the handsomely bound volume, *The Man From Snowy River and Other Verses*, which proved to be an instant hit. More than 1200 copies printed in the first run quickly sold out and the book was reprinted and reprinted again, selling a massive 7000 copies. The book's author, unmasked as Andrew Barton Paterson, was about to become a household name.

He was a feature at sporting events throughout the latter half of 1894, regularly riding with the Sydney Hunt Club or playing polo for Sydney. In October, he won a race on his polo mount Snowy. That day he also raced his bay mare Bellbird, and his roan mare Blue Bonnett. He finished the sporting year riding Albert in a steeplechase at the Australian Jockey Club's summer meeting on 29 December.

The new year started just as busily. There was more polo in the summer and hurdle racing in autumn. In one race, his mare Bellbird came down and broke a shoulder. The hunt season opened in May and Paterson, on board The Ace, joined 200 other sporting folk in the first of a series of hunts on most weekends over the next six months. One of his major events of spring was a point-to-point steeplechase in October. It was also in October that he attended a coming out party for a well-bred young lady named Alice Walker, who would eventually become his wife. First, though, came the difficult matter of the increasingly troubled engagement between Barty and Sarah Riley.

While Barty was riding to hounds in autumn, Sarah had left Melbourne on the steamer *Wodonga*, bound for Rockhampton, Queensland, and from there inland to the western pastoral town of Winton. There, Sarah's family was in partnership with the fabulously wealthy Chirnside family in a station named Vindex. Her arrival in Winton warranted mentions in the local papers and in late May she was reported to be a guest at the Winton Races. The women's pages noted she looked elegant in a 'very neat grey drillette costume and sailor's hat'.

In June, Sarah's friend Christina Macpherson left Melbourne— also on the *Wodonga*—bound for Winton, where she would join her brothers at the family station, Dagworth. She would also see Sarah, perhaps at a house party that was planned for Dagworth. It would be a welcome break for Christina. Shy, bespectacled and unworldly, she had been through a difficult period, having nursed her terminally ill mother throughout 1894. Christina travelled with her father, Ewen, and her sister, Jean, who was due to marry at Vindex in April of the following year. In the winter of 1895, as

Christina sailed north and Sarah continued a round of family and social outings in Queensland, Barty Paterson remained in Sydney, living the good life.

*

Christina Macpherson—Chris to her family and friends— earned her first place in Australian history when she was a baby. It was on 8 April 1865—when Christina was ten months old—that the notorious bushranger Daniel 'Mad Dan' Morgan raided the Macpherson family's station at Peechelba in northern Victoria and took everyone there hostage. Tall and heavily built, with a dark beard and a hooked nose, Morgan was widely feared in the pastoral districts on both sides of the Murray River and, when he raided Peechelba Station, the people he took prisoner had every reason to fear for their lives. But because little Christina cried out in her sleep that night, Morgan's blood-soaked career came to an end and several lives might have been saved.

Morgan had been on the run for almost two years when he raided Peechelba. His lawless reign over north-eastern Victoria and southern New South Wales had started when he badly wounded a police magistrate in a gunfight in August 1863. He followed this outrage with a series of raids on stations and mail coaches. Morgan delighted in robbing squatters, especially those he believed to have been hard on their employees. Soon, there was a price of £200 on his head. But by hiding in the bush and using a craggy outcrop of rocks as a lookout, he evaded capture, only emerging from the scrub to rob and plunder.

He went from Daniel Morgan to 'Mad Dan' in June 1864 when he raided Round Hill Station near Culcairn in southern New South Wales. After bailing up the station hands and their families, he lost his temper and shot a worker through the hand. Remorseful for a moment, the erratic Morgan sent another station hand, John McLean, to get a doctor. Moments later, Morgan changed his mind again and chased McLean down, shooting him in the back. The young man died that afternoon.

Less than five days after killing McLean, Morgan shot dead Sergeant David Maginnity near the hill town of Tumbarumba. The bushranger fled into the bush and the reward on his head rose to £1000. In September a party of police sent to catch him was fired upon near the town of Henty and Sergeant Thomas Smyth was hit in the shoulder and died later that month from his wound. Morgan claimed the responsibility for firing the fatal shot.

With so much blood on his hands, Morgan was more dangerous than ever. Throughout the first three months of 1865, he led six robberies on mail coaches or stations. Sometimes courtly and polite to his victims, he could also fly into murderous rages and his reputation for violent madness was cemented. He seemed to operate with impunity, prompting taunts in the New South Wales press that the authorities were incapable of catching him. In Victoria, there was a smug prediction that Mad Dan would meet his match if he dared to cross the Murray River. In April, the Victorians were proved right when Morgan raided the Macpherson home at Peechelba.

The bushranger quickly took control of the homestead, rounding up the Macphersons and their workers, and ordering them all into the dining room. He made himself at home, requesting refreshments from the kitchen and politely asking the women of the house to entertain their fellow prisoners on the piano. Morgan was in a courtly mood, but nobody in the room doubted he could explode at the slightest provocation. Late in the evening, he locked his male prisoners in a secure room and permitted some of the women to retire to bed. But when baby Christina was heard crying loudly in her bedroom, Morgan allowed a nursemaid to attend to the child. What he did not know was the station's co-owner, George Rutherford, lived in a house just a few hundred metres from the main homestead.

Instead of attending to little Christina, the nurse crawled out of the bedroom window and rushed to the Rutherford home to raise the alarm. Then she hurried back the way she had come, crawling back through the window and settling the baby. As she re-entered the dining room, the bushranger was none the wiser that his hours were now numbered. The homestead was soon surrounded by police and armed volunteers who watched the house until dawn. In the early morning light, when Morgan ventured into the yard to catch a horse, he was shot in the back and slumped to the ground. Aggrieved at the manner of his ambush, he complained: 'Why did you not give me a chance? Why did you not challenge me first?'

He died a few hours later. His beard was shorn off as a souvenir, his head was severed and sent to Melbourne for anatomical studies and his mutilated body put on public display in Wangaratta. Thanks to a crying baby, Mad Dan Morgan's violent reign was over.

About thirty years later, Christina Macpherson played a key role in a more significant moment in history when she partnered with Banjo Paterson to create Australia's most famous folk song, 'Waltzing Matilda'. The creation of the song sparked debate for years afterwards. For many years, the source of its music was unconfirmed and its words dissected, probed and disassembled. Was it a meaningless little ditty about the death of a sheep-stealing swagman or was it a cry of defiance against a greedy squatter and his henchmen, the troopers? These questions are a matter of speculation. Even the date of the song's composition is not known although it is widely accepted that it was written some time in 1895. If so, the date of its creation can be narrowed down by following the movements of the main players in that year.

Portrait of Christina Macpherson, ca. 1900. *Photograph courtesy National Library of Australia.*

Travel records and social jottings for 1895 show that Barty Paterson, Christina Macpherson and Sarah Riley can only have been together in western Queensland in the second half of the year. Sarah arrived there in May and Christina in June. Barty was busy on the polo field or hunting with the hounds on almost every weekend. But there are two windows throughout the second half of the year where his name is not mentioned in connection to sporting or social events in Sydney, leaving just two opportunities for travel—a period of four weeks in August and a similar period in November. It is most likely that 'Waltzing Matilda' was written at either of these times—yet one small entry in a railway ledger leaves open the intriguing possibility that Banjo, Christina and Sarah were all together at Dagworth Station, not in 1895, but in the stiflingly hot January of 1896.

The many unanswered questions about 'Waltzing Matilda' result from the controversy surrounding its origins. Something unsavoury happened at the time the song was composed but it was never publicly discussed by those involved. Some have called it a scandal, but it may have been no more than a misunderstanding, a case of inappropriate behaviour made worse by a sheltered young woman's naivety, and a suave and sophisticated man's underestimation of the emotions he had aroused. Suffice to say, by the social standards of the time, it was enough to create a lifetime of ill-feeling.

What is known is that during her visit to Dagworth, Christina Macpherson played a little-known Scottish folk tune on a type of autoharp known as a zither. The melody caught the ear of Banjo Paterson and inspired him to write words to go with the tune. He had no knowledge of music but Christina was an accomplished drawing room pianist. There was no piano at Dagworth but when Christina picked up the zither to play a marching tune she remembered by ear, she recreated a musical score that would be forever associated with Australia. Without Christina, Australians would never have sung along to the tale of the swagman who camped under the coolibah tree and drowned in the billabong. For her, and for Banjo, it was a monumental legacy but for both it came at a high personal price.

*

Paterson's visit to Dagworth followed an unsettled time in the pastoral industry. When Ewen Macpherson established Dagworth Station in 1883, the grass grew in a knee-high swathe across the western plains, and rivers of wealth seemed certain to flow forever into the squatters' pockets. But when drought inevitably returned, the creeks ran dry and the rich pastures were burnt away. Then, when the wool bubble burst, even the greatest of the land barons felt the pinch. The lesser princelings—those with less capital to fall back upon—felt it harder. Among them were the Macphersons who by the mid-1880s had fallen into an uncomfortable level of debt.

The squatters first tried to meet this squeeze in 1891 by cutting pay rates, sparking the great shearers' strike. At that time, an angry Henry Lawson warned in 'Freedom on the Wallaby' that the dispute would 'boomerang'. He was proved right three years later when the squatters again tried to employ non-union shearers on lower rates. It sparked the second round of the same fight. This time the strike was driven by union 'diehards', mostly in the Winton area of Queensland, and while it was not on the same scale as the 1891 strike, it was a significant battle in a violent class war that pitted workers against employers. In echoes of the first strike, thousands of workers laid down their shears and set up new strike camps and millions of sheep waited unshorn.

The pastoralists tried to bring in 'free' workers to do the job of the strikers. Equally desperate, the unionists took on the scabs, intimidating and threatening them at railheads. Men were bashed, shearing sheds torched and fences flattened. In reply, the pastoralists used the newspapers and the police to harass and undermine the strikers. The situation was deadlocked. Something had to give, and in August 1894 it came to a violent, anarchic head at a station on the Darling River in western New South Wales.

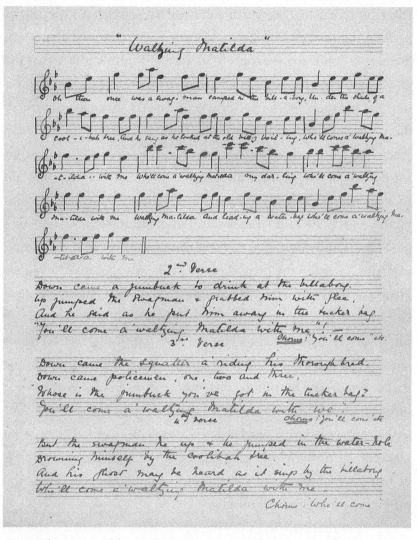

Original music and lyrics for 'Waltzing Matilda', in the handwriting of Christina Macpherson. *Image courtesy National Library of Australia.*

The owners of Tolarno Station were facing disaster. More than 400 unionists had blocked approaches to the station, driving away scabs and intimidating any who supported the pastoralists. With the shearing season almost at an end, the owners needed to break the blockade.

They decided to do it not on land, but on water. They would use the great inland highways—the west-flowing rivers—to bring non-union workers into the station and get the sheep shorn. It was a dangerous gamble that led to Australia's first and last act of inland piracy.

The paddle steamer *Rodney* embarked from Echuca on the Murray River early in August 1894. Bound for Tolarno Station with fifty non-union shearers on board, she was captained by Jimmy Dickson—a man particularly hated by the unionists because he had transported non-union workers in the 1891 strike. If the pastoralists hoped to keep the *Rodney*'s journey a secret, they were immediately disappointed. The boat had barely cleared the towering red-gum wharf at Echuca when unionists gathered on the riverbanks to hurl stones and insults at the *Rodney* as her single side wheel drove her towards a devastating confrontation.

The *Rodney*—built at a cost of £5000 and described as one of the finest boats on the river—churned her way downstream, smoke puffing from her stack as she ran swiftly with the current. River travel was the fastest way to reach remote inland destinations, but even the *Rodney* at full steam could not outpace the telegraph and, when she reached Swan Hill, more angry unionists had gathered to try to stop her. There were heated protests, but attempts to board and capture the free workers failed. Two days after leaving Swan Hill, the *Rodney* and her controversial cargo nosed their way into the Darling and powered upstream against the current, and against the wishes of thousands of angry men.

The boat reached Pooncarie without incident on the morning of Saturday 25 August, even though unionists had gathered at a camp nearby. But that evening, when the *Rodney* was tied up at a woodpile on the riverbank, the skipper Dickson received alarming news. Striking shearers a few kilometres further upstream had strung a wire across the river to snag the boat and stop the scabs from reaching their destination. Dickson decided to go no further that night, and he steered the boat into a billabong surrounded by a swamp of mud and reeds. The boat was tied to a tree but steam was kept up to the boilers in case a quick getaway was needed. Prudently, the captain assigned four men to the watch. He might have retired to his bunk that night confident his boat was in a good defensive position but, if so, he had underestimated the ferocity of his opponents.

In the dark hour after three o'clock in the morning, attackers with faces masked or daubed in river mud splashed their way through the murky waters of the swamp and stormed the *Rodney*. At the same time, other strikers rowed rapidly across the river to attack the vessel from the other side. On board, the watchmen sounded the alarm and a man rushed to release the rope that tethered the steamer to a tree. But he was met and stopped by an armed raider who threatened to shoot him. Unaware that the rope remained uncut, the captain rushed to the wheelhouse and ordered full steam astern but the boat remained firmly tied to the tree. As *The Barrier Miner* reported five days later, the fight for the *Rodney* was soon over:

> The steamer was then boarded by a few men, who took possession of her. The crowd subsequently swarmed in like ants . . . The first batch, after a struggle, held the captain. The others numbered 150, disguised and in gangs and according to one statement, hunted the 'free labourers' off and threw their swags into the swamp. Another gang, according to the same statement, looted the boat of portable goods, while a third gang poured kerosene over the vessel from stern to stern.

The passengers and crew leapt for their lives as the attackers struck matches and the *Rodney* burst into flames. She burned for six hours, drifting from bank to bank, as the attackers cheered and sang in the red firelight. Finally, the flames reached the waterline and the boat sank into the murky water of the river. The wreck of the *Rodney* lies there still. When the river falls, the rusted ribs of her hull emerge from the mud like the fossilised skeleton of a dinosaur. After more than a century, the wreck is mute testament to a time so volatile that ordinary workers became pirates and the rule of law fell victim to class warfare.

The piracy of the *Rodney* caused a furore. The newspapers declared it a 'union atrocity' and a 'diabolical outrage'. Worse, *The Brisbane Courier* feared it was 'the first instalment of an endeavour to bring about Socialism in our time'. In Melbourne, *The Argus* described it as an insurrection, and in Sydney, parliament was told the shearers were 'armed and desperate ruffians'. The resolve of the pastoralists and government was strengthened. Police and armed civilians were deployed to sheds to protect free workers. If anything, the destruction of the *Rodney* served only to harden opinions against the unionists—but still they fought on.

Two weeks later, police shot two unionists at a station near Wilcannia. The papers said the police had behaved with great courage to prevent a riot, but the union said its men were unarmed and shot without warning. It was in this environment that eight men appeared at the Broken Hill Court in September over the attack on the *Rodney*. Dozens of witnesses came forward to swear the men were innocent, and, partly because the pirates had been disguised, all eight defendants were acquitted. It was a major victory for the unionists, who tried to press home the advantage by mounting more attacks on woolsheds.

While sensational events in New South Wales attracted the headlines, the angry core of the strike was again in Queensland, centred on the Winton district. The trouble had started at Oondooroo Station in July, when unionists tried to intimidate the first man willing to work on the lower rate. As radical union leaders began to gather around Winton, a handful of sheds were burnt and pastures and wool stores destroyed. The government responded by sending in troops against its own citizens. It seemed the newspapers' fears of an insurrection were not without foundation.

But by late August, the strike was starting to fizzle out and Dagworth Station remained unscathed. Nonetheless, Bob Macpherson was heavily in debt and he had 80,000 sheep to shear. Trouble was inevitable when he announced his flock would be shorn by free workers on the wages and conditions set by the Pastoralists Alliance. Well aware that he was playing with fire, Macpherson decided to begin the shearing on the morning of Monday 3 September, and damn the consequences.

Late on the night of 1 September, sixteen men gathered at a billabong next to the dry bed of the Diamantina River upstream of Dagworth. Among them were the radical unionist John Tierney and a strange loner named Samuel 'Frenchy' Hoffmeister—both notorious diehards from the 1891 strike. Gathering up their arms, they set out from the billabong for the short walk to the Dagworth shearing shed. In flood, the Diamantina becomes a vast, shallow lake that surges across the plain, 2 kilometres wide in places, but it was dry on that cloudy, moonless night and the strikers had no problem following the empty riverbed downstream towards Dagworth. Silently, they crept up on the shearing shed, planning to take it by surprise and burn it to the ground.

But Bob Macpherson and his brothers were expecting trouble. They had gathered men and arms, and, with the help of a single policeman, they were ready to defend the shed against attack. As the defenders slept lightly in a cottage, the strikers crept down the riverbed and into the cover of a dry creek. At about half-past twelve on Sunday morning, the raiders opened fire without warning. Macpherson and his men leapt from their beds and took up their weapons as bullets punched ragged holes in the shearing-shed walls.

Muzzle flashes punctured the darkness. A voice rang out from the creek bed: 'Come out with your hands up, you bastards, or die!' Then, as bullets whistled overheard, one of the raiders dashed from the creek with a tin of kerosene and a handful of wax matches. Moments later, the oily smell of the kerosene wafted through the shed and then a match flared. With a *whump!*, flames erupted and quickly took hold of the dry timbers, incinerating about 140 lambs that had been brought into the shed the night before. The Macphersons tried to douse the flames but could do little in the face of the gunfire from the creek. It began to rain lightly, but it was too late. The shed was now a wall of orange flame.

Mission accomplished, the attackers melted into the darkness and retraced their steps up the bed of the river. In the glaring light of the fire, Bob Macpherson could only watch as a big part of his livelihood went up in smoke.

A manhunt began the next day. The attackers were quickly traced back to the strike camp at nearby Kynuna. But that day, before the police could close in, 'Frenchy' Hoffmeister died of a bullet wound in controversial circumstances. He escaped the squatters' justice, but the strange manner of his death ensured his name lived on in history.

Earlier on that rainy morning, Hoffmeister had put his swag in a tent at the camp and after lunch he was seen burning some papers on a camp fire. A fellow striker heard him mutter: 'That done, I am satisfied.' Then Hoffmeister wandered away and moments later at least one gunshot rang out. Hoffmeister was found lying on the wet ground with a bullet wound to his head. One of the most dangerous unionists in the battle against the pastoralists was dead. It seemed clear that the man who had been responsible for violent, armed raids on multiple shearing sheds had taken his own life. But some of his fellow strikers did not believe it was suicide and, today, some still believe the real cause of the striking swagman's death—supposedly at the hands of the squatters—was covered up.

Those who believe Hoffmeister did not take his own life cite the absence of a suicide note and his actions in the hours before his death. Even with the police closing in, he had shown no sign of distress. Shortly before his death, he had asked a mate to cover his two saddles so they would not get wet in the rain—a strange precaution for a man who intended to kill himself. And, crucially, one of his mates swore that he had heard more than one shot ring out when Hoffmeister died. Yet the striking swagman had been shot just once. It was enough to fan suspicions of a sinister secret.

An inquest was held later that month and the findings were very clear. Hoffmeister had committed suicide. The cause of death was indisputable—a single bullet wound to the head. If any other shots were fired then none hit their target. But the bullet that killed Hoffmeister entered his head *through the roof of his mouth*. If he was killed by a second party then he can only have been overpowered and the muzzle of the gun forced into his mouth before the fatal shot was fired. It seems highly unlikely that the tough shearer could have been so easily overwhelmed so close to his mates and it is hard to disagree with the inquest's findings. Strange, radical Samuel Hoffmeister—a man described even by his friends as 'a bit barmy'—can only have died by his own hand.

*

There was no sign of these traumatic events as Barty Paterson travelled towards Dagworth in 1895. He was well aware of the attack on the shearing shed and of the death of Hoffmeister, but as he completed his journey—probably finishing the last leg in a station coach pulled by four horses—he was impressed by the positive sights he saw around him. Aware that thousands of sheep were lost during a previous drought, he was pleased to note that 'there was grass everywhere, beautiful blue grass and Mitchell grass with the sheep all fat and the buyers all busy'. It was an encouraging sight as his coach rolled through a landscape of red-brown earth, stunted mulga and tall coolibahs framed against 'jump-ups'—flat-topped rocky outcrops that grew out from the flatlands.

Paterson arrived at Dagworth to find a square homestead of stone with an iron roof and wide verandahs. Surrounded by cottages and sheds, it was the thriving centre of its own little community. It was either here at Dagworth Station, or at Vindex Station to the south-east, that he would be reunited with Sarah Riley. Soon it would be time to commit to marriage or call it off.

In the meantime, however, Paterson was keen to see his new surroundings. He rode the grassy plains with Bob Macpherson, listening intently to stories about the shearers' strike and the death of Hoffmeister. Macpherson also showed his guest stone weirs that had been built across the bed of the Diamantina to the north of the homestead. It might have been this visit to the water-giving weirs—known locally as 'overshots'—that prompted Macpherson to recount an incident that had occurred some five years earlier, when a swagman killed a Dagworth sheep near one of the waterholes. When the swagman was seen with the sheep, he leapt into the waterhole to escape, but drowned.

Perhaps this sad story created a little spark in Paterson's mind, and maybe a conversation a few days later triggered a flash of inspiration that completed the picture. That conversation was said to have been held when the Macphersons hosted a house party at the homestead for Paterson and their other guests, who included Christina Macpherson and probably Sarah Riley. According to several accounts, including one published by Peter and Sheila Forrest in *Banjo and Christina*, when the station overseer, a man named

Carter, joined the guests at the dinner table, Bob Macpherson asked: 'Well, Carter, what did you see today?'

Carter is said to have replied: 'Oh, nothing much, only a swagman waltzing matilda [carrying his swag] down by the river.'

It was a throwaway remark, a casual observation that could have been uttered on any station across the land, but as Bob Macpherson later recalled, Barty Paterson's reaction to these simple words was remarkable:

> A few minutes later Banjo repeated the words 'waltzing matilda' and became very animated. He reckoned he could write a poem about it. Everyone gathered around him and he wrote it then and there. Christina was a good musician and she set it to music that same night. A few days later we all went to Winton. We called at the old Aryshire pub and we sang the song there.

The words that Paterson penned that day were marginally different to those known to Australians today, but the song clearly tells the familiar story of the swagman camping by the waterhole:

> Oh, there once was a swagman camped in the billabongs,
> Under the shade of a Coolibah tree;
> And he sang as he looked at the old billy boiling,
> Who'll come a-waltzing Matilda with me.

The light-fingered swagman soon grabs a thirsty 'jumbuck'—a sheep—that has wandered down to the waterhole and 'put him away in his tucker bag', but then the squatter arrives on his thoroughbred with three troopers in tow:

> Up sprang the swagman and jumped in the waterhole,
> Drowning himself by the Coolibah tree;

And his voice can be heard as it sings in the billabongs,
Who'll come a-waltzing Matilda with me.

The music that Christina Macpherson played as Barty Paterson wrote the words alongside her was based on her memory of a tune she had heard at the Warrnambool Races in Victoria's Western District more than a year earlier. It was 25 April 1894 when the Warrnambool Brass Band played the melody, a 'march' version of old Scottish folk tune, 'Thou Bonnie Wood of Craigielea', at that country race meeting. Christina did not know the name of the piece, but she had no problem playing it from ear.

Paterson later said Christina played the zither while the Dagworth party was taking a journey in a 'four-in-hand coach', but this seems unlikely. At the same time, Paterson also claimed that Christina later married her father's business partner, Samuel McCall McCowan. In fact, it was her sister who married McCall McCowan and Christina never married at all, so Paterson's recollection of the creation of 'Waltzing Matilda' must be taken with some scepticism. It is possible that his memory was clouded by a lingering prick of conscience. After all, his collaboration with Christina may have been the final, cruellest blow to his relationship with Sarah Riley.

Whatever happened between Barty and Christina at Dagworth remains unknown, but it is easy to imagine the musician and writer huddled over the zither, their heads almost touching as the words and music began to meld together. Barty was handsome and charming, and he knew how to flatter a young lady. Shy and naïve Christina had little experience of men and she welcomed the attention from the suave Sydney poet. They might have laughed together at the joy of creating something special. Perhaps they touched hands and shared smiles as the notes tinkled out into the quiet Queensland night, and, for Christina, who was still mourning her mother, it would have been a moving moment.

All of this might have happened, or none of it, but at some stage during the composition of 'Waltzing Matilda' a line was crossed, sensibilities were outraged and Paterson's visit to Dagworth came to an abrupt end. So, too, did his engagement to Sarah Riley.

Paterson perhaps saw his collaboration with Christina as harmless and may have meant nothing by it. But Christina's brothers saw it very differently. In fact, family history strongly suggests the ill-feeling created was so intense that Paterson was angrily ordered to leave Dagworth in disgrace.

There is no evidence to show that Sarah Riley was at Dagworth when the song was written but it seems likely that she was there, on the invitation of her friend Christina. If so, it must have been tremendously humiliating to witness the closeness between her fiancé and best friend. And even if she was absent from Dagworth, it would not have taken long for the news to reach her at Vindex. Either way, it was the final straw that ended a strained relationship. After seeing her fiancé enjoying the attentions of other women for seven years, Sarah had had enough.

In September 2006, Christina's niece, Diana Ballieu, recorded an interview at her home in Toorak, Melbourne, with the National Library of Australia's Robyn Holmes. As a young woman, ninety-three-year-old Mrs Baillieu had been very close to Christina, whom she described as 'a very sweet aunt . . . [and] rather a shy little lady in a lot of ways'. Diana Baillieu believed that shy, unworldly Christina fell under Paterson's spell, leading to the bitter confrontation with the Macpherson brothers. She said:

> He [Paterson] was obviously a lady's man and he not only
> sort of cast an eye upon, a flirty eye upon Aunty Chris, and

124

she'd been so lonely and innocent, it's no wonder she sort of fell for him. He was obviously a very, very attractive man . . .

Although Christina never discussed the incident at Dagworth, Diana Baillieu never doubted that her aunt was devastated by the misunderstanding with Paterson, who was 'probably the only bloke that ever made eyes at her'. Nor did she doubt that the Macpherson brothers angrily told Paterson to leave their property and never return. If so, how humiliating it must have been for the well-bred Paterson and the two fine ladies, Christina and Sarah.

Poor Sarah suddenly found herself single at the age thirty-two, with little hope of finding a new husband. Her long wait was over and her patience had gone unrewarded. Regardless of whether anything had happened between Barty and Christina, Sarah had been treated poorly. In the words of Diana Baillieu more than a century later, Paterson's 'seven-year engagement to Sarah Riley was a touch much, wasn't it?'

Nonetheless, Sarah soon rallied. She remained in Queensland for several months, visiting some of the colony's best families. In early February 1896, she stayed at Emu Park near Rockhampton and, on the twentieth, she was listed as a passenger on the mail train from Rockhampton 'to the west'. By then, the scorching heat of January had given way to torrential rain, causing widespread flooding in central Queensland. Sarah probably spent the next three weeks with her family at Vindex. Perhaps she even returned to Dagworth to make whatever amends she could with the Macphersons. Sarah, of course, was blameless in the Dagworth incident, but her friendship with Christina never recovered. On 11 March Sarah was back in Rockhampton, where she boarded the *Arawatta* for Sydney then Melbourne. That strange encounter at Dagworth Station ended in mystery and sadness—but it also left Australia with its greatest folk song, 'Waltzing Matilda'.

Australians have wondered about the origins of the song ever since. Was it simply a little ditty based on a station yarn about a sheep-stealing swagman? Or did it have deeper political roots, springing from the violence of the shearers' strike and the mysterious death of the rebellious Samuel Hoffmeister?

In later years, the theory of 'Waltzing Matilda' as an allegory of class struggle gained traction. It is true that Paterson usually wrote about ordinary folk and Hoffmeister's story might well have caught his fancy. But the poet's radical youth was now behind him and he was already a man of the establishment. It is hard to imagine him eulogising a red-ragger like Hoffmeister. In fact, Paterson only ever referred briefly to Hoffmeister, saying in a wireless broadcast in the 1930s that the 'woolshed at Dagworth was burnt down and a man was picked up dead'. He went on to say that the Macphersons held no malice towards the strikers and that he, Paterson, had seen the Macphersons 'handing out champagne through pub windows to these very shearers'. These are not the memories of a man who had supposedly written a protest song based on violence, arson and death.

Just as there was no one Man from Snowy River, and Clancy of the Overflow was based on an anonymous bushman with an unpaid debt, there was no sole swagman who 'waltzed matilda' for Paterson at Dagworth. The swagman of the song probably owed at least part of his creation to the sheep thief who drowned at Dagworth and was otherwise an amalgamation of the countless men who walked from station to station in search of work. It is likely that Paterson only ever saw 'Waltzing Matilda' as another bush tale, partly based perhaps on the stories he heard and the sights he saw during his sad, eventful visit to western Queensland in 1895.

Like many great works, 'Waltzing Matilda' tells the story that the listener wants to hear. For those who see its roots deeply embedded in the striking shearers' bitter fight for justice, it sums up the Australian value of a fair go for all, regardless of class or creed. But even those who see it only as a merry little tune with no real meaning sing it with the same pride as those who believe it is a war cry for equality. Some dislike the song, believing it to be a celebration of crime and cowardice, but more than any other it is Australia's song and is recognised around the world. Such is the legacy of a chance comment at a dinner table, an emotional connection between two women and a man, and the memory of countless swaggies who once waltzed matilda across every corner of the wide, brown land.

*

Intriguingly, passenger records show that an A.B. Paterson travelled by mail train from New South Wales into Queensland, crossing the border at Wallangarra on 3 January 1896. Five weeks later, on 8 February, the same traveller was on the train crossing back into New South Wales. If this traveller was indeed Banjo Paterson, then it leaves open the prospect that 'Waltzing Matilda' was actually created in the Queensland summer of 1896. Certainly the other main players in the saga—Christina Macpherson and Sarah Riley—were there at that time. Sarah did not leave Queensland until March, while Christina attended the wedding of her sister Jean at Dagworth Station in April. It is possible that the ill-fated party at Dagworth was actually held early in January 1896—but like much of the 'Waltzing Matilda' story it remains no more than speculation.

What can be said with certainty is that the song was created by Barty Paterson and Christina Macpherson. In about 1934,

Christina removed any doubt when she wrote to the music historian Thomas Wood:

Dear Sir

In reading your impressions about music in Australia I was interested to note that you had mentioned the song 'Waltzing Matilda', and thought it might interest you to hear how 'Banjo' Paterson came to write it. He was on a visit to Winton, North Queensland, and I was staying with my brothers about 80 miles from Winton. We went in to Winton for a week or so & one day I played [from ear] a tune which I had heard played by a band at the Races in Warnambool [sic], a country town in the Western District of Victoria. Mr Patterson [sic] asked what it was—I could not tell him, & he then said he thought he could write some lines to it. He then and there wrote the first verse. We tried it and thought it went well, so he then wrote the other verses. I might add that in a short time everyone in the District was singing it.

In the letter, Christina remembered that men were always travelling across western Queensland, some riding and some on foot. These travellers were usually given rations at stations but, because of the vast distances they had to cover, some helped themselves to stock or other goods. Christina remembered an occasion when Paterson and her brother Bob discovered the skin of a recently killed sheep at a waterhole. The way Christina remembered it, the remains of the unknown swagman's stolen meal became the basis for 'Waltzing Matilda'.

Paterson confirmed his authorship of the song in 1939—two years before his death—when he wrote a one-page letter on Australian Club notepaper to a school headmaster, Laurie Copping of Hall, near Canberra: 'A Miss Macpherson . . . used to play a tune which she believed was an old Scottish tune but she did not know the name of it. I put words to it.'

But for all its importance, 'Waltzing Matilda' brought little reward to its author. In 1902, Paterson sold the verse, along with some other 'old junk' to Angus & Robertson. The publishers then sold the rights to James Inglis & Co—the makers of Billy Tea, a company with the far-sighted idea of using the song to promote its product. The words were put to sheet music arranged by Marie Cowan, the wife of the company's general manager, using the tune first played by Christina Macpherson. In the process, the words were slightly changed.

Copies of the music were given away in every packet of tea sold. The tea company sent a copy to Paterson, who praised Mrs Cowan's work and wished her well. It is thought the sale earned Paterson just £5.

The song was immediately popular in the Winton area and might first have been performed at the town's North Gregory Hotel soon after it was written. It was sung at Gallipoli and on the Western Front during World War I but it did not become truly famous until 1938 when the internationally renowned baritone Peter Dawson recorded it on a gramophone record with the music arranged by Thomas Wood. Then, with the uniquely identifiable music and words pouring from wireless speakers around the country, it really was Australia's national song.

For the rest of his life, Paterson spoke little about 'Waltzing Matilda'. He was never one to push the virtues of his own work and his reticence to discuss the song he had co-created might reflect no more than the natural reserve that he brought to all aspects of his public life. It has been suggested that he simply did not like the song, or that as a happily married man it brought back memories he preferred to forget. The latter may be so, but the former seems unlikely. Late in his life, in a chat at his Sydney home with a journalist friend, Vince Kelly, Paterson reportedly said he had 'a greater affection for "Waltzing Matilda" than almost all his other verses'. If so, it is fitting that the song that delighted millions of Australians brought some pleasure to the man who wrote it.

8

GROWING PAINS

Paterson returned to Sydney, suddenly single and probably a little bruised by the unsavoury nature of the break-up with Sarah Riley. As he resumed work in his law office, he perhaps gave little thought to the song he had written with Christina Macpherson. Duty to his family still called and, by necessity, the unloved profession of law had to be practised. What his business partner John Street thought of the treatment of his cousin Sarah is not known.

On a mild spring night in October 1895, Paterson joined dozens of well-heeled guests at a spectacular coming-out ball for Alice Walker, at Rosemount, the grand Sydney home of her uncle. A well-bred young lady from Tenterfield Station in northern New South Wales, Alice was connected to some of the colony's finest and wealthiest families, and the guest list at her ball read like a who's who of Sydney society. Notably, most of the guests were unmarried. If, as seems likely, Paterson's visit to Dagworth Station had been made in August, then he, too, was single when he joined the other guests at Rosemount that spring evening.

He arrived to find warm light spilling from the many windows and music tinkling out from the ballroom. Servants bustled around offering champagne and wine, and bouquets of artistically arranged flowers made splashes of bright colour throughout the house. In the gardens, Chinese lanterns glowed softly in leafy, walled enclosures. Each newcomer was welcomed and then, when everybody had arrived, eighteen-year-old Alice was formally introduced to her 200 guests. After a sumptuous meal, an 'excellent band' struck up lively waltzes and finely dressed couples took to the floor.

Perhaps the handsome and worldly Barty danced with Alice that night. Maybe they even chatted lightly as they enjoyed a chaperoned stroll in the leafy gardens. Barty's days as a single man were a long way from over—his aunt Nora wrote at this time, 'Bartie [sic] has so many lady friends'—but the pretty, athletic debutante he met at Rosemount that night may well have caught his eye because they married eight years later and their long and happy union endured until his death.

In the meantime, his social life was a whirl. A week after Alice's coming-out party he joined hundreds of others at a garden party at Government House, and a week after that he rode in the final event of the Sydney Hunt Club's season—the point-to-point steeplechase from Blacktown to Prospect. Paterson dearly prized steeplechase victories but in this case he had to settle for second. On 14 December, he attended a performance in Sydney of *A Club Life,* a comic opera that he had co-written with the composer Ernest Truman. *The Sydney Morning Herald* said it was 'handsomely staged and for the most part brightly performed'. At the end of the opening night performance, the audience cheered as Paterson and Truman bowed on the stage.

In January 1896, the journalist and poet, Bernard Espinasse, published a revealing article about Paterson in the Melbourne journal

Table Talk. Espinasse discovered a reserved and private Paterson, a man with a deep well of humour and broad interests. Interestingly, Paterson told his interviewer that he regarded himself not as a poet, but as a 'versifier'. Espinasse agreed that his subject, so loosely built, with the legs of a horseman, certainly did not *look* like a poet . . .

> That is, till you looked at his face. And then possibly the first thing to strike you in the dark complexioned, mobile countenance would be the abundant evidences of humour. But the eyes are once more the windows of the soul. Quick moving, large and bright, they carry in their depths a light which promises well for the future of another and still better 'Clancy of the Overflow'.

It was this article that revealed the family racehorse as the source of the 'Banjo' pseudonym, answering a question that might otherwise have plagued Paterson fans for generations. Espinasse also discovered that Paterson often received gifts and letters of congratulations from bushmen. Many of these gifts were simply addressed to 'The Banjo, Sydney' but always reached their destination. And while Paterson was a hero to the rough-and-ready bushmen, Espinasse found a man with refined tastes:

> Mr Paterson (who, by-the-by is just into the thirties), is a moderate smoker, almost a non-drinker, and owns to a fancy for dogs. He has already spent a good deal of money on paintings by local artists, and intends to add very considerably to his present art gallery. One fine water-colour sketch of a mob of wild horses by Mahony occupies the pride of place on his walls . . .

Later that year, Paterson created one of his most enduring characters in 'Saltbush Bill'—'a drover tough, as ever the country knew'. This rugged character was reprised several times in years to come, appearing in a number of papers in 1897, 1898, 1903 and 1905, but it was another Bill—Mulga Bill—who best captured the essence of the changing times. In July 1896, 'Mulga Bill's Bicycle' appeared in *The Sydney Mail*, complete with illustrations. With typical Paterson humour, it tackled the new fad of cycling, but for poor Mulga Bill it was calamitous.

'Twas Mulga Bill from Eaglehawk, that caught the
    cycling craze;
He turned away the good old horse that served him
    many days;
He dressed himself in cycling clothes, resplendent to be seen;
He hurried off to town and bought a shining new machine;
And as he wheeled it through the door, with air of
    lordly pride,
The grinning shop assistant said, 'Excuse me, can you ride?'

Mulga Bill was reluctant to brag but did so anyway. None could ride like him, he said. In fact, he was rather gifted. Inevitably, Bill's first ride was a disaster. 'White as chalk', he rocketed down a mountain road, so badly out of control that even the wombats in their holes feared for their lives. When the bike struck a stone, Bill's maiden bicycle journey came to an inglorious ending in the waters of Dead Man's Creek. The bike remained in the creek and Mulga Bill returned to horseback. It was a funny tale that made people laugh but also hinted at a sense of nostalgia for the numbered days of the horse as the main means of transport.

Meanwhile, Banjo's real identity—already an open secret in the literary world—was now known to all. Newspapers described him as 'modest with much right to be otherwise' and noted his ballads could be heard 'wherever the white man has settled'. He continued to earn a few shillings by writing for *The Bulletin* and other journals, including *The Australasian Pastoralists' Review* and *Sketch*. Writing was his joy but the law still paid the bills.

He was now a sought-after figure in Sydney's arts and literary scene. In 1897, his interest in the arts was reflected in his appointment as co-editor of the literary magazine, *The Antipodean*. It was a high-quality, if sporadically produced, publication that—like the redoubtable J.F. Archibald—dared to suggest Australian artists or writers could stand alongside their Old World counterparts.

Those published in the December 1897 edition included the novelist Rolf Boldrewood (real name Thomas Browne) who wrote *Robbery Under Arms*, Ethel Turner, author of *Seven Little Australians*, and Paterson's rival, Henry Lawson. The 1898 edition—which included Paterson's 'Saltbush Bill's Second Fight'—was sold around the country for the price of one shilling and sixpence, and the advertising assured readers that it was good value for 'Banjo's contribution on its own'.

Sydney had a burgeoning bohemian scene in the 1890s, and Paterson could sometimes be seen in the company of clever, creative types at desirable locations. Among his friends were *The Bulletin* artist Phil May and the legendary bush poet and horseman, Harry 'Breaker' Morant. In June 1898, a society journalist Florence Blair, who wrote chatty articles on bohemianism in Sydney, reported that Harry Morant and Barty Paterson were often to be seen on Thursday afternoons at the studios of the artist Tom Robertson, surrounded by 'many jars and art objects . . . brightened by flowers and draperies':

> H. Morant looks like a man who has been used to horses all
> his life, has a sunburnt face and a non-society air, but 'Barty'
> Paterson as he is familiarly called, although the singer of bush

delights, is a thorough town man in appearance, thin faced and clean-shaven, always to be seen at Government House balls, Town Hall concerts and fashionable first nights, with a great passion for polo.

This portrait of Paterson as an important figure in Sydney's social circles was an accurate one, yet the presentation of him as a shining star of the bohemian scene does not gel with the memories of those who knew him. As the artist Norman Lindsay remembered in 1965's *Bohemians at the Bulletin*, Paterson tended to avoid mixing with writers, artists or 'other self-elected intellectuals'. According to Lindsay, Paterson preferred the company of men of action, rather than men of words. And while he had many acquaintances, he had few really close friends.

Lindsay felt the best word to describe Paterson's personality was 'sardonic'. He spoke with a slow drawl but never with an excess of words. His conversation was terse and factual and 'quite deleted of intellectual flourishes'. He was an aristocrat whose class status kept others at arm's length—yet he was not a snob. He judged a man by his achievements, not his pretensions. To Lindsay, Paterson was a man to respect, if not like. And despite an apparently mistaken recollection that Paterson suffered from bile, Lindsay remembered a man whose sharp intellect was matched by a fine physical presence:

[He was] a tall man with a finely built, muscular body, moving with the ease of perfectly co-ordinated reflexes. Black hair, dark eyes, a long, finely articulated nose, an ironic mouth, a dark pigmentation of skin due to the prime affliction of his life—bile. Every morning he suffered its effect of nausea till he had got rid of its accumulation. His eyes, as eyes must be, were his most distinctive feature, slightly hooded, with a glance that looked beyond one as he talked. If he focused it on you, it could be tolerant or completely ruthless, as he accepted or rejected you as a human being.

One man whom Paterson readily accepted was Harry Morant. Their introduction came by way of a letter from Paterson's uncle, Arthur Barton, a pastoralist from north-western Queensland who had hired Morant to break in some horses. Morant was heading to Sydney and planned to call on Barty. Barton felt it prudent to include a good description of the man who was visiting his nephew. Morant was a man, Uncle Arthur wrote, of manners, education and skill—he even claimed to be the son of an English gentleman—yet he was reckless, utterly fearless and not entirely to be trusted:

He can do anything better than most people: can write verses; break in horses; trap dingoes; yard scrub cattle; dance, run, fight, drink and borrow money; anything except work. I don't know what is the matter with the chap. He seems to be brimming over with flashness, for he will do any daredevil thing so long as there is a crowd to watch him. He jumped a horse over a stiff three-rail fence one dark night by the light of two matches which he had placed on the post!

Barely had Paterson finished reading the letter than Morant arrived at his office. Bronzed, clean-shaven Morant had the physical prowess of a consummate horseman and clear, confident eyes. He was a man after Paterson's heart and they hit it off immediately. Time 'passed on golden wings' that afternoon as they talked of stag hunting on Exmoor and 'ripping' cattle in the scrubs at the back of Dubbo. Morant so enjoyed the chat that he realised with a start that it was three o'clock and the banks were now closed. He needed to cash a cheque. Could his new friend oblige with a fiver? With thoughts of Uncle Arthur's letter fresh in mind,

Paterson politely declined. For his part, Morant 'bore no malice for the refusal'.

*

Paterson and his new friend had much in common. Morant was clearly of good stock, and, like Paterson, he was a bush balladeer. Both were masters of horses, although as a horse 'breaker' the Englishman Morant was second to none. It was this skill that provided the pseudonym he used for poems published in *The Bulletin*. Both men were accomplished steeplechasers and polo players. Each admired the other. But at the same time, their differences were profound. Sober-minded, respectable Paterson was a man who lived by the rules. Hard-drinking, womanising ne'er-do-well Morant lived by rules of his own.

When he arrived in Australia in 1883, the man who would be forever known as 'The Breaker' was already on the make. Exiled from his family in England, possibly over gambling debts, he was packed off to the colonies in disgrace. Soon he appeared in western Queensland as Edwin Murrant—the only son of the widowed matron of a workhouse in Bridgewater, England. But soon Edwin Murrant became Harry Morant—a subtle difference in surname that underpinned his claims to be the illegitimate son of one of England's most honourable gentleman, the dashing naval officer, George (later Admiral Sir George) Digby Morant.

The Breaker's claim to descend from one of the Empire's best and oldest families is borne out by the nature of his education. As a child of the workhouse, he was schooled in the arts of fighting, thieving and scamming. But he also received one of the best scholastic educations that money could buy. As noted by Nick Bleszynski in *Shoot Straight, You Bastards!*, a workhouse matron who earned just £40 a year had sent her son to a prestigious public school normally available only to the children of the elite. If Catherine Murrant could not pay to make young Edwin the mannered gentleman he became, then who did? There is a strong case that the benefactor was indeed the worthy George Morant, paying his dues for a moment of passion with a woman below his station back in the early spring of 1864.

Although Morant senior later vehemently denied paternity, there was no doubt that the twenty-eight-year-old Edwin Murrant, alias Harry Morant, was of good background. As events later showed, he entered the good graces of fine families in England and Australia with ease. Cultured and compelling, he could write a poem to charm a lady, or skewer a squealing heifer with a spear from the back of a galloping horse. The Breaker was a man of many talents.

He arrived in Queensland penniless and seemingly in disgrace. After a short stint as a horseman with a travelling circus, he drifted west to the sun-baked inland where his skills on horseback secured him a job as a stockman on a cattle station near Charters Towers. It was there that he met a striking Irish lass, the beautiful and spirited twenty-four-year-old Daisy May O'Dwyer.

They became Mr and Mrs Edwin Murrant in March 1884, but the marriage was doomed to be a short one. Daisy was not what she seemed, and nor was Edwin. Daisy claimed to have moved to Australia for health reasons but there was a cloud over her past. She had worked as a governess in Dublin but left Ireland suddenly after a scandal that might have related to the suicide of the young man of the house where she worked. Although she hid secrets of her own, she soon realised her new husband was not a good catch when he scammed his way out of paying the £5 fee for their wedding.

Things soon got worse. In April, Edwin appeared in court charged with the theft of a saddle and thirty-two pigs. He was acquitted of both charges, but the fledgling marriage was already in terminal decline and, five weeks after the wedding, Daisy threw him out. She went on to become famous as the anthropologist Daisy Bates, and Edwin, who changed his name to Harry Harbord Morant, began a new life that would end in front of a firing squad seventeen years later.

The newly single Harry raised hell across western Queensland. Constantly claiming a remittance would arrive from his people in England at any day, he drifted from town to town, often departing with creditors hot on his tail. On horseback, he had no fear. He performed breathtaking stunts for no more than a dare. Hard-riding and hard-drinking, he left a trail of dropped jaws, broken hearts and unpaid debts. He was a man to remember.

By 1895, Morant and Barty Paterson were on excellent terms. They exchanged letters in which Morant described his outback adventures to his office-bound friend in Sydney. Harry wrote of bloody hunts for cleanskin heifers through the scrub country, 'pig sticking' with a lancer's spear, battles with outlaw horses and a drunken escapade in which he was badly injured when he fell into a deep cellar. Although Paterson later turned his back on his one-time friend, in the halcyon days of the 1890s he undoubtedly admired and respected Morant—and was maybe a little envious of his dashing, irresponsible ways.

The passing years did not blunt The Breaker's enthusiasm for dangerous stunts. In 1897, he earned fame for his mastery of one of the wildest and meanest 'outlaw' horses ever to hurl a man from its back.

It was at the Hawkesbury Show, north of Sydney, in May that he tamed Dargin's Grey—the feared equine star of the lauded Martini's Buckjumping Show. The crowds shouted that day that Morant would be the subject of an inquest, 'sure as eggs', if he tried to mount the grey outlaw. But the crowd knew less about The Breaker than they did about horses and Morant tamed the beast despite breaking both stirrups early in his ride. The fickle crowd turned from forecasting Morant's sudden death to applauding his heroism. The way *The Hawkesbury Herald* remembered it a few years later, the triumphant Morant was both brave and humble:

> It was a popular victory. The 'Breaker' was carried shoulder high all around the ground. A collection was taken up, and a good sum realised, but when offered to Morant he smilingly remarked, 'Give it to the hospital'.

Meanwhile, it was a productive if rather haphazard time for Henry Lawson. He had returned to Sydney from Bourke in 1893 with hopes of finding permanent employment as a writer. It was an ambition he never achieved. Unable to get regular work, he freelanced prolifically, painted or laboured to make ends meet, and stayed with his Aunt Emma or in 'third rate hash houses'. In December 1894, his mother Louisa had published Henry's first book, *Short Stories in Prose and Verse,* and in 1895, Angus & Robertson agreed to publish his second. It was also in 1895 that he met Bertha Bredt, a trainee nurse and the daughter of a prominent feminist and social agitator. They married in 1896. It should have been a good match, but as always, Henry proved to be his own downfall.

Lawson was a key figure in the bohemian Dusk and Dawn Club, an exclusive Sydney-based circle for writers, artists and journalists. Its motto was 'Roost High and Crow Low', and its rules were printed in Chinese, supposedly to prevent offence to any of the 'Duskers'—some of whom were actually dead! These figures from history were nominated for election to immortality in the 'spiritual' division of the club. Shakespeare made it but Beethoven did not. The living members of the club were encouraged to play practical jokes, robustly critique each other's work and to drink a lot. Enclosed in his almost silent world and surrounded by like-minded souls,

Lawson revelled in the creativity of the club and found drinking broke down the barriers that set him apart from so many others. He could be as unappealing as any drunk, and the black dog of depression forever tailed him, but he was a man who valued his mates and they valued him.

Lawson's many friends forgave him his weaknesses and rallied around him when he fell. In March 1896, he lost one of those friends when Charles Lind shot himself at Manly. Lind left a note to Lawson that read in part:

> Harry, my boy . . . you have frequently heard me remark how I looked upon all in this world and all that is connected with it as a farce, more or less hideous, and a horrible farce, and I will simply add that now in the face of the inevitable I have no reason to alter my opinion. Good-bye, old chap.

A month after this devastating blow, Henry had a chance at a new beginning when he married Bertha Bredt. It might have been something of an omen that he had to borrow £10 to pay for the wedding. Almost immediately, the newlyweds moved to Western Australia to join a rush for gold but failed to strike it rich, or even find permanent work. After a short time living in a tent they returned to Sydney where things were looking up, thanks to the publication by Angus & Robertson of two of Lawson's books, *In the Days When the World Was Wide* and *While the Billy Boils*. Both were well received by critics and readers, and Lawson's star as a writer was further on the rise.

But his return to Sydney also meant a return to his old ways. It was a recipe for conflict. Bertha wanted family and domesticity. Henry wanted to write and drink with his bohemian friends. There were arguments. Henry wrote productively, but, as usual, he mismanaged the finances and the couple's income was uncertain.

Making it worse, Henry held a strange torch for Hannah Thorburn, a young woman who modelled for an artist friend. The nature of their relationship is not known, but Hannah cast such a spell over Lawson that she emerged in his later writings as a romanticised ideal of womanhood. For Bertha, it was all too much.

In desperation, she persuaded him to look for work in New Zealand, hoping that removing him from his usual haunts would save him from his demons. Armed with a letter of introduction from J.F. Archibald, Henry and Bertha arrived in Wellington in April 1897, where Henry secured a job teaching at a remote Maori school in Mangamaunu on the South Island. Bertha had extra reason to hope the isolation of the remote coastal community would save her husband from himself. She was pregnant with their first child.

But after an initial burst of enthusiasm, Lawson found Mangamaunu stifling. He struggled to relate to the Maori communities he was trying to serve and, in an alien culture, his creative well ran all but dry. It was another disaster. In October he and Bertha returned to Wellington where Bertha delivered little Joseph Henry (Jim). As soon as they were able, they moved back to Sydney, Bertha hoping that somehow it would be different this time. Predictably, it was not.

In Sydney, Henry was given a sinecure in the Government Statistician's Office. He soon lost the job, possibly because he found the process of clocking in and clocking out demeaning but, away from the vacuum of remote Mangamaunu, his art returned. Although he barely seems to have appreciated it, he owed much for this to his friends and colleagues. As always, Archibald continued to support him, while George Robertson was generous with advances and loans. And not least, his friendly rival, Barty Paterson, continued to help with free legal advice and negotiations with publishers.

In an anecdote that reveals his relationship with Lawson was a friendly one, Paterson later recalled paying a visit to the Lawson home in Sydney at around this time. He was pleased to learn from Bertha that Henry was working.

'What's he working at?' asked Paterson, 'prose or verse?'

'Oh, no!' replied Bertha. 'I don't mean writing. I mean working. He's gone back to his trade as a house painter.'

As always, the house painting was sporadic and the family continued to struggle financially. Under the pressure, Henry's drinking worsened. In November he was admitted, not for the last time, to a sanatorium for inebriates—a respite which seems to have slowed his decline. Bertha was supportive at first, writing regularly to her husband pledging her love and urging him to recover. It seemed to be paying off. When Henry was discharged he stopped drinking and a relatively stable period followed. He revised *In the Days When the World Was Wide* for a new edition to be published in 1900, and received some promising offers from publishers in London.

He became convinced that success lay overseas, a point he made clear in 'Pursuing Literature in Australia', a personal statement that appeared in the January 1899, edition of *The Bulletin*. In it, Lawson wrote negatively of a system that failed to financially reward Australian writers and concluded with bitter advice to young writers to leave Australia for London, America, Timbuctoo, anywhere—or else 'shoot himself carefully with the aid of a looking glass'. Unfairly, 'Pursuing Literature in Australia' did not acknowledge that most of its author's problems were self-inflicted, nor did it recognise the generous support he had received from Robertson or Archibald. It did, however, give a strong sense of Lawson's discontent at a world that failed to reward a man for his work.

It was a reality that might have occurred to Barty Paterson in June that year, when acting as Lawson's lawyer he secured £5 for Henry from *The Bulletin* for various works. On 20 April 1900, with the help of benefactors including George Robertson, Lawson sailed with his family to Britain. He later remembered it in verse as 'That wild run to London/That wrecked and ruined me'. In truth, however, his ruin had begun long before he went to England.

Paterson, meanwhile, had done some travelling of his own. In September 1898, he had sailed on the *Guthrie* to Darwin after accepting a commission to write a tourist guide encouraging travellers to visit the remote Northern Territory. It was an assignment he enjoyed. He later told a newspaper reporter the journey was inspired by 'that intense desire to get away into the wilds which you think few only have trod'. In Darwin, he played tennis against some locals and gave them a thrashing. But he was keen to see the bush and wasted little time in getting away to the 'wilds'. Soon he was shooting crocodiles and buffaloes on the hard fringes of the northern coast. Hunting the buffalo, he said, was 'about twice as dangerous as going to war'.

He joined a party of shooters at a buffalo camp, sleeping on the hard ground under a mosquito net and living on damper and buffalo meat. Riding a specially trained horse, Paterson bagged several large bulls by riding alongside the galloping beasts and firing from close range with a carbine. He earned praise for his shooting skills from Darwin's *Northern Territory Times and Gazette,* which said the poet from Sydney, did 'fairly well for a novice'. When he left the Territory on 28 October, Paterson took with him some buffalo horns. This pleased the *Times* which thought the souvenirs should be ample proof 'to some of the sceptics of the south that there *are* buffalo in the Northern Territory'.

Paterson saw the Territory as a place of massive, unrealised potential and, so far, a colossal failure. He noted that its aridness and extremes had combined to defy all efforts to develop it, yet its possibilities were endless. In an article for *The Sydney Morning Herald* in 1901, he noted that Darwin had a fine port within easy reach of Asian markets but it 'does not ship a single horse north and there is not even a freezing works—a thing that every little town in New Zealand has got'. His list of frustrations at the Territory's unfulfilled potential went on but he never lost faith in its possibilities. As late as 1935, he was still urging young men to go north.

His visit to Darwin prompted some nationalistic political rumination where he worried about the threat to Australian jobs from imported Asian labour. He warned the Territory was 'clamouring for the introduction of the cheap and nasty Chow' and that northern Australia was at risk of being overrun by Asians:

> Only eight days' steam from our Northern Territory there lies the great seething cauldron of the East, boiling over with parti-coloured humanity—brown and yellow men by the million, and they are quite near enough to us to do a lot of harm if their ideas run that way . . . Furthermore, our Northern Territory, practically uninhabited by whites, is just the place to suit these people. On those great sweltering, steaming, fever-laden plains, where the muddy rivers struggle slowly to the sea, the Orientals are in their glory. If they once get a good footing there, they will out-breed and out-multiply any European race.

This fear of Asian colonisation later materialised in some of his poetry. In 1923, he published 'A Job for McGuinness', a short poem telling of a white man's inability to find employment. Paterson wrote that McGuinness might only find work in a trench, with a gun in his hand, when the 'Chow and the Jap begin to drift down from the tropics'. In an era where White Australia still had decades to run, his concerns were shared by tens of thousands of Australians. It is worth noting that the motto of *The Bulletin* then—and for many years to come—was 'Australia for the White Man'.

One of the great political issues of the late nineteenth century was Federation. The ambitious idea that Australia might become one nation under a central government was an unpopular one for some, but it had powerful supporters. The influential New South Wales Premier, Sir Henry Parkes, was chief among them. A champion of a united Australian government since 1867, he had set the tide of change in motion in 1889 with a stirring speech at the town of Tenterfield in the colony's north. His 'Tenterfield Address' was a pivotal moment in the maturing of Australia.

Parkes arrived in Tenterfield by train on the afternoon of Friday 25 October. He was met with delight by the citizens. Hundreds gathered at the station to welcome him, all the stores were closed and a brass band played in the streets. The mayor gave a short speech in which he described Parkes as 'an ornament and delight to society'. Modestly, the premier replied that the townsfolk were too kind. He said the praise accorded to him fell short of his actual achievements but was undoubtedly heartened by the cries of 'No, no!' that rang out from the crowd as he uttered these self-deprecating remarks. Pleased with his reception, he retired to his hotel to prepare to deliver a speech at a banquet that evening.

In the speech, Parkes put an impassioned case for Australia's three and a half million people to have an army run by one government, railway gauges that were uniform across the land, a single customs service rather than many, and a national parliament with two houses ruling for the benefit of all. The vision was of a government for white men. The vote would be denied to Aborigines, people of Chinese and Indian descent, women and the poor, but Australians would be one in nationhood. Applause and cheers boomed out in the hall as Parkes called for a convention to discuss the formation of a federal government. It seemed Federation had popular support, at least in Tenterfield.

The first Federation convention, in 1891, drafted a bill for the national Constitution, but many in the colonies were unconvinced. Victoria was relatively enthusiastic, but there was strong opposition in free trade-minded New South Wales, while the smaller colonies were wary of centralised government and worried that a federal union would hit their tariff incomes. When Parkes was forced to resign the premiership in October 1891, his dream of a united commonwealth seemed to be fading away. But by the time of his death in April 1896, support for Federation had begun to grow. The slow pace of change prompted some newspapers in Sydney to declare federation 'as dead as Julius Caesar' but in that year another federation conference began. In 1898, referenda were held on a Commonwealth of Australia Constitution Bill. It won majorities in all six colonies, but only narrowly in New South Wales, where the idea still had strong opposition. Among the sticking points was a conflict between the two biggest colonies over where a national capital should be sited.

As the debate continued, Paterson poked fun at the stick-in-the-muds in New South Wales with 1898's 'Johnny Riley's Cow, a Ballad of Federation'. In the poem, Johnny Riley was 'down on Federation' because his cow kept crossing the Murray River into Victoria. Each time the wayward beast splashed across the border, poor Johnny had to pay fines to the Victorians. He thought Federation would be the ruin of New South Wales. But the cow, who was Queensland-bred, cared nothing for the squabble between Sydney and Melbourne and favoured Federation—'one people east and west—/And all may do as I do—travel where the grass is best'. It highlighted the silliness of a border separating people who were already one in identity.

In June 1899, Paterson took another shot at Federation opponents in New South Wales, with 'The Federal Bus Conductor and the Old Lady'. It urged 'the old lady' to stop talking and get on board:

Now 'urry, Mrs New South Wales, and come along of us,
We're all a-goin' ridin' in the Federation 'bus.
A fam'ly party, don't you know—yes, Queenslan's comin' too.
You can't afford it! Go along! We've kep' box seat for you.
The very one of all the lot that can afford it best,
You'll only have to pay your share the same as all the rest.

The stragglers, New South Wales and Western Australia, finally joined the 'Federation bus' and the colonies were officially united on 1 January 1901. Australia, at last, was a commonwealth. The vexed question of the capital was solved in 1908 by a decision to build it in a sparsely populated area known as Canberra, about half way between Sydney and Melbourne. Edmund Barton—a relative of Paterson's on his mother's side—became Australia's first prime minister.

By that time, much had happened in the life of A.B Paterson. He had been to the Boer War in South Africa and when Federation was declared, he was preparing for a voyage to China. Henry Lawson—who wrote rather disdainfully 'the men who made Australia had federated long ago'—was in London sinking further into torment, and Harry Morant was on a course towards infamy. Australia was coming of age and Paterson would be there to record its growing pains.

9
THE BOER WAR

While Australians were struggling with the complexities of Federation, the wider British Empire was becoming increasingly preoccupied by steadily worsening strife in another far-off colony—South Africa. In 1880, the Boers—descendants of independently minded Dutch settlers—had declared independence in the Transvaal in the country's north-eastern region, and inflicted a heavy defeat on a British force. It ended in an uneasy stalemate that saw the Boers granted their independence in the Transvaal and neighbouring Orange Free State. The discovery of a massive gold reef at the Witwatersrand in the Boer republic caused tensions to rise. The Boers were short of resources and manpower, and reluctantly decided to bring in 'uitlanders', or foreigners, to help exploit the gold find. Many of the uitlanders were of British stock and so many arrived that they threatened to outnumber the Boers, giving powerful numerical support to the British.

There was conflict between the Boers and the foreigners as an expansionist Britain eyed off the Witwatersrand gold as well as fabulous diamond riches in the Kimberley. The Boers saw a British invasion as inevitable and in 1899, they launched a pre-emptive strike. It led to a war that pitted the might of the British army with men from around the world against Boer farmers, either volunteering or commandeered to fight. It was, at first, a close-run thing.

As the threat of war loomed, the Australian newspapers were sure it would be a one-sided contest. Adelaide's *The Advertiser* said it would be a disgrace to be beaten by the Boers but there would be no glory in victory. Rival paper, *The Register*, felt the Boer fighter was not a match for his British counterpart and was confident the competitiveness of the Australian colonies meant a stream of men would lend 'their aid in support of the Empire'. Although the Boers soon proved to be much tougher opponents than expected, the papers at least got it right when they predicted enthusiasm from Australian volunteers. When war was formally declared on 11 October, men in cities, towns and villages across the country rushed to join up.

The volunteers' names were published in the papers and town bands played as the men boarded trains at crowded stations on the first stage of their journeys to the front. Australia was doing its duty to the mother country and the colonies competed to see who could be the best son. In Perth, *The Western Mail* acknowledged that the people of that colony were 'West Australians first and Australians second'. Even when it came to the send-off for the soldiers, the *Mail* said, the west did it better than the rest, and as for the quality of the men, 'we are pretty sure that none of the sections of Australasia can place a squad of finer physique in the field'.

For Paterson, the outbreak of war was an opportunity to pursue adventure as a writer. The way he told it later, he got his chance at a meeting with Sir James Fairfax, owner of *The Sydney Morning Herald*. Paterson offered to go to South Africa as a correspondent at his own expense, 'on trial for a month, which was just about as far as my finances would take me'. He proposed to write long and colourful 'letters' to the *Herald*'s readers, bringing them detailed coverage of Australia's adventure against the Boers. Fairfax could plainly see the benefits of having the famous 'Banjo' Paterson as a correspondent and he not only signed him up, he also gave him £100 towards his costs. By the end of October, Paterson was on board the troop ship *Kent*, with a commission to send back reports, photographs and observations for *The Sydney Morning Herald*, *The Sydney Mail* and *The Argus* in Melbourne.

The *Kent* sailed from Sydney on 30 October 1899 to Albany in Western Australia where she took on more men and horses. From there, under the light of a faint moon, she began the three-week journey across the blue water towards Africa. As the lights of Albany faded away behind the ship, Paterson said farewell to his homeland for the first time. Ahead lay battle with the Boers. A few days later, he noted in his diary, with tongue firmly in cheek, that the Boers were, by all accounts, 'only part human'.

A dry humour underpinned his early dispatches from the *Kent*. With no real action to write about, Paterson mined a productive field when he poked fun at the army. An ambulance unit was on board and Paterson took the opportunity to ask an orderly—a retired infantry sergeant-major—whether the Boers would fire upon the ambulances. The cynical old orderly was in no doubt: 'Of course, they'll fire on the hambulances,' he told Paterson. 'They 'ave no respect for the 'elpless. They've even been known to fire on the cavalry.'

The men settled into a shipboard routine, their days starting with reveille at six in the morning and ending in lights-out at nine thirty-five at night. Everything ran like clockwork—or should have, except that the men settled into little cliques and wanted little to do with outsiders. As Paterson recalled, the medics retreated to a section of the ship after commandeering as many hammocks as they could find; cursing Lancers fought and struggled in passageways; and the machine gunners and signal men squabbled over access to the deck for their training drills. 'Thus we fared across the Indian Ocean, toiling, rejoicing and borrowing gear and equipment—generally without the knowledge or consent of the lender.'

There was an outbreak of influenza on board and the sick men were treated with a mixture of quinine and rum. When the quinine ran out, the men learned the influenza medicine was now composed entirely of rum and almost every man on board lined up for the final treatment. It inspired Paterson to write a song he called 'The Rum Parade'. Performed to the tune of 'Ballyhooley', it was sung at soldiers' concerts after dinner, with toes tapping to the chorus:

> So it's forward the Brigade
> If they'll hold a 'rum parade',
> At Pretoria there's nothing can alarm ye,
> And it's easy to be seen
> If they leave the quinine,
> Ye'll be there before the blessed British Army.

The South African coast came into view on 30 November. The next morning, the ship steamed into Port Elizabeth, where Paterson was disappointed to realise that the arrival of the Australians excited very little interest. Thousands of men and horses from across the empire had already landed, 30,000 more were on their way and the Australian presence was regarded as inconsequential. 'The kangaroo,' he wrote, 'began to think that he was not such a very large animal after all.'

After an hour on shore, Paterson was ordered back on board and the *Kent* sailed for Cape Town—a place that struck him as 'very like

Adelaide, only that it is built on a steep hill'. There, they found the same indifference to the Australians until they visited an officers' club and learned their very own regiment, the New South Wales Lancers, had done sterling work in a battle the day before. Suddenly, the men from New South Wales were no longer outsiders and 'the kangaroo was himself again!'

*

Paterson soon discovered that the colonial abroad was something of a novelty. In Cape Town, he met the Governor, Sir Alfred Milner, 'my first world-wide celebrity'. At the meeting, Milner asked Paterson to take two English society ladies on a jackal hunt with a pack of hounds. When Paterson said he did not have a horse, the governor airily replied—with a hint that he regarded Antipodeans as natural stock thieves—'an Australian can always get a horse'. Sure enough, Paterson did find a horse and dutifully turned up for his hunting date with the ladies, who turned out to be the Duchess of Westminster and the wife of a lord of the realm. As he recalled years later, the assignment was not a hardship:

> Both were young and attractive women, beautifully turned out, and their features had all the repose that marks the caste of Vere de Vere [a reference to the uppermost level of Anglo-Norman aristocracy]. Both carried whiskey and water in hunting flasks and they both smoked cigarettes— accomplishments which had not, at that time, penetrated to the lower orders. Being handed over to the care of a casual Australian meant nothing in their young lives; in fact I don't think anything on earth could have rattled them. When you are a duchess, you let other people do the worrying.

Paterson was happy to play the 'bronco buster from the Barcoo' for the aristocratic ladies and he ensured they bagged their jackal. But it was impossible to miss the fact that there was a war on. This reality was driven home when he met his first Boer—a prisoner who had seen several battles. In peacetime, the prisoner had been a medical doctor, 'refined and educated', and not the monster that the propaganda painted the Boers to be. During a discussion at a hotel, the prisoner told Paterson he thought the Boers had had the best of the war because they fired until the last minute and then retreated. They lost ground, said the prisoner, but saved men.

The Boers indeed had the better of it, at least at first. Although numerically inferior to the British forces, the army of farmers soon showed they were formidable opponents. At the start of the war, during Black Week in December 1899, the British forces had suffered humiliating defeats in three encounters in just seven days. The Boers had modern rifles with smokeless cartridges, allowing them to fire from cover undetected, and the latest French field guns that could be mobilised quickly and brought to bear with deadly efficiency. More than 2500 British soldiers were killed or wounded. It was a shocking lesson that the war would not be won easily and that British tactics would have to change.

Those changes included the introduction of new weaponry and armies. By January 1900, Britain had amassed 18,000 men in South Africa, including Australians and other colonials, with more on the way from all corners of the Empire. It was the largest military contingent that Britain had ever sent overseas. It was also the first time that Australian soldiers were sent to fight in their country's name.

Paterson was keen to tell their stories to his readers at home but after landing in Cape Town, he was disheartened to learn that it would not be that easy. An army wary of newspapermen felt there were already too many reporters trying to cover the war and it was clear that getting to the front would be difficult. Luckily, Paterson's meeting with Governor Milner provided the break he needed.

When Paterson said he wanted to see the action, the governor had laughed and said the military was complaining that there would soon be more correspondents than soldiers at the front. Nonetheless, he agreed to help. Perhaps with gratitude for Paterson's help with the jackal-hunting expedition, Milner offered to write to the chief censor approving Australian reporters to cover the exploits of the Australian troops. It was enough to clear the hurdles, and on 4 December, Paterson was aboard a troop train, bound for the north and his first sight of armed conflict.

The troops were keen to get to grip with the Boers, whom many believed to be 'semi-savages'. Paterson, however, already had a different opinion of the enemy. He thought the Boer prisoners he had met in Cape Town were 'square sturdy men, much the type of our bushmen'. In a report to his newspaper readers, Paterson noted: 'We have as many people just as rough as they are.' It was not the last time that he saw the Boers as human beings, not so very different from Australians.

After a journey of almost forty-eight hours, the train stopped at the junction town of Naauwpoort, 'a frightful place—just a lot of galvanised iron houses and a dust storm'. The Boers were at Colesberg, 70 kilometres to the north. The heat at Naauwpoort was extreme and there was nothing to do. Fortunately, there were two other press men in town. After days of inactivity they decided to ride north towards the front. Not wishing to miss anything, Paterson, the rookie correspondent, decided to follow them. It gave him his first taste of war.

The reporters camped that night with some New Zealand troops and joined them the next day as they pushed across a plain towards a steep hill. As they reconnoitred the hill a shell suddenly fell and the troops scattered in the rocks. More shells struck the plain below and bullets kicked up spurts of sand as Boer marksmen tracked small parties of British soldiers crossing the open and exposed plain. The shells made a 'nasty screaming sound' but seemed to cause no more than a fright. It was quite entertaining to watch the action unfold on the plain below from the relative safety of the hill but later that day, when Paterson had to do the same, the reality of coming under fire was less amusing.

Meanwhile, a group of Australians had been sent to find the Boer guns. They had done so by the simple tactic of riding towards the enemy until he began firing at them. Having located the guns without loss, the Australians hurriedly retired to their camp, where Paterson joined them that night for a surprisingly good meal. His first experience of battle was over. It had been a dramatic day of barking seven-pounders, screaming shells and whizzing bullets, but many of the shells did not explode and most of the bullets missed their mark. The Australian losses that day totalled two or three horses and a shoulder injury to a sergeant who fell from his mount. As a first taste of war it was rather bloodless and came across in Paterson's account as something of an adventure. If so, it was a cruel misconception of what lay ahead. Before he left South Africa, Paterson would see a war where men and horses were torn to shreds and crying women and children were driven from the ruins of their burning homes.

*

Harry 'The Breaker' Morant had been thinking about redemption for some time. In a letter to his friend Barty Paterson in 1896, Morant had pondered the possibility of his family finding 'one prodigal turning up with a request for fine veal'. But the black sheep could not return home a wastrel. The war in South Africa seemed to offer a solution. As an officer and gentleman he might return to England and atone for the sins that had driven him away seventeen years earlier. There was, he hoped, even a chance of acceptance by the man he claimed was his father.

While Paterson was hunting jackals with titled ladies, Morant was making his way from Queensland to Melbourne. From there he drifted north, then west, following the Murray River on its winding journey to the South Australian coast. He arrived on the river's lower reaches early in 1898 and found work managing cattle at Paringa Station, a sprawling cattle property that ran north towards the arid meeting point of three states. The homestead, which stood on a cliff top overlooking the wide Murray, was occupied by the Cutlack family. Their son, Frederick, was a boy of twelve when Morant arrived that summer and his memories of that time provide some detail of The Breaker's final weeks in Australia.

It might have been coincidence that a well-respected Colonel Charles Morant had settled in the Murray-side town of Renmark, or it may have been a genuine case of Harry Morant making family contact for the first time since his exile began. Either way, he was soon able forge a connection that supported his claim of being the son of the English naval officer, George Morant. With a letter of support from Fred Cutlack's father, The Breaker presented himself to Renmark's Colonel Morant and was recognised as one of the family. Morant's excellent manners and supposed family connections were so impressive he was invited to visit the governor, Lord Tennyson, and his wife in Adelaide. Bastard son of a British gentleman or not, Harry was equally at home taking tea in a parlour as he was taming wild horses in the outback. Seeking to build a bridge, the colonel even went so far as to write to his supposed kinsman, George

Morant, in Devon. According to Nick Bleszynski in *Shoot Straight, You Bastards!*, the reply that returned was a firm 'no comment'.

The summer that Morant arrived at Paringa was a dry one and cattle that were roaming the outreaches of the station needed to be brought in before the last waterhole dried up. Morant and another man were sent out to bring the stock in. To the delight of young Frederick Cutlack, they took the boy with them. Frederick drove a spring cart carrying blankets and supplies, while Morant and the other stockman rode alongside. They made camp about 25 kilometres from the homestead and, in the hot days that followed, they brought in the thirsty cattle from remote outposts. As they worked, Morant sometimes entertained his companions with ballads and bursts of song. Cutlack recalled that one of those songs was an original ditty about 'The Adelaidies'. This work, never written down, was 'supposed to be rather strong stuff for my young ears'.

But the cavalier adventurer Breaker Morant still had bridges to mend and the promise of war remained his best chance. After noticing a recruitment poster in a pub window he decided to go to Adelaide and join up. He would serve in an Australian army and return home to England with his honour restored. But the 'wild' Harry was never far from the surface and before he left Renmark, he performed a stunt for which he is still remembered in the riverside town. On a dare, he rode a horse into the bar of the Renmark Hotel. That bar was known for years as 'Breaker's Bar'.

Fred Cutlack's last memory of Morant before he left Paringa to join the South Australian Mounted Rifles was of the Englishman boiling his quart pot for the last time on the banks of the Murray as he waited for a steamer to take him downriver to the railhead to Adelaide. When the boat arrived, Morant gave the quart pot to young Frederick. He also left the Cutlack family with a photo of

himself in army uniform and slouch hat. It is the image that defines
Australian memories of Breaker Morant today.

*

Through the first nine months of 1900, Barty Paterson filed long and
finely detailed reports of the war for his Australian readers. As the
British steadily pushed the Boer defenders north, Paterson described
a blizzard of artillery shells and bullets as the British charged across
open plains to attack kopjes (steep, rocky hills) held by fast and
mobile Boer forces. The enemy was all but invisible in the rugged
hilltops and often the British only learned of the Boers' presence
when shells or bullets from smokeless rifles fell among them.

Much of the Boer marksmanship was wide but British men and
horses fell in a bloody heap often enough. Paterson grew to respect
the enemy, who seemed to be able to vanish like spirits in the rocks
and brush of the kopjes. He saw acts of heroism and he saw men
die, uttering their last words for women at home who were about
to become grieving mothers or widows.

He was often close to the fighting. A good way to observe the
action was to position himself atop a non-occupied kopje from where
'one can see away on one plain the guns shelling a hill, on another
flank a mounted infantry force dismounting to pour fire into a
Boer stronghold, in another direction a cavalry patrol engaged in its
unhealthy occupation of "drawing fire" from concealed enemies'.
As this war played out across the hills and plains he spent a lot of
time riding between camps to learn the latest news for his letters
home. At times, he spent up to fourteen hours a day in the saddle.
With each dispatch, he fine-tuned the art of producing engaging,
descriptive prose that would be remembered as excellent reporting
of Australians at war. He underplayed his own risks, but the reality
was that being a war correspondent was a dangerous job. Seven

had died in the first month of fighting and Paterson's enthusiasm for being in the thick of it could easily have made him the eighth.

The rookie correspondent's reports naturally focused on the conflicts that he observed. He described cavalry advances over the plains and artillery and rifle attacks on Boers entrenched on the steep and rocky kopjes. He saw men fall to bullets and shells but noted the Boer marksmanship was poor and the damage could have been far worse. Amid the chaos of battle, he also turned his attention to the people and places he saw. Through the eyes of an Australian who loved the bush, he brought the African countryside to life for his readers at home.

The Boer homesteads lacked verandahs and looked 'barn-like' but the farms were otherwise absurdly similar to those at home, right down to sheep and horse yards and gardens. The sun-baked veldt with its dusty karoo bushes reminded him of Australia's spinifex country. He noticed the Boer farmers—who raised sheep, cattle and ostriches—overcame a lack of timber by burning dried blocks of manure. He thought the ostrich, 'who never seems contented or happy', was the great mystery of South Africa, but was unimpressed by the springbok. He described the weather as perfect, like the 'best possible Australian day, sunny and clear, with a brisk invigorating breeze blowing' and he believed the Boers to be fair fighters, their young men to be very like young Australians and their young women just like girls from any Australian country town.

On 13 March, the British captured Bloemfontein, the capital of the Orange Free State, in a victory that proved to be 'ridiculously easy'. The leaders of the town had decided not to fight and persuaded the Boer defenders to melt into the hills in retreat. With the city open and apparently undefended, Paterson took a chance that accorded him a place in the history of the war.

As the British shelled a column of Boers making for the hills, Paterson and two other press men competed to become the first Britons to enter Bloemfontein. Unsure whether any defenders remained to fire upon them, the correspondents galloped over a beautiful green flat and into the town. Paterson's Australian-bred black colt was a superb animal and it carried him first into Bloemfontein, his two colleagues following closely behind. As they rode into town they were welcomed by the residents, who 'all shook hands with us, and hoorayed as though they liked having their town captured'. Paterson overcame his usual modesty to describe this remarkable incident in a short but powerful paragraph to his Australian readers:

> I don't like to say too much about the race into Bloemfontein, but when we three correspondents decided to go into the town there was considerable risk of capture, but we were so anxious to be first in that we raced with whips going for at least three-quarters of a mile, and my black horse landed me first in Bloemfontein, a distinction to be proud of, and one that there are many claimants for, but the fact remains that we were the first to be seen in the town, and we guided the Mayor out to see Lord Roberts and surrender the town.

Later that month, Paterson met the great English poet and writer, Rudyard Kipling in Bloemfontein. It sparked in Paterson a lifetime of admiration for Kipling, 'a little, squat figured, sturdy man . . . [with] nothing of the dreamer about him'. The great writer was a bundle of nervous energy who talked in a rapid chatter about the war and the future of South Africa. Three days later, Paterson attended a correspondents' dinner in honour of Lord Roberts. Paterson was seated that night next to Kipling, and as they dined, Paterson asked the Englishman for a memento of their meeting. Kipling scribbled down extracts from two of his poems, 'The Long Trail' and 'The Flowers' on the menu for the evening meal. According to Paterson's granddaughters, Rosamund Campbell and Philippa Harvie, the former poem was their grandfather's favourite, and the autographed menu became one of his most treasured possessions.

At around this time, Paterson met a young newspaper correspondent who was destined to become one of the greatest men of the century. His name was Winston Churchill, an aggressive, aristocratic young man, who 'drank a big bottle of beer for breakfast every morning'. An aspiring politician, twenty-five-year-old Churchill had had one unsuccessful run at parliament in Britain and told Paterson he had only become a newspaper correspondent to gain enough public recognition to be elected when he ran again. A 'man to be feared if not liked', Churchill told Paterson he intended to plaster *The Morning Post* with cables of his own heroics and 'when I go up for parliament again, I'll fly in'.

Churchill had graduated from Sandhurst as a junior cavalry officer but was never popular with his superiors. The army, Paterson recalled, was prepared to bet that Churchill would either go to jail or become prime minister:

Churchill was the most curious combination of ability and swagger. The army could neither understand him nor like him; for when it came to getting anywhere or securing any job, he made his own rules. Courage he had in plenty . . . but, like the Duke of Plaza-Toro, he felt that he should always travel with a full band. As one general put it, 'You never know when you have got Churchill. You can leave him behind in charge of details and he'll turn up at the front, riding a camel, and with some infernal explanation that you can't very well fault.'

The British continued their northward march and captured Johannesburg on 31 May 1900. On 6 June, Pretoria—the capital of the Transvaal—fell in another relatively easy victory. Many observers thought the taking of the city meant an imminent end to the war. They were soon proved wrong. The British might have the population centres, but the hard core of the Boer resistance had not been defeated and the nature of the war was changing. Steadily retreating into the rugged north, the Boers gave up on set-piece battle and started to become highly effective guerrilla fighters. It meant that British tactics would eventually have to change.

Paterson had caught an early glimpse of how those tactics might evolve when he wrote in April that the Boers would give up if their farms were tightly squeezed. If the government gave notice that all stock would be confiscated from farms where the owner was absent—fighting the British—then the men would return from their commando units in the wilds, and the war would come to an end. It was a harsh observation that he had cause to regret in June, when he saw the British burn down the house of a Boer commandant:

> . . . when you see it done it is a different matter. When you really see women and children turned, homeless and crying, out on the open veldt—well, you want to be home and done with the war. Let us hope that it may be the means of bringing the war to an end.

In his last dispatch from the war, dated 11 August, Paterson said the Boers were heartily sick of the war and hundreds would surrender if not for the new policy of sending prisoners overseas to Colombo or St Helena—a fate they dreaded. Earlier prisoners had been treated too leniently when they were allowed to return to their farms because many had simply taken up arms again to re-join the commandos in the veldt, he wrote. Many on the British side thought the answer was to ensure no Boers should be left on farms while the war continued. Sterner measures were needed against those who laid down their arms only to take them up again, and Paterson expected those steps to begin sooner rather than later. He could not have known then that the British commander, Lord Kitchener, would eventually end the war with draconian force against South African men, women and children.

By then, though, Paterson's war was over. In August he suddenly left South Africa and returned home to Sydney. He had experienced months of danger and adventure. He had seen combat at close quarters, putting himself at high risk so that he could get as close to the action as possible. He had seen men die and civilians mistreated. He had even been hit in the ribs by a ricocheting bullet but escaped injury. As the Boer 'bitter-enders' retreated further into the northern Transvaal, he hoped for an end to the war within months. He had had enough.

During his nine months in South Africa he had produced powerful and colourful word pictures, not only of the fighting, but also of the land and its people and culture. He had found a people—the enemy—who were remarkably similar to Australians, not the primitive monsters the propaganda painted them to be. His empathy for the Boers can have done him no favours with the army or the government, and it has been suggested that his insistence on discovering them as human beings had something to do with the suddenness of his departure. However, he had earned the right to go home with his head held high. His 'trial for a month' at the South African war was a triumph for journalism and for humanism.

The war he left behind was very different from the one he had joined. By late 1900 the Boer 'bitter-enders' were ambushing British troops, blowing up trains and bridges and destroying telegraph stations. In February 1901, after the scattered Boer commanders refused peace terms, Kitchener responded by scorching the earth. If the Boer fighters would not surrender, they would be flushed out of the veldt in a 'series of systematic drives, organised like a sporting shoot'. In a devastating total war, even their families would become casualties of the conflict.

The British torched Boer farms, razed their crops and slaughtered their livestock. Wells were poisoned and the earth salted. Weeping women and children were driven from the smoking ruins of their homes and herded into concentration camps of canvas and wire. There, they died in their thousands of disease and malnutrition. A network of stone or concrete blockhouses sprawled across the Transvaal, protecting roads, bridges and railways. And, in the field, the dirty war continued.

*

While Barty Paterson was beginning a new stage of his life at home in Australia, Breaker Morant was in the thick of the fighting in the Transvaal. After enlisting as a private in Australia, he had been promoted to corporal and by the time he landed in Cape Town in February 1900 he had become a sergeant. He was on the road to redemption at last. In baking heat, his unit was soon sent north towards Pretoria. Morant the desert horseman felt quite at home as he rode the veldt to what he hoped would be glory in war and a new beginning at home.

His superb horsemanship and educated manner made him stand out and he soon came to the attention of Major General John French who gave Morant the perfect job—a dispatch rider, or galloper, charged with delivering urgent messages between columns of the army as it advanced. The Breaker might not have been trusted with the loan of a £5 note, but on horseback few could equal him and he was mentioned in dispatches for his reliability as a messenger.

The celebrated British war correspondent Bennett Burleigh also employed Morant as a dispatch rider. The dashing horseman played an important part in ensuring Burleigh's coverage of the war reached his readers at London's *The Daily Telegraph*. This job ensured Morant was in the midst of the action. It has also been said that he was a regular visitor to an army hospital, where he had affairs with the nurses and left them with broken hearts.

In October, Morant accepted a transfer to the Transvaal Constabulary. With the transfer came a lieutenant's commission. At last, the reckless ne'er-do-well had earned recognition that reflected his gentlemanly heritage. He gladly accepted the commission but requested he first be granted leave so that he could return to England. He had become close friends with Captain Percy Hunt, a gentleman from a good family in England. Their bond was a deep one, with the added advantage that Hunt could offer Morant entry into British society. Things were looking bright for Morant as he prepared to leave. Showing the regard in which he was held by his military colleagues, he received high praise in a letter from his former commanding officer with the Mounted Rifles, Colonel C.J. Reade:

> Your soldierly behaviour and your continual alertness as an irregular carried high commendation—and deservedly—from the whole of the officers of the regiment. I trust that in the future we may have an opportunity of renewing our pleasant acquaintance.

It was time for The Breaker to go home to whatever he had left behind. It was a defining moment. After an exile of eighteen years, he would be home in time for the Christmas of 1900.

10

RULE .303

Harry Morant was returning to England on his own terms and his spirits were high when he landed at Plymouth late in the northern autumn. If he approached the esteemed George Morant for a rapprochement then the olive branch was rebuffed, but the prodigal son at least seems to have been welcomed back into Devon society. Cashed up with army pay, he was there to enjoy himself. He hunted foxes and stags, played polo, caught up with old friends and, as always, made new ones.

Morant was determined to make the most of his return from exile. He even found time for romance. In a pledge that strengthened their growing friendship, Morant and Percy Hunt are said to have become engaged to two sisters—the daughters of a local squire—on the same day. Bonded by experiences of war and a love of hunting, the young soldiers spent much of that winter together. Breaker Morant, the daredevil drifter who had atoned for his sins in the hard Australian outback, seemed to be finding his feet in Devon's green and pleasant fields. But as winter came to an end, so too did

Morant's cash resources and whatever business had brought him home remained unresolved. Early in spring, his friend Captain Hunt returned to South Africa and a few weeks later Morant followed him.

Morant did not take up his commission with the Transvaal Cavalry. Instead, soon after his return to South Africa in April, he applied to join his friend Percy Hunt in a newly formed anti-guerrilla group, the Bushveldt Carbineers (BVC), led by an Australian, Major Robert Lenehan. Morant had ridden a racehorse owned by Lenehan in Sydney and the major was well aware of his recruit's prodigious skill on horseback. Morant was a perfect fit for the irregular band of soldiers charged with fighting the Boers under the new rules of guerrilla warfare. He gained his lieutenant's commission and was immediately sent north, first to Pretoria and from there, to Pietersburg.

At first, he served with distinction. In this war of raid and counter raid, Morant's unit played the Boers at their own game. Light, mobile and ruthless, the Bushveldt Carbineers were horseback commandoes who harried the Boer forces and disrupted their supply lines. They stole the Boers' food and lived off the land. Completely at home in this country that so resembled inland Australia, Morant rode into battle with a rifle at his side and books of classic poetry in his saddlebags.

He led a squadron that raided Boer farms, often attacking at dawn after riding through the night. Throughout the winter of 1901, he captured many prisoners and the Boers learned to fear him. He was popular with his fellow officers, and enjoyed hunting expeditions and polo games in Pietersburg in his leave time. His commanding officer, Major Lenehan, later described him as 'just the man for the work'.

As the Carbineers drove further into Boer-held territory, they set up a base in a frontier area north of Pietersburg. This base—a stout, fortified farmhouse—was known as Fort Edward. The commandos of the Bushveldt Carbineers would use it to harry the Boers in a war that was becoming increasingly desperate. Fast, mobile and intimately familiar with the terrain, the Boers staged lightning raids on men and infrastructure. The British built a network of concrete blockhouses linked by hundreds of kilometres of barbed wire and systematically cleared Boers from each sector. Disguised in British khaki or abusing the white flag, the Boers trapped the British in murderous ambushes.

Morant later claimed that around this time, he received orders from his friend Captain Hunt to shoot all Boer combatants dressed in British khaki, even if they surrendered. Morant said those orders were also issued by Captain Alfred Taylor, the sadistic BVC officer who was known to the native Africans as 'Bulala'—killer. Despite believing those orders originated from Lord Kitchener himself, Morant said he initially refused to follow them, and only did so after a traumatic personal experience. It is these supposed orders that define the debate over whether Morant was a murderer or a scapegoat.

A turning point came for Morant in July, when a Boer commando derailed a troop train near the town of Naboomspruit, and slaughtered all but four of the men on board. Among the dead was Lieutenant Alexander Best, a friend of both Morant and Hunt. The savage nature of Best's death deeply distressed Morant, who had by now experienced several bloody months of irregular warfare. It was a precursor to an even more distressing killing that pushed him over the line that separates soldier from accused murderer.

Morant's downfall began on the night of 5 August when his friend, Captain Hunt, led an attack on a Boer farm, hoping to capture the Boer commando leader Barend Viljoen. With seventeen men, Hunt charged the farmhouse after dark, pouring fire through the windows. But Hunt had dramatically underestimated the number of men defending the post. Fanned out inside the house, the Boers replied with a hail of bullets. One slammed into Hunt's chest as he stormed the house and he collapsed backwards into the yard. The Carbineers were driven back and had to leave their captain where he lay. Hunt died several hours later and, in the dead of night, the surviving Boers fled under the cover of darkness.

Hunt's naked body was recovered the next day. There were reports that he had been cruelly mutilated. When the news reached Morant, he was devastated. For the rest of his war, he was a changed man.

One of Morant's fellow officers was a former artillery gunner from coastal Victoria, Lieutenant George Witton. Like Morant, Witton had worked his way up through the ranks to earn his commission in South Africa. And, also like Morant, he would earn notoriety for what happened in the tumultuous weeks after the death of Captain Hunt. Witton later published his account of the confused and bloody events of 1901 in his book, *Scapegoats of the Empire*. In it, he said Morant became 'like a man demented' after learning of Hunt's death.

According to Witton, Morant broke down as he tried to address the troops, and his commander, the feared Alfred Taylor, stepped up to urge the men to avenge Hunt's death and 'give no quarter'. Encouraged, Morant immediately led a patrol to catch the fleeing Boers. Led by a guide, the patrol charged over the veldt, halting only every four hours to rest the horses before mounting up and racing off again at a brutal pace. Morant rode at the head of the column, his mood veering from sullenness to fury. When the patrol became lost, Morant erupted into a rage against the guide, cursing and threatening him until he feared for his life.

Breaker Morant, 1865–1902. *Photograph courtesy State Library of Victoria.*

At nightfall, the patrol rested at a native kraal for a few hours before resuming the pursuit by the pale light of a new moon. Late the next afternoon, they met up with the men of Hunt's unit at a mission station. The men told Morant that they had recovered and buried the body of his friend. They said Hunt's neck had been broken and his legs slashed with a knife. His bloodied and bruised face was imprinted with the marks of hobnailed boots, his clothing was gone and his genitals amputated. Morant was convinced that his friend had not been honourably slain on the battlefield but murdered and desecrated by a cowardly enemy. His blood sizzled in a dangerous mix of fury and grief.

At daybreak, news came in that the fugitive Boers were headed for a district called the Waterberg. A gloomy and sullen Morant set out immediately at the head of forty-five mounted men, stopping only once that day to rest the horses. The men travelled light and carried no food. At sunset, the patrol caught up with the Boers who had bunkered down for the night in a laager—a temporary stronghold of circled wagons set up in a hollow between a series of kopjes. The patrol was perfectly placed for an ambush, but as Winton remembered, Morant could not contain his impatience:

> Morant was excited and eager to make an attack. He sent Lieutenant [Henry] Picton with a party on his right flank, but to Morant, in his excitement, the moment seemed like hours. Before Picton could get his men into position, and just as I arrived at the foot of the kopje with the rear guard, Morant opened fire on the laager.

The quiet of the African evening was shattered by the roar of gunfire. Chaos reigned for a few moments and when the shooting stopped, the patrol rushed into the laager to find the Boers had galloped away, leaving behind their wagons and goods. Dead and dying horses were strewn around the camp. A search found one Boer—a man named Visser—hiding under a wagon. He had been shot in the heel.

According to Witton, Morant wanted to shoot the wounded man immediately but 'he was prevailed upon not to do so, as the firing might attract the Boers'. Instead, Visser was placed in a wagon and the men of the patrol spent that cold night, sheltering below a kopje, their bellies rumbling in hunger. Early the next morning, word reached the patrol that they were urgently needed at Fort Edward, which was under threat from Boer attack. They were to return with haste. Before leaving, Morant questioned the prisoner Visser and claimed to have found him in possession of a British army shirt and a pair of trousers that had belonged to Captain Hunt. According to Witton, Morant informed his fellow officers that he intended to shoot Visser at the earliest opportunity. The patrol then burned the Boer wagons and rounded up their oxen before setting out for the fort.

At eleven o'clock that morning, they halted near a river where they slaughtered one of the captured oxen and had their first food in more than twenty-four hours. After breaking their fast it was time to deal with the prisoner Visser. Morant convened a 'drumhead' court martial and put the case against the prisoner. 'This man,' Morant said, 'has been concerned in the murder of Captain Hunt; he has been captured wearing British uniform and I have got orders direct from headquarters not to take prisoners, while only the other day Lord Kitchener sent out a proclamation that all Boers captured wearing khaki [British uniforms] were to be summarily shot.' Morant later described this order as 'Rule Three Oh Three', a reference to the .303 rifles carried by the Carbineers.

Morant then ordered the formation of a firing squad headed by Lieutenant Picton. The injured Visser was taken from a wagon and placed in a sitting position on an embankment about 20 metres from the firing party. The order was given and bullets spat from the massed rifles. Visser collapsed to the ground, still alive. Calmly, Picton finished him off with a single round from his pistol.

As commander of the patrol, Harry Morant had committed the first act that would earn him infamy in Australia. But had he cruelly ordered the murder of Visser or was he simply following harsh directives from a British command determined to win an increasingly desperate guerrilla war? It is a question that is still being debated today.

*

The Bushveldt Carbineers had been wracked by morale problems before the killing of Visser but, following his execution, tensions between the officers and men threatened to erupt into mutiny. After months of savage guerrilla fighting, the unit was a seething mess of hostility. Some of the troops particularly resented Morant for his efforts to discipline them. It was in this environment that he oversaw the deaths of more Boer prisoners.

On 23 August, Morant led a patrol to intercept a party of eight Boers who had been captured and were being brought into Fort Edward. Before leaving, Morant met with Captain Taylor and announced his intention to shoot the incoming prisoners. Taylor supposedly said nothing to dissuade him. That afternoon, Morant's patrol rode out to take custody of the prisoners.

As Morant's men returned to the fort, they met a British missionary of German descent, Daniel Heese, who was travelling in a wagon with an African driver. Heese attempted to assure the prisoners that they would not be harmed but a short time later—within just a few kilometres of the fort—Morant ordered the patrol to halt. The prisoners were lined up on the side of the road and questioned. When one said he was aware that Captain Hunt was dead, all eight prisoners were shot dead on Morant's orders. As the bodies lay in the dust, Morant supposedly said: 'That's for

Captain Hunt.' It was later alleged that some of the prisoners were wearing clothing that had belonged to Hunt.

Appalled, the missionary Heese continued on his way, rejecting Morant's warning against travelling alone. Six days later, Lieutenant Handcock found the bodies of Heese and his driver in long grass not far from the fort. Heese had been shot in the chest. Morant and his men had a strong motive to kill the missionary, who was a witness to the killing of the Boers, but there was no evidence to prove they had done it. Nonetheless, Morant and Handcock would be held accountable for it.

There was more killing to come. On 7 September, word reached the fort that another party of Boers was coming in to surrender. That afternoon, a patrol lead by Morant and Handcock found three Boers in a wagon. All three—an elderly man and his two sons—were shot dead. The youngest, who was seriously ill with fever, might have been only fifteen. None of the three was armed. Four months later, on trial for his life, Morant would claim he was following orders from the top.

Before that, though, Morant again distinguished himself in the field. When news reached the fort that the notorious Irish-Boer freebooter and train wrecker, Veldt-cornet John Kelly, was planning raids on the British in the Spelonken district north of Pietersburg in September, Morant asked to be sent after him. An intriguing exchange said to have taken place between Lenehan and Morant raises questions over whether standing orders did indeed exist to kill Boer prisoners:

Lenehan (in reply to Morant's request): 'But we particularly want this man brought in alive.'
Morant: 'Alive! Don't you know what a bloody scoundrel he is?'

Morant and Witton set off with thirty men on 16 September. Six days later, they caught up with Kelly, who was camped with his men and some women on the Thsombo River near the Portuguese border. As there were women present, Morant refrained from firing on the camp and instead surrounded the camp and laid low. At half-past four on the morning of 23 September, the patrol rushed the camp and took everyone prisoner, including Kelly. All were safely returned to Fort Edward. It was a spectacularly successful raid that cleared the area of its last Boer guerrillas.

Hoping these heroics would lift the cloud of the previous Boer killings from his head, Morant took two weeks' leave to finalise the affairs of his friend Captain Hunt. But wheels were now inexorably in motion. On 21 October, Morant and six of his fellow Carbineer officers—including Handcock and Witton—were arrested after allegations about the killings were made by some of their men. They were held in solitary confinement while a case was assembled against them. The Australian government was not advised of their arrest and they were not given access to legal counsel until the day before their first court martial started at Pietersburg on 16 January 1902.

The cases against them would begin with the shooting of the prisoner Visser, and then the killing of the eight Boer prisoners. The hearings into the deaths of the three Boers and the missionary Heese would be held in February.

Their last-minute defence counsel was Major James Thomas, formerly a solicitor from Tenterfield. His hopes of saving the men boiled down to their claims that orders had been made to give no quarter to Boer prisoners. In evidence, Morant said those orders had come down through his dead friend Captain Hunt from Lord Kitchener's military secretary. Of the killing of the prisoner Visser, Morant said he had been captured wearing British khaki and was shot after a drumhead court martial. Later in the hearing, he tried to absolve the men of Visser's firing squad from blame when he said: 'They were following my orders and thought they were obeying Lord Kitchener's [orders].'

Morant added that he had not followed those orders until his best friend Captain Hunt was brutally murdered by the Boers. Under cross-examination, Morant was asked whether the drumhead court martial of Visser had followed the King's Regulations. Morant's reply was scornful and to the point:

> As to rules and sections, we had no Red Book, and knew nothing about them. We were fighting Boers, not sitting comfortably behind barb-wire entanglements. We got them and shot them under Rule .303.

On the morning of 23 January, proceedings were halted in dramatic fashion when a party of Boers attacked the fort at Pietersburg where the trial was taking place. Remarkably, Morant and his co-accused were taken from the cells and handed rifles. They helped to repel the Boer attack and, having done so, were promptly returned to custody and the case against them continued. At its end, the court retired without delivering a verdict

The case of the eight Boers started on 3 February. In a statement to the court, Morant said he knew the eight 'belonged to the same gang that had maltreated and dishonoured the body of my friend and brother officer [Captain Hunt]'. He said the Boers were train wreckers and that he had previously been reprimanded for bringing in prisoners alive. However, the treatment of Hunt's body had made him decide to do as other officers had already done—followed orders and shot prisoners. Handock, Witton and Picton also told the court that they had received orders not to take prisoners.

Their counsel, Major Thomas, argued the eight Boers were marauders and their killings should not be regarded as a lawless act at a time of war. The prosecutor, however, said the prisoners should have received a proper trial and that 'it is seldom justifiable for a combatant to take the law into his own hands against an unresisting foe'. The case concluded and again, the verdict was reserved.

The case of the three Boers followed—the two men and the 'boy'. Throughout, Major Thomas argued valiantly for Morant and the other accused men, citing the existence of orders to kill Boer prisoners and the gruelling nature of irregular combat as their defence. Copies of Australian newspapers quoting Kitchener as saying Boers captured in British uniforms should be shot were tendered to the court.

The case of the murder of the missionary Heese, started on 17 February. The prosecution alleged Handcock shot the missionary on Morant's orders. Morant and Handcock denied it. The evidence against them was thin and on 19 February, they were found not guilty of Heese's murder. It was the case that had most worried them and their acquittal fanned hopes that they would be cleared of the other charges. That night, two members of the courts martial panel delivered champagne to the men's cells. It seemed that Morant and the others would soon be free.

But their hopes were dashed. A few days after the Heese verdict, Morant, Handcock and Witton were found guilty of murdering Visser and the eight Boer prisoners. All three defendants were sentenced to death, and were taken to a prison in Pretoria to await their execution. In a sign of hope, however, the court strongly recommended mercy for Morant on three grounds, including 'extreme provocation by the mutilation of the body of Captain Hunt'. Mercy was also recommended to Handcock and Witton.

Witton's sentence was commuted to life imprisonment, but there was no mercy for Morant or Handcock. Kitchener had personally signed the execution order and had no intention of letting either man live. On 26 February, Morant and Handcock were informed the sentence had been upheld and that they would die at dawn the next day. That afternoon, they could hear the sounds of their coffins being constructed in the prison workshop. Meanwhile, Major Thomas rushed off to see Kitchener in the hope of getting a stay, but was told the field marshal was away and would not return for several days. That night, Morant and Handcock had a last supper in their cell and before dawn on 27 February, they were taken out of the fort to face a firing squad.

Morant and Handcock both asked for their blindfolds to be removed so they could face the men who would end their lives. Morant asked for a last cigarette and threw it away half smoked. He gave his cigarette case to the officer in charge of the firing squad and uttered his famous last words: 'Shoot straight, you bastards! Don't make a mess of it!' Then the rifles barked and the brave, reckless Harry Morant died instantly, his eyes still open and his mate Handcock dead beside him.

*

On the day of the execution, a highly distressed Major Thomas wrote a letter to a friend in Australia, saying the deaths of Morant and Handcock had 'broken' him. Thomas said the men died bravely but they were politically doomed 'through the iniquities of the court of inquiry'. Poor Thomas was so bitter he could barely express his feelings but he was certain the executed men were not guilty. Thomas never recovered psychologically from the trial and execution of Morant and Handcock. Although he retained respect in his home town of Tenterfield, Thomas became bankrupt and was disbarred from the law. He died poor and alone in 1941.

The Australian newspapers reported the shooting of Morant and Handcock as 'sensational news from South Africa', but few questioned whether the verdict was just. Melbourne's *Argus* said the executions were 'the eulogy of British fairness', while in the new House of Representatives in Canberra, Prime Minister Edmund Barton—who had been told little by the British Government—said it 'would be unwise to come to any conclusions . . . in view of the conflicting evidence'. Barton added that he had been privately briefed on the matter but could not make any authoritative statement on what he had learned. It seemed that many Australians were happy to accept the British had done the right thing.

But a brave journalist, W.T. Goodge, could not hide his outrage at the death of his friend, Harry Morant. Pointedly, Goodge referred to the 'assassination' of Morant and Handcock, and said he would never believe Morant had murdered unarmed Boers in such a cowardly fashion:

> He [Morant] pulled the bandage off his eyes when he faced the rifles, and the British Government blew his brains out. That's all right; I don't blame the British Government; they can't blow out their own brains because they haven't got any, and there's nothing like trying to please the enemy all the time you're at war, even if you have to make a regular circus of court martialling and shooting your own men.

It was widely reported that Morant was the son of the British admiral, George Morant, until the admiral indignantly published letters denying any connection to the 'offensive statement' that he had fathered such a scoundrel as Harry Morant. The admiral, according to the papers, was a venerable old gentleman who had made his name as a 'pirate exterminator in Chinese waters' and his word was not to be doubted.

In Sydney, Barty Paterson at first refused to believe the worst of Morant. In April 1902, he wrote an article for *The Sydney Mail*, in which he said Morant was a rogue but it was inconceivable to think he would take the life of an unarmed man. In May, he wrote to *The Bulletin*, saying, 'I find it hard to believe that he killed anybody for gain. Reckless ne'er-do-well he was, but one finds it very difficult to think of him as a murderer . . .'

It is clear from Morant's letters to Paterson that The Breaker had warm feelings for his fellow poet. Morant wrote to Paterson of things that interested both—hunting, horses and the bush. In Sydney, they had played polo together and enjoyed each other's company at artistic haunts. It seems strange, then, that when Paterson had his final say on Harry Morant, his memories were not kind ones.

In his *Sydney Morning Herald* reminiscences in 1939, Paterson recalled that Morant had once conned a gymkhana committee out of £10. In the same report—which did not mention that Morant was a fellow balladist—Paterson also wrote a rather distorted account of the events that had led to Morant's death, revealing his belief that Morant had been an underdog whose 'one day of power . . . went to his head like wine'. These rather mean recollections did Paterson no credit and sparked an angry reaction from some of his readers.

Frederick Cutlack, who as a boy had known Morant, wrote a strong letter to the *Herald*, criticising Paterson for not remembering Morant by his pen-name, 'The Breaker'. Cutlack, at least, was prepared to put his name to the defence of Morant.

Perhaps he [Morant] deceived some people, and left them angry; but he was known in all the back country from Queensland to the Lower Murray, and great numbers of other people of careless habits—or even some of scrupulous rectitude—loved him in spite of his faults.

No angel, Morant was nonetheless liked and admired by many. Perhaps a murderer, perhaps a scapegoat, his life and death made him part of Australian folklore—no mean feat for an Englishman who spent only half of his short life in Australia—and he deserved better from his one-time friend Barty Paterson.

It has been suggested that Paterson's final shot was the result of jealousy for a man who was his equal in the saddle, a fellow poet, and, despite his waywardness, a man of immense charm and bravery. It is possible, however, that Paterson's rather sour recollections were simply reflecting an older man's natural conservatism, written at a time when the Empire he admired was once again on the brink of war. Whatever the reason, it would have been better for Paterson to have either tackled the issue of Morant's guilt or innocence—or said nothing at all. After all, Harry Morant had then lain in his African grave for almost forty years and could not defend himself.

Morant and Peter Handcock lie in Africa still. Their grave marker is inscribed with a line from Matthew: 'A man's foes shall be those of his own household.' In 1910, Kitchener unveiled a war memorial in Handcock's home town of Bathurst. Handcock's name was not on the memorial, prompting unproven claims that Kitchener had insisted on it being removed. It took more than half a century for this omission to be reversed and the name of brave, simple Handcock was added to the memorial in 1964, restoring to him some measure of posthumous honour.

George Witton was sent to prison in Britain where he suffered serious illness on at least two occasions. After strident protests, he was released from prison in 1904 but not pardoned. His book, *Scapegoats of the Empire*, was published in 1907, but few copies were available, prompting claims that the book had been suppressed by the government. It became more widely read after it was republished in the 1980s. Witton worked as a dairy farmer in Victoria and Queensland and remained bitter towards the British until his death in 1942.

Today, efforts continue to gain a posthumous pardon for Harry Morant. Although he undoubtedly had blood on his hands, a view persists that he was the victim of British injustice. Murderer or victim, he remains as much a part of Australia's identity as other flawed men who died by order of the Empire. Like Ned Kelly, Breaker Morant polarises opinions today, and like Kelly, The Breaker died game.

//
WORLD TRAVELS

Paterson returned from the war in need of a job. He remained a sleeping partner in his legal firm with John Street, but his practice of the law was effectively over. He found peacetime in Australia unsettling after the excitement of the war and his thoughts turned to how he could turn his experiences into an income. The answer lay in taking to the road for a series of lectures. He began a national tour on 21 September 1900 in Sydney, where a big crowd turned out to hear him. He was not a natural orator—some observers said his voice was rather monotonous—and he was plainly nervous to be standing at the lectern, but he was a hit with his audience.

Attired in evening dress, he spoke in central Sydney and at Parramatta before moving on to country towns. People turned out in droves to hear him, paying between one and three shillings, depending on the quality of their seats. His lectures included a 'lantern show'—slides of the photos he had taken in South Africa—and his material ranged from the tragic to the humorous. On most nights, he played to a sell-out crowd.

In February 1901, Paterson toured regional New South Wales, gaining confidence as he went. He won applause in Goulburn and praise in Bathurst. In Tenterfield, he almost lost his composure when the audience gave him a standing ovation before his talk had even started. Once or twice he was jeered for being 'pro-Boer', but the audiences were deeply moved when he spoke of the sufferings of dead and dying men on both sides. He knew what his crowd wanted to hear and there was applause when he praised the 'resourcefulness and cool effrontery of the Australian soldier'. The Sydney newspapers admired 'his flashes of wit' and his humorous anecdotes of the lighter side of war left his Bathurst audience 'in a happy mood'. Eternally modest, with a sense of the ridiculous, he might have chuckled at a report that poked fun at his famous pen-name:

> Banjo Paterson was in a western town recently lecturing. Now, Banjo is not real good on the platform; in fact, he's dismal, as all first-class pen jostlers are. One man came out at the intermission and was asked if he was going back. 'Going back?' said he, 'why, Gawd spare me days, I went there and stood him magging for a blanky hour and the beggar never played the blanky banjo once! What right's he got to go round the country calling himself "Banjo" Paterson?'

Banjo continued the tours with lectures in Melbourne before crossing Bass Strait to speak in Hobart and Launceston. His Tasmanian audience was struck by his 'distinct Sydney-side accent' and liked what he had to say. The crowd at the Academy of Music Hall in Hobart was so impressed on his first night that many returned to hear him again the next. Then it was off to New Zealand before finishing the tour in South Australia in October.

The tours were lucrative, but the pace exhausting. The rigours of the road wore him down and when he was en route from

Tasmania to New Zealand, he wrote to the publisher George Robertson, saying he was in 'miserable health . . . [and] can't get enough exercise':

> I think as soon as this tour is over I will be off to China or else buy a pig-farm in the country and never move off it . . . The lecturing is not so bad but the lonely travelling is awful. Anyhow the money is good which is the main thing . . .

Good money notwithstanding, he gave up lecturing after New Zealand and turned his thoughts briefly to a career in parliament. He had made his first tentative foray into politics ten years earlier but changed his mind. He tested the waters again on the night of Tuesday 28 May 1901, when he visited the town of Burrowa near his childhood home of Illalong to address a big crowd at the town's hall.

Paterson told his potential constituents that he was there to explain his political views and, if they met with approval, he would stand. If they did not like his views then that was bad luck. He would not change his ideas. This plain speaking impressed his straightforward country audience and there was applause as he began to explain his beliefs. Paterson reprised some of the themes expressed in 'Australia for the Australians', and it seems clear that his protectionist position was largely formed by the failure of his own family to make it on the land. The audience applauded when he expressed a view that there were too many large estates and not enough small farms, and there were cries of 'Hear! Hear!' when he called for the government to buy the large estates and subdivide them. The applause died away when he opposed the Labor Party's call for a minimum wage of seven shillings a day, but he was back on firmer ground when he said it was important to keep alien labourers, especially the Chinese, out of Australia.

It seemed that A.B. Paterson was just the man his potential electorate wanted. But there was a problem. It was not that the locals disagreed with him; it was that everybody was already on the same page—including the sitting local member. Soon after the meeting, Paterson wrote to the *Burrowa News* to say he would not stand for the seat because 'my politics differ so little from the present member that I cannot see any justification for opposing him'. The Honourable Member for the Burrowa district must have breathed a sigh of relief to learn he would not be challenged by a candidate of such fame. For his part, Paterson announced he was likely to run for the Protectionist and Democratic Party in a seat held by a 'free trader'. This never happened.

The newspapers, however, were broadly supportive of the idea of Banjo as a politician. In June, Grafton's *Clarence and Richmond Examiner* possibly underestimated the political sophistication of rural voters when it noted: 'If he puts up for a country electorate, the fact that Kipling said he rode like an angel may secure his election.' In October, *The Bulletin* was full of praise for its celebrated contributor:

> If 'Banjo' Paterson wanted a testimonial to his demeanour on the battlefield he could get it from the Victorian Colonel Hoad. The Colonel says that 'Banjo' seemed to have no notion of physical fear, and was constantly in the thick of the fighting. He was also one of the most popular correspondents on the field: officers liked him, and the correspondent who is popular with the officers has a good time.

Perhaps it was his natural reserve, but for some reason, Paterson abandoned his flirtation with politics and decided to revisit journalism. Luckily, he was able to call upon an acquaintance in a high place. Sir James Reading Fairfax, owner of *The Sydney Morning Herald*, shared Paterson's passion for developing inland Australia and saw him as the right man to lead the charge. Fairfax offered Paterson a commission to write a series of articles titled 'Good Districts'. This job saw Paterson traverse the coast of New South Wales, writing about agricultural opportunities ranging from dairying in the south to the potential for tropical fruit production in the north.

Fairfax was pleased with Paterson's work and asked him to investigate the potential of an industry that would eventually revolutionise life on the hills and plains west of the Great Divide. Irrigation, said Fairfax, was 'one of the most important matters for this country', and Paterson was dispatched on a mission to write about the possibilities of bringing permanent water supplies to the hot and dry western plains. He soon found there was an Irrigation Section within the Public Works Office—but precious little had been done to get the water flowing. The men charged with examining this great project, however, were delighted that someone was taking an interest in their work, and, pulling dusty files and maps from pigeon holes, they urged Paterson to stir up the politicians and the public.

Soon the *Herald* sent a photographer on 'a frightful climb through granite gorges' to get a picture of a rugged valley between two mountains near Yass. It was thought that these peaks—Mount Barren Jack and Black Andrew—could bookend a massive dam to catch the cold, fast-flowing waters of the Murrumbidgee River. In this way, a significant part of the driest inhabited continent on Earth could be virtually assured a regular supply of water. Thirty years later, Paterson recalled the idea of damming the great, west-flowing rivers was immediately popular:

> Politicians at a loss for a catch-word found themselves repeating at their meetings, 'I believe in irrigation, and the Barren Jack dam,' and in a few days the public became dam-conscious so to speak. The late E.W. O'Sullivan was then Minister for

Public Works—a man of large ideas and one that kept his ear pretty close to the ground for indications of public opinion. Like Horace, he stepped nobly up to the bridge, and said: 'I will build the Barren Jack dam,' and that, as the Americans say, was all there was to it.

Work started in 1907. It was a massive project that saw a light rail line built to ferry in materials and an army of workers to the remote and mountainous construction site. The workers lived in huts of tin and hessian, labouring through icy winters and scorching summers. During the construction, the dam's name was changed from Barren Jack to Burrinjuck, a decision, according to Paterson, designed to make the area sound more appealing to 'English settlers'.

Water began to flow to new irrigation farms in the Murrumbidgee Valley in 1912 and when the dam was declared completed sixteen years later, large parts of inland Australia were well on the way to being permanently watered. The dam had cost about £1.7 million to build and Australia now had one of the world's biggest freshwater storages.

Meanwhile, eager for more adventure and hoping to reprise his role as a war correspondent, Paterson arranged with Fairfax to travel to China to cover the simmering Boxer Rebellion. In July 1901, he sailed on the steamer *Changsha*, with the aim of visiting China and Japan before taking the Trans-Siberian railway to St Petersburg. He would supply stories and photographs for the *Herald* and *The Sydney Mail*, and, if by fortune a war broke out, he would be 'at hand to act for the *Herald* as occasion may require'.

Still single, and now aged thirty-seven, Paterson sailed from Sydney on 29 July 1901. There was an irony in his hope that China's Boxer Rebellion would lead to another chance to report on a war. The so-called Boxers—the 'Society of Righteous and

Harmonious Fists'—were revolting against foreign imperialism in China and Christianity in general. Their nationalism might have appealed to Paterson but for his mistrust of Asians. He expressed a thought—perhaps facetiously—that covering a war in China would be a hazardous assignment as the 'Chinese impaled correspondents on bamboos'.

The rebellion was subdued before he could get to China but, even before his ship left Australian waters, a new opportunity seemed to beckon. When the *Changsha* reached Darwin in mid-August, the *Northern Territory Times and Gazette* suggested that Paterson might still find himself at the centre of a major confrontation in the east:

> There is . . . said to be a strong impression prevailing south that the much-talked-of collision between Japan and Russia may shortly become a reality, and that the graphic colonial war correspondent who forwarded such lively pen-pictures from South Africa is now being sent east in order that he may be conveniently on hand in the event of the expected eruption taking place.

China and Japan managed to avoid war at that time but Paterson did not let the outbreak of peace stop him from developing his skills as a correspondent. He took a keen interest in the people he saw at each port and he recorded his observations at each one, starting with Thursday Island—a 'place with more nationalities than there were at the Tower of Babel'. He scored a journalistic coup when he arrived in the Philippines—'the land of Uncle Sam'. Noting that 'a war correspondent can no more pass up a general than a woman can a bargain sale', Paterson was thrilled to secure an interview with the American general, Adna Chaffee.

Chaffee had been sent to China to help suppress the Boxers before becoming the governor of the Philippines, where he led the fight against Filipinos rebelling against American rule. Paterson enjoyed a long chat with the 'grisly looking old warrior' and filed a report that graphically illustrated the general's problems in trying to tame the peasant-soldiers of the islands. Paterson was proving his merit as a war correspondent—even if he did not have an Australian war to write about.

The *Changsha* left Manila in fine weather and had a clear passage to Hong Kong, despite the captain's fears that a typhoon might strike. It was early September when Paterson sailed into a Hong Kong harbour so crowded with junks that a shipmate thought the Chinese were holding a regatta. On the seventeenth, a guide took him to the coastal city of Yantai, then known in the west as Chefoo, where he planned to meet up with the famous correspondent for *The Times* of London, George 'Chinese' Morrison. As he travelled overland, Paterson was impressed with the abundance of fruit and flowers he saw, and was pleased to buy food and silk at bargain prices. The Chinese were happy to take his money, but as he remembered later, they did not make the white man feel welcome:

Neither man nor beast in China has anything but hatred for the foreigner. As we pass through the little villages and tumbledown humpies of the cultivators the men scowl at us; the dogs snarl and slink off with every symptom of terror and disgust; the cattle snort and shiver if we pass near them; and the mules will watch us uneasily till we go away. The people hate us with a cold intensity that surpasses any other hate that I have ever heard of. A fat Chinese shopkeeper, who speaks English, says, 'Poor Chinaman only good for chow [is only fit to be eaten]. What does Chinaman savvy?'

Paterson already knew Morrison by reputation. In 1880, as an eighteen-year-old, the Geelong-born Morrison had walked along the coast from Melbourne to Adelaide and then sold his diary of this walking tour to a newspaper. A year later, he canoed down the Murray River from Wodonga to the river mouth—and, for good measure, walked back to Geelong. Then he went to north Queensland to report on the Kanaka 'blackbirding' trade for *The Age*, walked from the Gulf of Carpentaria to Melbourne in what he described as 'a pleasant excursion' and set out to explore inland New Guinea, only abandoning the journey after being speared in the face and abdomen by natives. The spearhead was surgically removed a year later. Undeterred, Morrison continued to wander the world, working as a surgeon and a missionary before becoming *The Times'* man in China. As Paterson noted with characteristic understatement, 'a man like that takes some stopping'.

His meeting with Morrison was uncomfortable at first, at least for Paterson. His initial impression of the famous correspondent was of a 'tall, ungainly man with a dour Scotch face and a curious droop at the corner of his mouth'. Their introduction was marred by Morrison's insistence on talking mainly about women. Straight-laced Paterson never spoke publicly about women or sex and he thought Morrison's conversation hinted at an 'unbalance in his mentality'. But when the conversation was steered towards the Boxer Rebellion, war and investment in China, Paterson found the meeting a revelation. He later recalled Morrison as one of the three 'great men of state' that he had met. The other two were Cecil Rhodes and the incomparable Winston Churchill.

Soon Paterson left China for England. He was unable to go to Russia as planned because sea ice had frozen his intended route, but his visit to London proved to be a high point of his travels. There he caught up with that other great man, Rudyard Kipling, experienced British bohemia with his friend, the artist Phil May, and very nearly made his dream of reporting for *The Times* come true.

*

Henry Lawson, meanwhile, had done some travelling of his own. On the night of 4 April 1900, he was farewelled at a banquet in Sydney, ahead of his move to London. *The Bulletin*'s A.G. Stephens proposed a toast for Henry, saying he was sorry to see him leave but hoped he would return when success befell him. Lawson responded—perhaps with a drink to break his sobriety—by saying that books no longer needed to be published in England to be successful and that Australians were learning to appreciate works written and produced in their homeland.

Two weeks later, Henry, Bertha and their two small children sailed on the *Damascus* for London. When they arrived, things got off to a promising start. Henry was represented by a leading literary agent and was contracted to produce books for William Blackwood, the editor of *Blackwood's Edinburgh Magazine*. Newspapers back at home suggested this contract yielded a very healthy advance of £400. A 'special correspondent' in London met briefly with Lawson and filed an optimistic story for Australian newspapers:

> Mr Lawson has experienced the usual Australian stupefaction at the intense ignorance and lack of understanding of Australian matters that are so widespread in England . . . 'No Australian story complete without a bushranger' has long been the motto of the magazine editor, and England is heartily sick of the Australian bushranger of gentlemanly antecedents . . . and that is why Henry Lawson will print well and sell well in London.

At first, this optimism was justified. It was a productive time for Lawson. He soon found his feet and wrote some of his best works, including the Joe Wilson series of short stories. Joe was a character very like the author—sensitive, sad and doomed to meet disappointment. Lawson might have been describing himself when he later said Joe's 'natural sentimental selfishness, good nature, "softness" or weakness—call it which you like—developed as I wrote on'.

He later told an Australian reporter that he spent time in London, following police to learn all of the great city's 'misery, sin and heroism'. He might have taken some licence with this account as the family stayed only a couple of weeks in London before moving to the village of Harpenden in Hertfordshire. There, Lawson visited a low, thatch-roofed pub where he enjoyed drinking with farm workers but was dismayed at their insistence on calling him 'sir'. It was impossible for them to understand, he said, why this term of respect from an equal would sit uncomfortably with an Australian.

While in England, Lawson also helped to launch the career of another great Australian writer, Miles Franklin. Henry had taken a copy of Franklin's first novel, *My Brilliant Career*, to London in the hope of finding a publisher. William Blackwood reluctantly agreed to publish it, on the condition that Lawson provided a preface. He did so, writing in part:

> I don't know about the girlishly emotional part of the book.
> I leave that to girl readers to judge; but the descriptions of
> Bush life and scenery came startlingly, painfully real to me,
> and I know that, as far as they are concerned, the book is
> true to Australia—the truest I ever read.

My Brilliant Career was published in 1901 and went on to become an Australian classic. Despite its success—or more likely because of it—the book brought only limited happiness to its author. Members of Franklin's family were outraged at seeing themselves reflected negatively in the novel's characters. Some of her relatives even threatened to sue. The artist Norman Lindsay, who met a young Franklin at *The Bulletin* offices soon after the book was published, said Franklin's 'stuffy, scandalised Victorian relations' scared her so much that she was forced to flee to England.

Meanwhile, Henry once again made a mess of his financial affairs. Soon he was broke and fell to hounding publishers for extra advances or accelerated royalty payments. Much of the money that came disappeared in the pub. The strain on Bertha was immense and in March 1901, she was admitted to a London hospital for treatment of mental illness, probably severe depression. A census taken at the end of the month listed Bertha as being a 'lunatic' under treatment while Henry was shown as living in a three-roomed flat at Clovelly Mansions with their one-year-old daughter, Bertha Louisa. Their son Joe was not listed on the census but the papers showed a servant named Lizzie Humphrey was sharing the flat. It is possible that Henry and Lizzie—who was described in a newspaper gossip column as an 'attractive domestic'—were romantically involved, which could help to explain Bertha's breakdown.

The details of whatever went wrong remain clouded, but in May 1902, Henry wrote to *The Bulletin* to say that Bertha and the children would return to Australia in June and he, Henry, would follow them when he completed work on a new book. The letter explained the depth of his latest decline:

[I] have been wonderfully successful from a literary point of view, but my health has completely broken down, and I must come home for a year or so. Some of my stories are being translated into German. I know London as well as I know the Bush, and propose to write of London for the Australian papers and of Australia for the London papers.

Bertha and the children sailed from Southampton on the German ship, the *Kahlsruhe*, and Henry followed in the sister ship, the *Gera*. He met up with his family at Colombo and they sailed together for Adelaide. But this journey was the last they would take together. The straws that held together the unhappy marriage of Henry and Bertha finally collapsed somewhere between Colombo and Adelaide, and, when the ship docked in South Australia, Henry disembarked alone. He caught a train to Melbourne—while Bertha and the children remained on the ship for the final leg of their journey home to Sydney.

*

Barty Paterson, meanwhile, had found London to be everything he had hoped for. In stark contrast to Lawson's experience in the same city, Paterson had enjoyed glittering nights at plays and musicals in the West End and suppers with celebrities in fine restaurants. He had arrived in October 1901, just in time to catch a wave of artistry with a handful of Australians at its crest. Chief among them was Phil May, the former comic artist with *The Bulletin*.

An Englishman, May was wonderfully eccentric, immensely talented and forever broke. He was delighted to see his old friend and colleague Barty, not least because he had bought a horse he had not seen in a year and he wanted someone to ride it. May—'an extraordinarily skinny man with a face like a gargoyle'—was always buying things he did not need and spending far more than he earned. The horse was just the latest in his collection.

The shining lights of the city's bohemians gathered most Sunday nights at May's home in St John's Wood for a celebration of creativity. The host sang sentimental ballads in a pleasant tenor voice while operatic stars hit high notes and actors schmoozed with promoters and financiers. May was regarded as 'a kind of Aladdin' in the theatre world because it seemed he only had to rub a lamp to find jobs for performers, and they all pressed him to get them meetings with producers and promoters. Many of the artists left the May home on those Sunday evenings secure for a few more weeks after finding a job in a new show—thanks to Phil's good graces.

May owned a bulldog—'the cheeriest, kindest, slobberiest bulldog that anyone ever saw'. Phil's wife insisted he take the dog when he went out to the pub at night, in the hope that the responsibility for the animal would bring him home before daylight. It tended to be a forlorn hope. Everyone wanted to buy Phil a drink and he rarely refused. After enjoying himself for a few hours, he often called for a cab to take the dog home. As Paterson recalled in a book of personal reminiscences, *Happy Dispatches* (1934), the dog's outings proved to be an expensive business:

> The dog loved riding in cabs, and evidently had the idea that when he entered a cab he had bought it; for if there happened to be nobody at home when he arrived there, he would refuse to leave the cab and the cabman had to sit on the box and wait, perhaps for an hour two, until Mrs May came home. No wonder that Phil was chronically hard up!

In November, Paterson went to the offices of *The Times* for a job interview. At first, he was treated with the disdain one might expect for a mere colonial in the offices of the great newspaper but, after being kept waiting for an hour, he finally met with the manager, Moberly Bell—'a fine big personable man'. Paterson was pleased with the interview and wrote to George Robertson in Sydney to say that he expected to be appointed Australian correspondent for *The Times*.

Paterson had been rather down at not being able to travel to Siberia as planned, but a chance to work for one of the world's great papers was an incredible opportunity. He hoped to 'put some new ideas into English heads about Australia'. Unfortunately, he was too optimistic and the job at *The Times* did not eventuate. He had to be content with writing verses for the *Pink 'Un*—a small bohemian publication which at that time was fighting a losing battle against the rise of the motor car.

A disappointed Paterson found solace—as well as his own introduction to the motor car—when he went to stay with Rudyard Kipling at his 'unpretentious house' at Brighton. Barty did not know what to expect of Kipling but imagined a great literary genius must be seething with vice—a magnet for women, drink and trouble. Instead, he was almost disappointed to discover that Kipling and his charming American wife were unremarkable to the point of being ordinary. The only hint that Kipling was a great man came from the crowds of tourists, mostly Americans, who thronged about outside the house, hoping to get a look over the wall or an autograph from its famous occupant.

Kipling owned houses in New York and Cape Town and told Paterson he was keen to live in Australia. Kipling had visited Australia once and although he knew little about the country, he did a good job in summing up its inhabitants when he told Paterson: 'You people in Australia haven't grown up yet. You think the Melbourne Cup is the most important thing in the world.'

Kipling 'hated publicity as his Satanic Majesty is supposed to hate holy water' and therefore did not enjoy the attention of the autograph seekers. To avoid them, he had his car brought into the front garden so he could dash from his front step into the car and cruise past the crowds in splendid seclusion. He owned a series of British-made Lanchester cars and he received a new one just in time for Paterson's visit. The great writer never actually drove the car, but it came with a chauffeur in overalls. Paterson and Kipling clambered into the back and in scenes conjuring up images of Toad of Toad Hall, they hurtled over the Sussex Downs, scattering 'tourists right and left':

> Away we went through the beautiful English lanes, where the leaves swirled after the car and one expected to see Puck of Pook's Hill peering out from behind a tree. We passed military barracks, where Mulvaney, Ortheris and Learoyd [fictional characters in Kipling's *Soldiers Three*], with their swagger canes, were just setting out for a walk. We saw the stolid English farm labourers putting in the oak bridge that would last for generations. We saw a sailing ship ploughing her way down the Channel, and noted 'the shudder, the stumble, the roll as the star-stabbing bowsprit emerges'. It was like looking at a series of paintings and here at my side was the painter.

Paterson's stay with Kipling was a highlight of his journey and their glorious outing in the motor car that day was an experience Paterson never forgot. Just three years later, he would join a marvellous motoring adventure of his own, travelling all the way from Sydney to Melbourne in a remarkable convoy of cars and motorbikes. It was fitting that one of his last engagements in London was to recite a verse, 'The Lay of the Motor Car' at the Yorick Club in London. His time in England was at an end and soon he was aboard a ship, the fog-bound lights of London and the green and pleasant fields of the English countryside lying abeam as he headed back to the sunlit shores of home.

Kipling might have been correct when he said Australians had not yet grown up, but Paterson had left behind a growing community of Australian artists in London—men and women who were showing that Australia, the brash child of Empire, could hold her own on the world stage. Australians were proving themselves on sporting fields and in theatres, galleries and concert halls. Some of the best and brightest were doing it in London. Among those bohemians with Australian connections who remained behind was the kindly, chaotic, hedonistic Phil May whose merry life was destined to be a short one.

Paterson landed in Sydney in April 1902, with fond memories of his old friend. They never met again and May never returned to Australia. He died in August 1903, aged just thirty-nine. He left a lifetime of pleasant memories for his many friends and a mountain of debt to his many creditors. In an obituary, the *Australian Town and Country Journal* honoured Phil May as a man without an enemy—despite his many unpaid bills. The paper remembered how May had been so poor when he returned from Australia to London that he had slept under bridges and begged for broken biscuits in pubs, but even when he achieved greatness he never lost his head at the adulation he received. The *Journal*'s obituary summed up the impact he had on the artistic community with its final lines: 'The kindly natured race of Bohemians, scattered like the Jews in all parts of the world will feel a sense of personal loss in the death of Phil May.'

May had died leaving nothing for his widow, but the staff at *Punch* gave her a collection of May's original drawings and people rushed to buy them. Mrs May cleared about £3000, thanks to the generosity of an artistic community that so admired her late husband. 'The Bohemians of London may have had their weak points,' wrote Paterson, 'but they were prepared to pay their tribute to the greatest Bohemian of them all.'

*

Paterson's footloose days as a single man were almost over, but there was to be one last hurrah before he settled down into marriage and a permanent career in journalism. A month after his return from London, he was asked by Sir James Burns of the trading firm Burns, Philp & Co to accompany a group of settlers seeking to find a foothold in the wild New Hebrides (now Vanuatu) in the South Pacific. For Burns, it was a strictly commercial enterprise; his firm had bought thousands of hectares of rich land from the island chiefs but competition from French investors and hostility from some of the tribespeople threatened the venture.

Burns—whom Paterson described as being 'as near to an empire builder as we ever saw in these parts'—believed possession would prove to be nine tenths of the law and that his firm would stand the best chance of locking in its land purchases if he had men 'on the spot'. Paterson thought it sounded like an adventure and he agreed to visit the islands as a reporter for *The Sydney Morning Herald*.

With a group of missionaries and settlers as shipmates, Paterson sailed for the South Pacific, via Norfolk Island in May 1902. He described his fellow travellers as 'Australian Pilgrim Fathers in search of the land of the golden cocoa-nut'. He became friendly with the settlers—'hard-handed, anxious-faced men'—whom he felt were born adventurers. They were the type, he later said, who would set off anywhere at the drop of a hat just for the sake of going somewhere new.

They found a paradise at Norfolk Island—a place so abundant in sub-tropical riches that some of the settlers wanted to remain there instead of completing their journey to the New Hebrides. But even paradise has its pitfalls and a lady passenger on the ship was taken aback when she turned on a tap that emitted a stream of cockroaches, 'all in the highest health and spirits'. Otherwise, Norfolk Island was a sleepy place. According to Paterson's wry observations, even the horses had to be prodded into action with a nail in the end of a board. The people were similarly disinclined to haste. Paterson wrote of meeting a dentist who showed 'several scars in his arm which he said had been made by sticking a knife into himself . . . to find out whether he was dead or alive'.

Another paradise was found in the New Hebrides. The settlers were delighted with the riches of the land and the mission-aries—many of whom were doctors—divided their time between preaching to the natives and tending to their illnesses. The French and Australian settlers got on well and discovered they had more in common than they had expected. Paterson felt the island settlement would prosper, and reported as much to Sir James when he returned to Australia in June. In the end, Paterson was proved wrong. The settlement failed as a commercial enterprise, partly because trade tariffs were erected and also because various governments never got around to making decisions.

Paterson had only just returned to Sydney when he received some tragic news—his younger brother Hamilton had been killed in an explosion on a boat off the coast of New Guinea. Hamilton had recently overseen the installation of an oil-fired engine on the converted cutter *Endeavour* and was working on the engine when a Malay crew member took a naked flame too close to spilt fuel. The fuel exploded, blowing the boat apart. The Malay man was killed instantly and twenty-five-year-old Hamilton died two days later. *The Sydney Morning Herald* reported that Hamilton was a former Sydney Grammar boy and a champion rower who 'was of a particularly fearless disposition'.

In the wake of this loss, Barty undertook another lecture tour, and when he visited the town of Tenterfield he resumed his acquaintance with the well-bred young lady, Alice Walker. It had been seven years since Barty had attended Alice's coming out party in Sydney but each had surely made an impression on the other because they married less than six months after Paterson's visit to Tenterfield in late 1902. It was a happy union that lasted until Barty's death almost forty years later.

12

NEWSMAN

While Paterson was sailing for the New Hebrides, the war that
had made his name as a correspondent was declared over. After
three years of increasingly savage fighting the British were the
victors, but their reputation was blackened by the brutal tactics with
which they won. Kitchener's scorched earth policy—the program of
systematically destroying Boer farms while rounding up thousands
of civilians for internment in concentration camps—was horrifyingly
cruel and savagely effective. By the end of the war, more than
26,000 white men, women and children had died of malnutrition
and disease and an estimated 14,000 native Africans had died in
separate camps. The British had won control of the former Boer
republics, but at a terrible cost.

In Australia, the worst drought since European settlement was
in its penultimate, hardest year. The so-called Federation Drought
had cured the land to its rocky bones. The ground cracked open,
creeks and rivers became meandering scars of dust and pastures
were burnt away, leaving only sunbaked earth. Millions of sheep

and cattle died and farmers walked away from land that had become all but worthless. Work dried up along with the farmlands and the wandering bushman was in dire straits.

Yet, at the same time, Australia was continuing to grow up. Just one year after Federation and now tempered by war, Australians were learning to make decisions on their own. One of those decisions made the young nation among the most politically enlightened in the world. On 12 June 1902, the national parliament passed the Commonwealth Franchise Act, instantly giving most women (indigenous women excepted) not only the vote, but also the previously unthinkable right to stand for public office.

Many men, and some women, felt women were too weak and too prone to hysteria to be trusted with the serious business of choosing a government, far less being a member of one. It was thought that even those who could control their emotions would be too easily distracted by the more pressing business of managing homes and rearing children. But some forward-thinking women had been quietly proving they could mix it with the men, and of course they managed to do it without hysteria or weakness. It was a sign of changing times, but there were still many hurdles to leap. Conservatives noted with disapproval that some of these uppity women even dared to drink and smoke and ride bicycles!

Suffragette meetings had been held in Melbourne and Sydney throughout the 1880s and 1890s as the push for equality gained momentum. Activists told a meeting in Sydney that Iceland, which had already enfranchised women, was a land with 'no illiterate person to be found, no prison, no police, no thieves, and no army'. It was suggested Australia could become the same utopia if women were allowed to vote. But not every woman wanted that right. In South Australia—which had given voting rights to women way back in 1894—four women presented a petition to parliament saying political equality deprived women of the special privileges they had hitherto enjoyed.

But the tide of change could not be stemmed, thanks largely to the efforts of early feminists such as Louisa Lawson, publisher of *The Dawn* newspaper and mother of Henry. Rather bitterly, Louisa wrote in 1890: 'Men govern the world and the schemes on which all our institutions are founded show men's thoughts only.' Nine years later, she helped to found the suffragette Dawn Club in Sydney and three years after that, Australian women became some of the first in the world to win the vote. Thanks to the drive and dedication of a handful of brave women like Louisa Lawson, the country built on the masculine legend of the bushman had allowed women at least some of the same political rights as men.

*

Barty Paterson, who had declared in his diary in November 1902 that he was 'henceforth a journalist', had undoubtedly watched the women's suffrage debate unfold in the newspapers. He may have got some of his information from the light and lively Sydney paper, *The Evening News,* which enjoyed the debate over the women's issue. For every outraged letter writer who spouted that women desired to be submissive to their husband's political views, the *News* had allowed another to express a view that women had as much right to have a say in the affairs of state as their menfolk. In April, the paper had printed a long story about Ida Evans, 'the state's first lady lawyer', and in September, three months after the Franchise Act, the *News* carried a front-page interview with Miss Rose Scott, one of the leading architects of female suffrage.

It was at *The Evening News* that Paterson landed his first full-time job in journalism. In January 1903, he was appointed not as a reporter, but as the editor. It was a lofty position for one so relatively inexperienced, but the lawyer-turned-newspaper-man applied a simple philosophy to the job. 'The best editors are not necessarily trained journalists at all,' he later said. 'What they need is not the ability so much to write but also the ability to be right.' Paterson could do the former very well, but as editor he sometimes fell short on the latter.

At first glance, the racy *News* does not appear to have been a perfect fit for its conservative new editor but he seems to have jumped in enthusiastically. The headlines in his first month in the chair ranged from the dramatic ('Boat bottom up; A lad's gallant act') to the sensational ('Priest murders his sweetheart') to the trivial ('Unexpected chickens: Hatched by the heatwave'). Late in the month, the paper got slightly carried away when it reported thirty people were in hospital in the town of Forbes, suffering from typhoid fever. The *News* published a correction after the aggrieved mayor of that town pointed out that there were, in fact, only nine cases of the disease.

It was only a minor setback for the new editor. From his inky, untidy office, dominated by a paper-littered roll-top desk and crowded with overflowing pigeon holes, Paterson rather laconically went about bringing his own style to the paper. In doing so, he won the affection of his fellow 'ink-slingers'. Fifty years later, Claude McKay, a reporter who began his career under Paterson, recalled how the paper's sub-editor, a round and ruddy chap who got himself invited to every banquet in town, was put on a strict diet by his doctor. The devastated sub-editor unleashed a tale of woe on his boss:

I am not to eat cabbage, Barty. I'm fond of cabbage dished up and cut across, with pepper and butter. And I'm fond

of mashed potatoes, with plenty of pepper and butter. I'm
ordered to have neither . . . I can give up cabbage, Barty, but
I can't, I can't . . . I can't give up mashed potatoes!

McKay always remembered his editor's 'long, weather-beaten face
lighting with that attractive, humorous smile' when he recounted
the hungry sub-editor's anguish.

According to McKay, Paterson hated to be alone in his office,
where he sat alone with 'an habitual look of bewilderment'. When
visitors arrived, Paterson welcomed them like a long-lost brother,
leaning back in his chair and comfortably yarning as if there were
no deadlines and no paper to produce. Somehow, under this casual
guidance, the paper hit the streets three or four times every day.
But what most endeared Paterson to his staff was a decision to pay
contributors by the line, which meant a reporter could earn as
much as a guinea for a full column of copy. He also hired a political
cartoonist—a rarity for the time—and injected some of his own
interests into the pages. These changes included increased coverage
of sport, especially horseracing, and the introduction of a series of
stories on native wildlife.

Paterson understood what readers wanted and the *News* won the
evening circulation battle but he lacked the killer instinct that an
editor needs. His paper was scooped several times by the opposition,
which labelled Paterson 'Banjoey' and his paper, 'The Snooze'.
Sometimes, the paper's problems were self-inflicted. In one edition,
the artist Lionel Lindsay drew a cartoon of Rome with seven hills,
an organ grinder and monkey atop each one. Sydney's Italians were
outraged. The celebrated Sydney artist Antonio Dattilo-Rubbo
was so angry that he challenged Lindsay to a duel. Luckily for
Lindsay, the duel never proceeded but *The Daily Telegraph* was quick
to pounce:

All the Dagos in the metropolitan area are after [Paterson's] scalp in consequence. In Thursday's issue of the 'Snooze' Banjoey rises to explain that it was only a joke. 'A sense of humour does not seem to be characteristic of the Italian people', claims the plaintive humorist. The famous Banjoey himself is not an Italian. His frozen humour, however, is characteristic of imitation hokey-pokey compounded from the mountain snows amongst which he sought his saddened inspiration.

This was unfair. Whatever shortcomings Paterson had as a newspaper editor, there was nothing wrong with his sense of humour. Not that everybody saw the funny side of his newspaper's writings. In May 1903, the *News* had to apologise for offending a popular rugby union player, James 'Bull' Joyce by describing him as 'ferocious' and 'a ruffian' on the field. Joyce—who was a champion forward and goal kicker for Glebe and had also represented Australia—was actually an even-tempered and fair player and his friends at the Glebe club were quick to rise to his defence. When a delegation of outraged rugby players made a forceful visit to the offices of the *News*, there was nobody there to meet them. In its apology a week later, the *News* stated that all the staff just happened to be out at the time. The *Star*, however, implied that 'Banjoey' and his colleagues had bolted down the fire escape as the footballers barged through the front door.

An editor's job is never an easy one and Paterson found his to be demanding and stressful, although it might have helped that his personal life was now on a settled path. On 8 April 1903, at the age of thirty-nine, he had married Alice Walker at her family home, Tenterfield Station. The region's leading citizens packed the town's Presbyterian Church to see the couple take their vows. The women's pages in the newspapers reported the bride wore a trained gown of white crepe-de-Chine with a shirred skirt and a bodice decorated with Brussels lace. The veil was fastened with a diamond star. Alice's sister Bessie was the only bridesmaid. She wore a pearl crescent brooch that was a gift from the bridegroom. Barty's best man was William Kelly—a minister in the Federal Government and a member of fashionable clubs in Sydney and Melbourne.

Many of the station workers had known the bride since she was a child and, showing the affection in which she was held, they 'tastefully decorated' the church before returning to the homestead to await the arrival of the happy couple. The reception at the homestead was an intimate affair with only the staff and close friends and family present. A gossip column in the papers rather tastelessly reported that 'numerous and costly presents were given'. Touchingly, the station workers presented Alice with a silver salver, and the ladies committee of the Presbyterian Church gave the newlyweds two silver trinket boxes.

Following an afternoon tea, Barty made a short speech of 'well-chosen words' of thanks and then the couple departed, Alice strikingly attired in a dress of electric blue and a white felt hat trimmed with large pink roses. They had their honeymoon in the mountains near Cooma.

They made their first home at 'West Hall' in the Sydney suburb of Woollahra. In February 1904, they welcomed their first child—a girl. It made news in gossip pages around the country with *The Barrier Miner* in Broken Hill suggesting 'the little stranger should be called Banjo-sephine'. Not surprisingly, the proud parents did not take up this suggestion and named their little girl Grace. Now, with Barty's career as a newspaperman settled and his family started, his professional and personal life seemed fulfilled.

*

The new century had been less kind to Paterson's fellow 'deity of *The Bulletin*'. Henry Lawson's return from London had brought more strife to his troubled, alcohol-plagued life. While Barty's married life was just beginning, Henry's was coming to an end. At the same time as the Patersons said 'I do', Henry's long-suffering wife was saying 'I don't'. In April 1903, she successfully applied for a judicial separation, leaving her troubled husband alone and with two children to support financially.

It was the latest shattering development in Lawson's downward spiral. In December the previous year, he had leapt in despair from a cliff at Manly and was found at the water's edge, semi-conscious and in great pain from a broken ankle and a large wound over his right eye. The papers said the cliff was about 30 metres high. It was a tragic low point in Henry's troubled life, but Paterson later recalled the incident in humorous tones, showing that Lawson was able to see the funny side of his own misfortune:

> Lawson had an experience which happens to few people. He fell over a cliff at Manly and was reported dead. There was no time to make inquiries, so a section of the Press came out with very flattering obituary notices, which Henry read with great interest and enthusiasm. I asked him what he thought of these final 'reviews;' and he said that, after reading them, he was puzzled to think how he had managed to be so hard up all his life!

Lawson's *Children of the Bush*, published in 1902, had been well received and his Joe Wilson series, most of which was written in London, would be remembered as some of his greatest work. These bittersweet, semi-autobiographical tales reflected the memories of a man who watched the dreams of youth destroyed by the gritty reality of failed middle age. As the grim years of the new century marched on, Lawson's life began to more and more closely mimic his art.

The loss of his family had taken what little stability that remained in his life and he had retreated further into alcohol and depression. He drifted around the inner suburbs of Sydney, working a little and drinking a lot. Sometimes he could be seen at Circular Quay waving a tin cup and begging for donations. He liked to gather threepence from each mark and, when he had collected a few shillings, he would retire to a pub where each threepence could purchase a long glass of beer. It was during one such begging excursion that he performed a heroic act.

Just after lunch on 27 December 1904, Ettie Thrush, a married woman, gently placed her baby on the North Shore wharf and then leapt into the water, hoping to drown. Without hesitation, Henry Lawson jumped fully clothed into the harbour and held Mrs Thrush above water until she could be helped to safety. She was taken to hospital and her baby to an orphanage. When asked why she had jumped, Mrs Thrush replied, 'I have got my troubles.' It was a sentiment that Henry could fully understand for he had more than enough troubles of his own.

Whatever money he scraped up was never enough and he frequently defaulted on his family support payments. Bertha loved Henry, and despite his faults, she had tried to rebuild their relationship after their return from London. She was supportive of him during his treatments at the asylum and held out hope that he could mend his ways. But as time went by, she became increasingly desperate as Henry repeatedly failed to support his children and she fell into deeper hardship. It did not help that she loathed Henry's mother Louisa. Fed up, in 1903, Bertha refused to let Henry see his children unless he could prove he was no longer a 'low drunkard'. By July 1905, her situation had become so dire that she brought him to court on a charge of wife desertion. Eight weeks behind in his payments, he was sentenced to pay £12 5s 6d, or spend three weeks and three days in prison. Virtually penniless, he was sent to Darlinghurst Gaol that afternoon.

When hard times struck, Lawson was always quick to press his publishers and friends for money and he rarely faced a harder time than his first day in prison. He immediately wrote from his cell to Fred Shenstone of Angus & Robertson, asking for a 'pound or two' in advance for his next book. He also asked Shenstone to rally his friends for support, but for once, his friends could not help him and he served his full term. Later, he described the grim convict-era Darlinghurst prison as 'Starvinghurst' because of the lean rations behind the high walls. It was there that he wrote a poem he called 'One Hundred and Three'—his own prison number. It gives an insight into his sense of bitterness.

> The clever scoundrels are all outside, and the moneyless mugs
>   in gaol—
> Men do 12 months for a mad wife's lies, or Life for a
>   strumpet's tale.
> If the people knew what the warders know, and felt as the
>   prisoners feel—
> If the people knew, they would storm their gaols as they
>   stormed the old Bastille.

But, as unpleasant as prison was, it was not enough for him to mend his ways. There was more trouble ahead. His friends never gave up on him but they were fighting a losing battle.

*

While Lawson was struggling with alcohol, prison and family troubles, Barty Paterson was preparing to embark on another exciting journey—the first-ever motoring trial between Sydney and Melbourne. Organised by a canny thinker from the Dunlop rubber company, the 1905 trial tested man and machine in a feat of endurance. Nothing like it had ever been seen in Australia. For Paterson, who had been a fan of the motor car since taking a ride with Rudyard Kipling four years earlier, it was an opportunity too good to pass up.

He assigned himself to accompany a friend, Colonel Jack Arnott of the biscuit company, in a twenty-horsepower Innes car that could whiz along at a staggering speed. Although the car would complete the job started by the steam train and kill off the horse as the main means of transport, Paterson was excited by its prospects. He also noted the potential of the car to meet a great Australian passion—having a punt. He wrote in *The Evening News* at the time, 'The only objection to the cars is that they frighten the horses, but the Australian looks upon a race of any sort as a sacred thing.'

The reliability trial was a grand enterprise that saw the first petrol-driven cars and motorcycles complete the 572-mile (920-kilometre) journey from Sydney to Melbourne. Over five days, the twenty-three competitors, including one 'plucky' woman driver from South Australia, would cover the huge distance of more than 100 miles (160 kilometres) a day. It was not a race, but rather a test of attrition to see how the machines and their drivers would hold up to the challenges of distance, rough roads and mechanical misfortune. The competitors would earn points by reaching each stage of the journey in the best time. Those who avoided crashing, breaking down or coming to a humiliating halt in deep gullies that were scored across what passed as roads would be the winners. It was, said *The Sydney Morning Herald*, a chance to learn 'everything pertaining to the general excellence of motors'.

The fleet of motorcycles and cars gathered in the Sydney suburb of Ashfield before dawn on the morning of 21 February. The flat-capped and moustachioed motorcyclists set off first, the spluttering and backfiring of their machines punctuating the early morning darkness. The cars set out soon afterwards, their drivers and passengers cloaked in caps, goggles and heavy white driving coats. Hundreds of people turned out to see this strange armada roar its way through the quiet city streets. The small boys among the onlookers were particularly excited, and shouted for the drivers to 'shake her up' as the engines growled and the unfamiliar odour of exhaust gases hung in the air.

The motorcyclists quickly roared ahead while the going was easy but they slowed down when they reached the Razorback, a long and steady climb south-west of the city. The first of the cars, including Paterson's, soon caught up and then passed the motorcyclists, who had dismounted and were trying in vain to coax their machines back to life. This came as no surprise to Paterson. He could ride a horse as if he were part of it, but the motorcycle held little appeal. He thought the 'man who rides a motorcycle for pleasure, would go to the infernal regions for pastime'.

In a story for *The Evening News*, under a subheading, 'The History of the Haste Wagon', Paterson wrote that the car was like an untiring horse. He described how he and Arnott roared through a cloud of dust, the air filled with the aroma of half-dry gum leaves as the homesteads and distant blue hills slid past in an exhilarating blur. The first car rumbled into the town of Goulburn, 200 kilometres from Sydney, just before midday, having completed the journey in less than six hours. The rest of the field trundled into town during the afternoon to be greeted by 'a singing, jabbering mass of small boys, agriculturists and local oracles, all explaining to each other all about motor cars':

> As each fresh car comes in there is a wild rush, and the small boys push each other nearly under the wheels, and just as the throng is thickest a Yankee driver, with a face like granite, sends two thousand pounds' weight of priceless mechanism in amongst them, and the mob scatters and drifts up and down the street, fingering the cars that are waiting by the road side filling up and making adjustments before being handed over. Each fresh chauffeur is a thing of less beauty than the last, and Goulburn has not got reconciled to their peaked caps, their goggles, and their iron features.

Day two of the trial sorted the contenders from the pretenders when the road from Goulburn to Yass deteriorated rapidly. In some places, deep gutters had been scored across the surface and cars began to drop out with bent axles and ruined tyres. The attrition did little to dampen public enthusiasm for the spectacle; it seemed that almost every person standing on the roadside had a Dunlop scorebook in which each vehicle could be checked and ticked off as it passed. Paterson wrote that most of the onlookers were thrilled to see the dashing machines roaring along the road—with one exception 'who cursed us with great fluency'.

Paterson and Arnott also suffered a setback when they shattered a wheel on a cross-country short cut. It threatened to derail their journey until some flour mill mechanics at Albury saved the day by bolting stout lengths of timber to the broken wheel. The 'lady driver', Mrs Thompson, was another to suffer a mishap near Albury. She ran off the road but was towed out by 'yokels' and arrived in the border town late that evening. The road behind had been littered with bits and pieces from the flying cars. Tools, driving coats, oil cans and gloves were lost to the wind, the drivers in too much of a rush to stop.

The day finished with a victory for the horse when one of the cars broke down and had to be drawn into town behind a 'horsed trolley'. The mayor welcomed the competitors with an official celebration. Most were battered and bruised and would have preferred to rest, but turned up anyway to spare the mayor's feelings. The competitors needed all the rest they could get. The New South Wales papers said the roads south of the border were appalling. One driver agreed, observing that motoring on Victorian roads was like 'driving over an old graveyard with the tombstones sticking up'.

Of the twenty-three cars that set out from Sydney, seventeen made it all the way to the finish line in Melbourne. Among the last to arrive were Paterson and Arnott. Late but not defeated, they limped into Melbourne just in time for the welcoming speeches to the rest of the fleet. Thousands of people turned out to see the cars arrive and, although there was no clear winner, observers noted the motor car would prove to be the transport of the future.

It was not the last time that Paterson would take a motoring journey with Jack Arnott. In February 1906, they drove from Sydney to the Burrinjuck area, where they enjoyed some excellent fishing for trout. From there, they travelled to the town of Tumut where Paterson disappointed locals by telling the editor of the *Tumut Advocate* that he preferred the town of Yass to Tumut as a possible site for the future national capital. After a short stay in Tumut, Paterson and Arnott drove to the Yarrangobilly Caves in the Snowy Mountains before visiting Jindabyne for more fishing. Then it was home to Sydney, where his wife Alice was expecting their second child.

13
BACK TO THE BUSH

Although the sub-editor, Claude McKay, remembered that his boss 'had no instinct whatsoever' for news, Paterson managed to produce *The Evening News* paper several times each day while retaining the goodwill of his staff and readership. In his spare time, he worked on a project dear to his heart. For some ten years he had been collecting old bush songs with plans for a book of the same name. He travelled far and wide to collect these songs, doing much to ensure they were rescued from obscurity, as a rapidly changing Australia moved away from its bush traditions.

Eventually, fifty-five works were published in the book early in 1906. Among them were 'Bold Jack Donahoo', 'Five Miles from Gundagai' and 'The Wild Colonial Boy'. The book's cover featured a bullocky singing as he led his beasts along a quiet country road. A little ditty printed on a bottom corner extolled the virtues of 'stringybark and green hide'.

Old Bush Songs was welcomed by reviewers, who already had a sense of nostalgia for an Australia that was fading away. Adelaide's

The Register urged readers to part with a half-crown to buy a copy while, in Perth, *The Daily News* predicted a new generation of bushmen would enjoy the book and 'the old-timers would cry over it'. Readers must have had the same yearning for the old days because it was a hit, selling about 5000 copies in its first year.

Claude McKay's memory of a relaxed Paterson as editor was misleading. The pressures of the job were taking a toll and soon after the release of *Old Bush Songs* he left *The Evening News* to become the editor of the *Australian Town and Country Journal*. The weekly *Journal*, with its focus on rural readers, seemed to be more his style.

Meanwhile, life on the home front could not have been better. On 9 May, Barty and a heavily pregnant Alice attended an interstate tennis match at Double Bay and five days later Alice gave birth to a little boy, at the family home in Woollahra. They named him Hugh—a brother to Grace—now aged two.

Paterson continued to edit the *Journal* for another two years but even at the slower pace, his health declined. He tired easily and caught cold often. As his nerves frayed, and with the children growing, his thoughts turned increasingly towards a life on the land. Although he had lived most of his adult life in Sydney, his heart remained in the country, especially his beloved upper Murrumbidgee region in the steep foothills of the Snowy Mountains, and he hoped to make his family's home there.

The opportunity came late in 1907 when a station called Coodra Vale, at Wee Jasper south-east of Yass was offered for sale. Made up of about 40,000 acres (16,188 hectares) of steep, rocky country, it was just what Paterson was looking for. 'I want my children to grow up loving the country and the horses like I did,' he said, 'and Alice is only too happy about it.' Also, their new home would be closer to Melbourne and therefore 'easier to get to the Cup'. More importantly, the change would be good for his health. The strain of editing two newspapers had taken a toll and, in January 1908, he wrote a letter of resignation from the paper.

In March, he formed the Coodra Vale Company with some partners and sold the family home, West Hall. To augment his capital, he wrote in June to his publisher, George Robertson, asking him to make an offer for the copyright for 'The Man From Snowy River' and other works. The letter gave a sense of Paterson's growing sense of claustrophobia in Sydney. He told Robertson that he hoped to get 'some decent work done' when he returned to the bush, and also that he always felt seedy in Sydney.

Not everyone wished him success. In October, as the family moved into their new home, an old foe in the *Catholic Press* sneered that Paterson the 'horse poet' had become 'something of a cocky-grazier in the Barren Jack district':

> Here was a man who caught the popular taste with his first work, and slumped badly with his later efforts. He was never a poet at any time, but in 'The Man From Snowy River' he strung together horsey rhymes with pleasing facility. This was a type of verse specially suited to the backblocker and the stable boy, but Australia is not as horsey as it was, or at least its taste has improved so that it is satisfied with a very thin sprinkling of the horse poet's productions.

Paterson might have taken some consolation in knowing that thousands of book buyers disagreed. In any case, it was Paterson himself who claimed to be a 'versifier', not a poet, so the criticism was rather mean-spirited. Also, by his own admission, his new home was in the backblocks, a land, he said, that had been 'left over when the rest of the world was made'.

The family's new home was a sturdy, square cottage with a wrap-around verandah on a narrow flat between steep foothills. The

Goodradigbee River chuckled over a shoal of rocks at their front door and a long, green flat stretched away to either side. The river was useful for watering stock but it also offered potential in a newly emerging tourism business. Since the construction of Burrinjuck Dam, the clear, winding Goodradigbee and other local streams had become sought-after destinations for fly fishermen casting for wily mountain trout. Paterson and his partners in Coodra Vale hoped to take advantage of this growing interest by offering accommodation to anglers, who could now motor from Sydney to Wee Jasper in a day or two.

Most of all, 'Coodra' was serene and beautiful, and although 'as a station prospect [it] was best avoided', it was a good place to raise a family. And for Barty, it was like the closing of a circle. In his 1939 recollections for *The Sydney Morning Herald* he described a rural idyll at Coodra Vale, a perfect picture of the bush that reflected the memories of his own childhood home at beloved Illalong:

> As the sun was setting, the lyre-birds came out of their fastness and called to each other across the valley, imitating everything they had ever heard. Gorgeous [lorikeets] came and sat in rows on the spouting that ran around the verandah, protesting shrilly when their tails were pulled by the children. Bower birds with an uncanny scent for fruit would come hurrying up from the end of the garden when the housewife started to peel apples, and would sit on the window-sill of the kitchen, looking expectantly into the room.

But the beginning of their first summer there was anything but idyllic. In December it was already unbearably hot and rain was a distant memory. On 3 January, a hot wind swept in from the west, raising a thick cloud of fine, blinding dust. A small fire that broke out near Mount Barren Jack was fanned by the dusty wind and

BACK TO THE BUSH

before long the flames were galloping across the paddocks, turning dry grass to ash. Soon the fire ran into the bush and that night the hills were alight in a red line more than 30 kilometres long.

As the fire bore down, families wrapped their children in wet blankets and ran for their lives, leaving all they owned behind. The air was thick with smoke and the sun blazed orange in a hot, dirty sky until it seemed as if the whole world was burning. It was a fire that only nature could stop. By 5 January, it was burning on Coodra Vale. Luckily, the Patersons were not there but a party of visiting anglers had to leap into the river for shelter, leaving their sulkies to burn on the bank.

The next day, the weather finally changed and a light but consistent rain fell. It was not enough to quench the fire but it was enough to halt its advance and the worst was over. Left behind was a blackened scar of ruined homes, dead trees, flattened fences and charred animals, their scorched carcasses still smoking in the ash.

In hindsight, the Patersons might have seen the fire as an omen for their experiment on the land but they were determined to make a go of Coodra Vale, and to provide the rural life they wanted for their children. Besides, Barty still hoped the new surroundings would inspire some good writing. He did find time to write, producing a lengthy treatise on a subject close to his heart, *Racehorses and Racing*. This guide to the sport of kings provided its author with personal satisfaction but it held little commercial appeal and to Paterson's disappointment it was not published in his lifetime. However, his experiences at Coodra Vale had long term spinoffs when he published 'The Mountain Squatter' in 1915. Described as one of Paterson's finest ballads, it as an ode to sheep and the clever 'collie pup' that rounds them up. It finishes with a sentiment familiar to any stockman who has owned a good working dog: 'The cash ain't coined to buy/That little collie pup.'

The family's life on the land did not mean they were cut off from the finer things. Although not wealthy, they lived as 'gentlemen squatters' and frequently travelled to Sydney for sporting and social events. On 10 April 1909, they went to the races at Randwick and a week later they were guests at a vice-regal ball, hosted by Lord and Lady Dudley, at Government House in Sydney. Beautiful, charming and fiercely determined to get whatever she wanted, Lady Dudley had a special cause—to set up a network of bush nurses to provide care to the poor and isolated across Australia. The scheme was hotly opposed by country doctors, but Lady Dudley was equally intent on making it happen. Soon after the ball at Government House, she summonsed Paterson to a meeting to ask for his help:

> You are well known among the bush people and I want you to organise a trip for me through all the back-blocks towns. I will live in the Governor-General's train, and I will address meetings and ask for subscriptions in every centre, even in the small places. I will get £20,000 without any trouble. Will you help me to do it?

Paterson admired her pluck, but was disturbed by the thought of her speaking night after night 'in smelly little country halls with the thermometer at a hundred and ten'. He knew Lady Dudley's plan would fail because the local doctor in each of those towns would pressure wealthy people not to donate. As it happened, the tour never took place, although Lady Dudley did manage to get nurses working in some parts of the country. Paterson felt ashamed at not taking part in the scheme but it was not the last time his path would cross with Lady Dudley's.

In August, Barty and Alice returned to Sydney to attend the funeral of Barty's grandmother Emily 'Mama' Barton, who had died at Rockend at the age of ninety-one. Newspaper obituaries recalled her 'exciting experiences' when the Aborigines from the Yass district had invaded Boree Nyrang station some sixty years earlier. She was buried in a plot she had chosen next to the family vault at St Anne's churchyard in Ryde. A poem that she wrote remains as testament to the love that she felt for her children and grandchildren and to the importance of her waterside home as a hub for her far-flung family:

> When to this my cottage home,
> Sons from far stations come;
> When each well-known voice I hear,
> Speaking words of hearty cheer
> And the sunburnt hands I hold
> Or the stalwart frames unfold
> While loving looks around I see
> Life has still charms for me.

In January the next year, Barty and Alice had their own brush with death. Two years after the region was ravaged by fire, the fickle summer weather delivered devastating flash floods. The Patersons, with Alice's brother Douglas Walker, were attempting to cross the Murrumbidgee River when a wave of dirty water roared down the narrow valley. The buggy was swept away and its occupants hurled into the torrent. Alice and her brother clung to branches to keep their heads above water while Barty bravely climbed on to the backs of the terrified horses and cut them loose from the buggy. Horses and humans made it to safety but the buggy surged downstream and its owners never saw it again.

There was a certain irony in Paterson's alarming encounters with the elements in a land he loved so much. More than twenty years earlier, inspired by his passion for the upper Murrumbidgee, he had written 'A Mountain Station'—a wry ballad that cited the misfortunes of a squatter who took a chance on a high-country property:

> I bought a run a while ago,
> On country rough and ridgy,
> Where wallaroos and wombats grow—
> The Upper Murrumbidgee.
> The grass was rather scant, it's true,
> But this a fair exchange is,
> The sheep can see a lovely view
> By climbing up the ranges.

The mountain squatter in the poem went the way of many before him. His sheep were eaten by dingoes or stolen by the neighbours and his cattle were swept away in a flood. Paterson undoubtedly hoped life would not imitate art and that his mountain station would be a success. But like the fictional squatter, the Patersons were besieged by dingoes that defied a so-called dog-proof fence and the volatile mountain rivers varied from raging flood to sullen sluggishness, depending on the rain—or lack of it.

Coodra Vale was not a financial success and, like his parents before him, Paterson learned the hard way that farming was a good way of turning a small fortune into an even smaller one. The fictional mountain squatter in the ballad sold his troublesome property and, in late 1911, the Patersons did the same when Barty agreed to hand over his share of the station to his partners.

But the failure at Coodra Vale had not extinguished his dream of a life on the land. In March 1912, the family moved north to a smaller property at Bimbi, south-west of Grenfell in central-western New South Wales. Their new station, Glen Esk, had a picturesque homestead surrounded by vines and fruit trees. In wet years, a shallow lagoon in front of the house filled with water, attracting hundreds of water birds and other creatures. When the family arrived, however, the region was in the grip of yet another drought and the lagoon was probably no more than a dusty depression lined with thirsty trees.

The Patersons continued their gentleman squatter lifestyle and were often absent from the new home. In April they were among a big crowd who rugged up in cool weather to enjoy the races at Randwick and in May they travelled to the central-west town of Forbes for the Picnic Race Club ball at the town hall. They were back in Sydney in July, again rubbing shoulders with the governor when he hosted a party for 200 children at Rose Bay. A month later, the Patersons attended a ball on board the P & O Company's luxury cruise ship, the SS *Medina*. On this glittering occasion, the ship was decorated with bunting, palms and coloured lights, and the cream of Sydney society danced on the promenade deck.

It might have been Paterson's attendance at such events that prompted Perth's *Daily News* to describe him at around this time as a 'stout, staid Tory' who was no longer the lively bohemian of his youth. It was a bit unfair. Certainly, the middle-aged Paterson was no longer an angry young man and he was undoubtedly quite comfortable in society's upper levels, but that did not necessarily mean he was disengaged from the country people, about whom he had written so much. In August, he and Alice returned to Bimbi to attend a plain and fancy dress ball. They shared a fine supper with the locals, some of whom wore their most imaginative costumes. Among the revellers were gypsies, soldiers and native Americans. One brave gentleman came dressed as a 'half woman and half man'.

The fun of the ball masked the hard times for the local farmers. The drought continued to bite, a problem that hit the Patersons just as hard as their neighbours. Sheep died and wheat yields were poor. Then things took an even worse turn when careless picnickers started a fire in the nearby Weddin Mountains in January 1913. The fire burnt for about two weeks, reaching Glen Esk by month's end. Paterson is thought to have been among about a hundred men who helped to stop the flames from reaching the village of Bimbi.

The family stuck it out at Glen Esk for a few more months. In April, Barty was appointed as a horse judge at the Grenfell Show— probably his last public function in the district. By October, the family was on holiday in Camden near Sydney and, in November, they attended a party at Yaralla, the grand home of Alice's aunt, the millionaire philanthropist Eadith Walker. By then, the experiment in life on the land was over and they moved back to familiar surroundings at Woollahra. Although their time at Bimbi was not a financial success, it is credited with inspiring some of Paterson's later poems, including 'Song of the Wheat' and 'Whisper from the Bland'.

Despite the failure of their farming ventures, they were financially secure enough for Barty to make a living as a freelance journalist while completing his treatise on racing. There followed a quiet period in the family's lives. Nobody, of course, could have known that the assassination of an obscure aristocrat thousands of kilometres away would soon plunge the world into turmoil.

14
THE WORLD AT WAR

Archduke Franz Ferdinand, heir to the Austrian throne, cut quite a figure as he stepped ashore at Sydney's Farm Cove in the autumn of 1893. Handsome and square-shouldered, he looked every bit the European prince as he was welcomed to Australia on his tour of the world. Although he spoke barely a word of English, he made his pleasure known as he visited a meat-packing plant and witnessed a sheep-shearing demonstration.

Later, accompanied by scores of attendants and dignitaries, the archduke toured western New South Wales for a hunting expedition. The archduke was very impressed by Australian animals. He was so impressed, in fact, that he set out to kill as many of them as he could, and he was followed by a team of taxidermists as he laid waste to a legion of kangaroos, wallabies, emus and wild turkeys. He even shot a platypus. Each specimen was gathered for preservation and transportation to Austria, much to the disappointment of the Australians in the shooting party, who had hoped for a nightly meal of roasted turkey.

Apart from a regrettable incident in which a zealous landlady on Thursday Island in the Torres Strait had refused to let the archduke drink a beer outdoors on a Sunday, the archduke's visit had been a great success. When he sailed out of Sydney in late May, he declared through an interpreter that after Austria, Australia was his favourite country. The women, he said, were 'superlatively beautiful' and the men 'light-hearted and unconventional'. Australians were flattered by this regal praise but, as Franz Ferdinand's warship sailed through the heads at Sydney bound for New Caledonia, none in Australia could imagine that the next time he made national news in his second-favourite country it would change the world, and, in doing so, accelerate the transformation of Australia from a British colony to a young nation in its own right.

Two decades after the archduke's visit to Australia, Europe was simmering with tension. Extreme nationalism was rife and an arms race had seen the hurried building of war ships and other weapons. At the heart of the unrest was the Balkans—where Franz Ferdinand's Austro–Hungarian empire was competing with Russia and Serbia for territory and influence. Austria–Hungary had infuriated Serbia by annexing Bosnia-Herzegovina six years earlier; a growing Turkish military threatened to stifle Russia's hopes of achieving greater influence in the Balkans; and, in France, many still burned with the desire for revenge after the German annexation of Alsace–Lorraine following the Franco–Prussian war in 1870. The great powers, including Britain, were tied to this time bomb through a series of complicated alliances that promised military support to any ally that might be attacked.

A spark in the wrong place could ignite the powder keg. That spark was struck when Franz Ferdinand and his wife Sophie visited the Austro–Hungarian troops in Bosnia and Herzegovina in 1914.

It was a risky venture. Serb radicals had already made several attempts on the lives of high-ranking Austro-Hungarian officials and, as a strong supporter of combining Slavic lands under the control of his crown, the archduke was at the top of the hit list for extremists. It was into this volatile environment that the royal couple arrived in Sarajevo on the bright and sunny morning of 28 June.

Franz Ferdinand and Sophie alighted from a train at Sarajevo station shortly before ten o'clock. There they were met by six cars which would transport the couple, their retinue and a small security force first to a brief inspection of a nearby military barracks and then to a reception at the town hall. Dressed in military uniform capped by a hat adorned with green peacock feathers, the archduke travelled with his wife in the back of the third vehicle, an open-top sports car with the top neatly rolled down at the back. After the visit to the barracks, the lightly defended motorcade made its way towards the town hall where Franz Ferdinand was scheduled to deliver an address. He may well have been nervous about the visit. According to one account, he had said to a family member a few weeks earlier: 'I know I shall soon be murdered.' His fears were well-founded.

As the motorcade made its way towards the town hall, a team of three assassins was lying in wait along the riverside road, the Appel Quay. The first assassin blended in with the crowd at the front of a café. He was armed with a bomb. Further along the route, the second attacker had a bomb and a pistol. Leaving little to chance, a third killer, Nedeljko Cabrinovic, waited near the bank of the Miljacka River, a small bomb hidden under his clothes. The mastermind of the plot, Gavrilo Princip, was a few streets away, awaiting news of the archduke's death.

The motorcade passed the first two assassins without incident. Either their nerve failed or they could not get a clear shot at the motorcade because neither pistol nor bomb was deployed. The plot was at risk of failure. But the third terrorist, Cabrinovic, was made of sterner stuff.

As the cars passed his riverside ambush point, Cabrinovic hurled his bomb at Franz Ferdinand's open-topped car—but his aim was poor. The bomb bounced off the car's folded-down top and fell to the street. Seconds later it exploded, injuring about twenty bystanders and damaging the fourth car in the convoy. The archduke and his wife were shaken but unharmed. The motorcade, now down to five cars, continued on its way.

After the official function at the town hall, the rattled archduke changed his plans and decided to visit some of those wounded in the bombing at the Sarajevo hospital. Again, Franz Ferdinand travelled with Sophie in the back of the third car. It seemed the attempt on his life had failed. The course of the entire century might have changed then, but for a simple case of human error. Franz Ferdinand's driver thought the convoy was travelling to the hospital as first intended. Nobody had told him that the royal party's destination had changed. Instead of travelling directly along the Appel Quay to the Sarajevo hospital, the driver turned the royal car right into Franz Josef Street.

Gavrilo Princip—'Gavro' to his friends—had heard the bomb explode and initially thought the plot had succeeded, but when he saw the motorcade on the move, he knew the archduke was still alive. Bitterly disappointed, but still hoping to make his kill, Princip waited outside a delicatessen on Franz Josef Street. Moments later, the driver of the royal car realised he had taken the wrong turn and brought the car to a halt in the street, directly in front of Princip. The car was immobile in the street, the royal couple horribly exposed in the back seat. Princip seized his chance.

Drawing his pistol from a pocket, the assassin fired two shots from a distance of about 2 metres. One bullet tore into Franz Ferdinand's neck. The other punched into Sophie's abdomen, just above her right hip. A thin stream of blood ran from the archduke's mouth and his head fell forward. Next to him, his wife slid off the seat and collapsed on the car floor, her head resting on her husband's knees. 'Sophie, Sophie, don't die,' said the mortally wounded archduke, 'Live for our children!' Then, as the driver finally regained control of the car and began to race towards the governor's house for medical treatment, Franz Ferdinand uttered his last words. 'It's nothing,' he said, repeating the phrase several times, his voice growing fainter each time. 'It's nothing, it's nothing . . .'

The archduke was terribly wrong. Sophie was dead when the car arrived at the Governor's residence and Franz Ferdinand died ten minutes later.

Gavrilo Princip—who tried unsuccessfully to poison himself after the shooting—later said he only wanted to kill the archduke, not start a war. But the assassination was to have global consequences, costing millions of lives. Although the terrorists were quickly caught, anti-Serb riots broke out in Sarajevo and in several cities across Austria and Hungary. A diplomatic storm brewed as Austria made impossible demands on the Serbian Government. Serbia was ordered to suppress anti-Austrian propaganda and submit to an independent investigation into the assassination, or face the military might of Austria and its close ally Germany. But proud Serbia was defiant. Instead of bowing to the threat, the Serbs mobilised their army. On 26 July, Serbian soldiers crossed the Danube River into Austro-Hungarian territory. The situation was slipping out of control.

Two days later, with the recalcitrant Serbs still refusing to yield, the Austrians declared war. Then, what should have been an isolated

European conflict grew rapidly. One by one, the powers were drawn into the maelstrom. Germany and Italy, as signatories to an alliance with Austria, had no choice but to join the war on Serbia. Russia—which was bound to support Serbia and was also allied to France and Britain—was worried by the threat of a pre-emptive attack from Germany—a fear that proved valid when Germany declared war on Russia on 1 August. Two days later, Germany was also at war with France. Although the Austro-Germans expected Britain to remain neutral, on 4 August, Britain and its dominions declared war on Germany and Austria.

Most people thought that the war would be over within six months. But the mechanised warfare of the twentieth century was very different to that of the past. Soon to be known as the Great War, the European squabble grew into a global conflagration that lasted for more than four years and changed the course of the century. An estimated 17 million people were killed and about 20 million injured. From the heart of the conflict in Europe to the dustiest, most distant colonies of the Empire, young men flocked to the bugle call to lay down their lives in the 'war to end all wars'. Australians were among the most loyal of supporters and they died in their thousands.

*

Barty Paterson took a great interest in the war. In September 1914, he visited an army training base at Kensington near Sydney, where he was appalled to learn that the men were in dire need of warm shirts, socks, pyjamas and undershirts. A newspaper columnist known as 'Fanella' wrote that Paterson appealed to the public to 'give it now'. According to 'Fanella', the soldiers could expect to face weather bleaker than a night on a Scotch moor, and Paterson's appeal was the 'most sensible remark that has been uttered for a fortnight'.

But Paterson's thoughts were turning towards playing a more direct role in the war. These thoughts made news as far away as Perth, where the *Sunday Times'* 'Peeps at People' column incorrectly reported that he was being held back from the war by 'indifferent health, a wife and a bunch of children of assorted ages and sexes'. The columnist was right, however, in claiming that Banjo was keen to reprise his role as a war correspondent.

Now aged fifty, Paterson's health was fine and his family was not holding him back. At a time when thousands of men were leaving their homes, families and jobs to fight in Europe, Paterson also felt the call to arms. If Alice did not support him in this hope, she at least did not oppose it and, in November, Barty sailed with a fleet of troop transports, bound for London, from where he hoped to find his way to the front as a war reporter. It was a bold and somewhat risky gamble; he had made no arrangement to get to the front and had as little idea as the next man on what to expect when and if he got there.

He wasted no time in filing reports for Australian readers, however. On 20 November, *The Argus* ran his account of the fleet's uneventful journey over smooth seas, stopping at ports he did not name—presumably for security reasons. Despite the lack of real news to report, his story brought to life Australia's sense of pride at being part of this great venture for the Empire. It was, he wrote, 'the greatest national undertaking yet attempted by Australia' and one that he hoped would lead to a lasting peace.

While he was at sea with the troops, some real news happened. It was, in fact, the most spectacular moment of Australia's war so far. Since September, the German light cruiser *Emden* had been prowling the Indian Ocean and had captured or sunk more than twenty British and allied ships. The *Emden* had also destroyed millions of tonnes of oil in a spectacular raid on the Indian port of Madras. On

28 October, disguised as a British ship with a fake fourth funnel, the *Emden* raided Penang in British Malaysia and sank a Russian cruiser. Then, as quickly as she had arrived, the *Emden* slipped out of Penang harbour and escaped.

Now, with a flotilla of allied warships on her tail, she was the most hunted ship in the world. It was only an encounter with the Australian cruiser HMAS *Sydney* that would halt her depredations.

On 9 November, the *Emden* reached the Cocos (Keeling) Islands where her skipper planned to attack an allied wireless station, but the alarm was raised and the *Sydney*—which was just 90 kilometres away—was dispatched to take on the German raider. The two ships sighted each other at quarter-past nine in the morning and twenty-five minutes later, the *Emden* fired the first shots. A total of fifteen shells slammed into the *Sydney*, but only two exploded. Several men were seriously wounded. The *Sydney* could have taken a pounding, but she was faster than the German ship, and carried bigger guns. Under the command of Captain John Glossop, the *Sydney* widened the distance between the two ships and brought her heavier guns to bear. She began to pump dozens of shells into the German raider from a range of about 9 kilometres. The sailors on the German ship were cut to shreds. A gun crew was blown apart with one direct hit and the decks were slippery with blood, yet still the brave Germans fought on.

Even when his guns were silenced, the German captain would not surrender. He gave orders to beach his burning ship on North Keeling Island. Around him, his men continued to die as the shelling continued but the *Emden's* battle flag still flew. That afternoon, a reluctant Captain Glossop fired more shells into the beached *Emden*, until her decimated crew finally hauled down the flag and the battle was won.

It was a victory that fired the Australian troops en route to the front with a patriotic fervour. Australian sailors had struck a blow for their Empire and their country, and the *Sydney* would go down in naval history. Within two years, as the war continued to rage, no less than three Australian films would celebrate her victory.

The defeat of the *Emden* was also a victory for the hopeful war correspondent Barty Paterson, who got a scoop on Australia's biggest story of the war so far. On board his troopship, Paterson had become friendly with a tall, athletic lieutenant named Jack Massie, an international cricketer whom Paterson later described as 'strong and rugged as an ironbark tree'. Massie was a member of a highly regarded family from Sydney and through his excellent social connections he was acquainted with Captain Glossop. When the troopships arrived in Colombo, Massie arranged a meeting with Glossop so that Paterson could 'get some stuff that the other correspondents wouldn't get'. The result was a scoop telling the inside story of the battle, as told by the victorious skipper.

Paterson and Massie found Glossop out of uniform and enjoying a quiet drink on his own. The modest captain was unexcited that he had 'woke up to find himself famous' and put his victory down to his ship's superior speed and firepower. Nonetheless, he agreed to be interviewed and the result was a story that was published in Australian newspapers in late December. It gave a detailed and concise account of the battle—not a bad effort for an author who was more at home on the back of a horse than the deck of a ship.

It was also a sensitive story that paid tribute to the honour of the German captain and acknowledged the suffering of his men. But it was Paterson's interview with Glossop that enabled the writer to provide a small but stirring detail that fed the already soaring pride that Australians felt in their feat of arms. The story, with the sub-heading, 'What the boy said', told of a remarkable moment early in the battle when a shell hit the *Sydney*, killing a man who was working on a range-finder. This anecdote—published in newspapers around Australia—summed up the way that Australians wanted to see their fighting men:

> When the man working the range-finder was killed his body was thrown on top of a 16-year-old boy, who was sitting behind him working with a telescope. The boy was stunned by the concussion, but as soon as he came to himself he struggled to his feet, throwing the dead man's body from him. He made no comment on the somewhat strenuous proceedings. He simply said, 'Where's my blanky [bloody] telescope,' and, grabbing it off the deck, he fixed it on the *Emden* again as if nothing unusual had happened. His remark deserves to become historical.

Years later, Paterson reprised his interview with Glossop in his book *Happy Dispatches,* a series of biographical stories about the important people he had met. Again, this account captured the underlying humanity of the men who fought and died in that historic sea battle. Paterson provided graphic details of the carnage inflicted on the German crew, but he also told of the regret felt by Glossop of having to fire shells into an enemy ship that had already been defeated.

Glossop had signalled the stricken *Emden* after she was beached, asking whether she would surrender, but her crew had signalled in return that they did not understand the message. 'What was I able to do?' the captain asked rhetorically. 'If they were able to flag-wag in Morse they were surely able to haul a flag down. We understood there was another German warship about and I couldn't have the *Emden* firing at me from the beach while I was fighting her mate.'

The captain finished his discussion with Paterson and Massie, with recollections of the blood that was shed on the *Emden*. He told how the survivors had been driven all but mad by the flesh-tearing blasts of the *Sydney*'s guns, of the stench of explosives and the torment of the German sailors who were fly-blown with wounds and dying from drinking salt water. 'I have seen my first naval engagement, Massie,' said the captain, 'and all I can say is, thank God we didn't start the war.'

*

Paterson arrived in London in December to find a city in chaos. It was, he wrote in his diary, a 'stricken city, cut off from all reliable news, with everybody working feverishly to organise an army overnight'. The opposing armies had already become dead-locked in France and Paterson was keen to get there so he could report firsthand on the war. He hoped his successful reporting en route to London, combined with his proven track record as a war correspondent in South Africa, would be enough to get to the front. The problem was that everybody else wanted to get there, too, and the British authorities had little interest in letting reporters get anywhere near the fighting.

On 14 December, Paterson visited the War Office where he found lots of people trying to do their bit for the war but achieving very little. The place was packed with old soldiers and civilians who all wanted to get to the front but were struggling to progress beyond the waiting rooms. Everybody was snagged in an impenetrable, overwhelmed bureaucracy. Whether it was a civilian who wanted to donate a car to the army (provided he could drive it to the front), a retired colonel who wanted to give £1000 worth of gifts to the troops (only if he could distribute them at the front) or an entertainer who wanted to sing comical songs to the soldiers (at the front), their efforts to join the war were blocked in London. All of these well-intentioned people were passengers in a war, Paterson wrote, and 'in a war like this there is no room for passengers'.

In desperation, Paterson once again tried to use his excellent connections to break the deadlock. He called on an acquaintance from Sydney, the New South Wales agent-general in London, Sir Timothy Coghlan. A veteran public servant, Coghlan could slice through red tape like a surgeon wielding a scalpel. Coghlan said he could get Paterson to France but warned 'if you write one word for a newspaper, or if you tell anybody that you've ever been inside a newspaper office, you'll deserve all that's coming to you'. It was half of what Paterson wanted. If he could at least get to France then he would be in the box seat should reporters be allowed to the front. With Coghlan's help, Paterson would get across the channel, and, in doing so, he would be reunited with another of his important connections.

The formidable Lady Rachel Dudley, whom Paterson had met five years earlier, had done what the retired generals and generous civilians had failed to do and had made it to Paris, where she oversaw the opening of an Australian hospital. Wealthy Australians in London had flocked to her cause. Rich men had sent cheques and, in some cases, even their wives, to help establish the hospital. Lady Dudley was unfazed by dogged opposition to the hospital from the British army and even successfully insisted on choosing her own man to head it. Coghlan advised Paterson that a vacancy had arisen there for an ambulance driver—a perfect pretext to get the would-be correspondent closer to the fighting. Paterson jumped at the chance and requested a passport that afternoon.

While he waited for the passport to be processed, he took a short trip to Ireland. He was impressed by the friendliness of the Irish and the beauty of their land. He noted that it was a land of trouble 'yet the first thing that struck me was the politeness and good humour of the people'. The visit was a chance to indulge his love of horseracing and he stayed at a stud near Dublin, where he learned as much as he could about Ireland's thoroughbreds. During his stay, he took part in an Irish hunt through a glistening landscape of dewdrops and mist. But the Irish interlude could only be a short one; the war continued and his passport was ready. On 23 December, he arrived in France, ready for his new job as an ambulance driver.

The Australian hospital had been set up in two buildings—a chateau and a golf club in the town of Wimereux, north of Boulogne. Paterson was pleased to see familiar faces at the hospital, among them its new head, Colonel William Eames, whom Paterson had known in South Africa. Paterson also renewed an acquaintance with another Boer War medico, Dr Alexander MacCormick. Eames and MacCormick were among several medical professionals who had been studying in London when the war broke out. They seized the chance to work at an Australian war hospital, but so far it was a hospital without many patients. During this quiet time, the hospital staff honed their golfing skills on the links next door.

Paterson spent Christmas Day dining with medical men, including some of Britain's finest specialists, but was still no closer to the action. That soon came to him, however, when a flood of wounded British soldiers arrived from the Front. As an ambulance driver, it was Paterson's responsibility to get the wounded men to hospital.

Soon, all of the beds were full and grievously injured young men lay on stretchers in the hallway as the staff worked double-time to care for them. Paterson admired the stoic bravery of the young Britons. In *Happy Dispatches*, he remembered Lady Dudley's privately run hospital could afford better food than military hospitals, and was therefore a favourite with the 'Tommies', even if it was something of an ordeal to get them there:

> We used to meet them at the railway station with the ambulances and drive them over those infernal cobbles, bumping and jolting their wounds and shattered bones; but there was never a whine out of the Tommies. If we apologised for the roughness of the trip they said, 'It doesn't matter, sir, so long as you get us there.'

When the injured soldiers reached the hospital, they got the best care that Australian doctors and nurses could provide—although they did have to endure the ministrations of Lady Dudley, who defied the wishes of the matron and insisted on washing the faces of the dirtiest men. But Paterson could not help admiring the determination of Lady Dudley, whom he described as a wonderful woman. 'She should have been a general,' he wrote in *Happy Dispatches*, 'for no doubts assailed her and no difficulties appalled her.'

Paterson had now done his own small bit for the war effort but, as 1915 dawned, he realised that he had little or no chance of getting to the front as a reporter. His dream of reprising his career as a war correspondent was dashed, and in January he reluctantly decided to sail home to Australia.

15

'METHUSALIER'

Early hopes that the war would soon be over were proved horribly wrong, as British and German forces became deadlocked in a series of costly battles that claimed small tracts of French or Belgian land at a terrible cost. The armies faced off in lines of trenches. Artillery barrages cut men on both sides to shreds and countless more died in pointless infantry advances across 'no man's land', as generals used to the glorious cavalry charges of the past ordered men to advance into the teeth of machine-gun and rifle fire.

As the stalemate continued, Paterson's frustration grew at his inability to bring the story of history's greatest-ever human conflict to Australian newspaper readers. But not everyone shared his vision of himself as a war correspondent. As he was sailing home from France, an anonymous letter writer to *The Bulletin* vented bitter spleen at the poet and would-be war reporter:

> So 'Banjo' Paterson is on his way back to Australia, his job as war correspondent over. The mystery was that any newspaper

employed him at work so manifestly out of his line. The ideal correspondent—Henry Lawson—is still hanging about Sydney. Henry has his known defects. There is little of the ascetic about him. But, under the stern discipline of military life, his consumption of cakes and ale could be limited, if not shut off altogether. What priceless pictures he could then provide of Tommy Cornstalk's habits, whims, prejudices, failings and virtues!

Lawson, however, was too busy fighting his own war with a beer glass to entertain thoughts of visiting the front. He had bought a room at Mrs Byers' Coffee Palace in North Sydney, where he lived in between spells in prison or hospital. The patient Mrs Byers would become his dedicated housekeeper and friend for the rest of his life. Although he continued to write, his best work was behind him, and his prose and poetry became even more haunted and melancholy. He shuffled through the streets of Sydney, begging for handouts and drinking himself slowly to death.

The year of 1914 started well enough for Lawson, when Angus & Robertson re-published four of his works, including *While the Billy Boils* and *Joe Wilson and His Mates*. The newspapers applauded this news in January but, in April, Henry was in trouble again when he faced court on charges of being drunk and disorderly and using foul language in front of two ladies. He admitted to being drunk, but denied insulting the women. The court convicted him of both charges and fined him a total of fifteen shillings. When the guns began to fire in France, Lawson both opposed the war and supported it but had no intention of becoming part of it.

What neither Paterson nor Lawson knew in that Australian autumn was that Paterson's former war correspondent colleague, Winston Churchill, would soon turn his formidable mind towards a military engagement that would become part of Australian folklore. The determined Churchill had achieved the first stage of his political ambitions by becoming the First Lord of the Admiralty in 1911. In February 1915, he oversaw an ambitious plan to forge a sea route from the Aegean Sea to Russia by a naval attack on the Dardanelles Strait in Turkey. When the navy was repelled, Churchill came up with the idea of opening the strait through a land invasion to capture Turkish forts that lined the narrow waterway. The site for the invasion was a place that few Australians had heard of—a dry and scrubby peninsula known as Gallipoli.

*

Joseph Stratford was a big man, his upper body toned and hardened by the demands of his job as farm labourer and canecutter in northern New South Wales. At thirty-four, he was older than most of the men around him, but he was well liked for his loyalty and bravery. When the burly Stratford leaped from a landing craft early on the morning of 25 April 1915, he was weighed down by a heavy pack and rifle and he quickly sank into the choppy water lapping the edge of an obscure beach, some 20,000 kilometres from his home. He shrugged off his pack and struggled to shore. As he found his footing on the rough beach, Joe Stratford became one of the first Australians—if not the very first—to land at Gallipoli on the Turkish coast.

Stratford charged up the beach as machine-gun bullets began to cut the men around him down. With bayonet fixed, he ran at a Turkish machine-gun nest, defying the hail of lead that spat from the muzzle. Some accounts of Stratford's landing suggest he bayoneted two Turks before falling to the ground, his muscular body shredded by bullets. His remains were never found. Another 2000 Australians would fall dead or wounded at Gallipoli that day.

Joe Stratford never knew it, but his death would make him part of a legend that inspires and saddens Australians a century later.

Stratford and his fellow soldiers landed north of Gaba Tepe, in an area later known as Anzac Cove. Many believe the troops had landed in the wrong place. Instead of storming a beach at the foot of a relatively accessible slope, they had landed beneath a series of steep and rugged ridges. To fulfil their mission, they would have to fight their way up these lightly defended but formidable peaks. It was a deadly challenge.

The Gallipoli invasion was supposed to be a fast raid that would open the way to knock Turkey out of the war but it took eight months of brutal fighting, costing more than 110,000 lives, before ending in defeat for the invaders. Some of those who survived were sent to an even greater field of industrialised slaughter, the Western Front in France and Belgium.

Back in Australia, Paterson was doing his bit in support of the war effort. While the fighting raged at Gallipoli, he penned an open letter to the troops in the form of a poem that was distributed to the soldiers on a printed card. 'We're All Australians Now' told of the country's pride in the young men from around the country who had put down their tools and swags and picked up a gun to fight for their homeland.

The poem correctly observed that 'We have, through what you boys have done/A history of our own' but rather optimistically stated that old rivalries between the states and even older conflicts between the English, Irish and Scots were consigned to history by the bravery of the men at Gallipoli. In true Paterson fashion, however, the final stanza neatly summed up the country's growing sense of nationhood:

And with Australia's flag shall fly
A spray of wattle bough,

To symbolise our unity,
We're all Australians now.

Paterson's pen was at least as mighty as a gun when it came to supporting the war, but he yearned to be part of the action and he became increasingly interested in plans to form a Remount Unit to manage the horses sent to the Light Horse troops on the peninsula. Based at Maribyrnong in Victoria, the unit was formed in September 1915, and the army began to look for volunteers. Experts in horsemanship were needed—vets, blacksmiths and farriers were in demand, and men who knew horses and could lead other men were especially sought after. Paterson knew more about horses than most and he was by birth and inclination officer material. He was a perfect fit for the job.

The army felt the work would be fairly easy in a physical sense and set an age limit of fifty for the unit's recruits. Paterson had turned fifty-one in February, but like so many other Great War volunteers he got around that problem simply by lying about his age. He gave his date of birth as 17 February 1866—two years after his real birth—and listed his address as care of the Australian Club in Sydney.

Still physically fit—his army records listed his height at 5 feet 10 inches (1.8 metres), his weight at 11 stone 10 pound (74.4 kilograms) and his eyesight as 'good'—he was accepted as an officer and given the rank of lieutenant. He was soon transferred to Maribyrnong to join his unit and was promoted to captain. On 12 November, he sailed on the *Orsova*, bound for Egypt and another adventure.

The Remounts were, by Paterson's admission, an unlikely military unit. Few of them knew anything about army drills. Those young enough to fight had hesitated to enlist because they felt they could not handle drilling and 'the rest did not even know a sergeant-major from any other major'. Most of the officers were over-age and the younger men were 'roughriders'—jackaroos, bushmen, former jockeys and buckjumpers who rode outlaw horses at country shows. The late Breaker Morant would have been a perfect fit for this rough-and-ready bunch.

As military men they were, Paterson said, 'about Australia's last hope'. But as masters of horses they were second to none and they needed every ounce of their skills to tame animals that would have been more at home on the rodeo circuit than fighting a war. Paterson's crew was known to the army as the Sixth Squadron of the Second Australian Remount Unit. With typical Australian humour, the men preferred to call themselves the 'Horse-dung Hussars' or, more fit for polite ears, the 'Horsehold Cavalry'. The aggregate age of these roughriders and their well-seasoned officers spawned a third and enduring nickname, 'The Methusaliers'. Whatever they were called, this motley bunch was expected to turn an equally motley collection of horses into combat steeds for the real cavalry.

The voyage of the *Orsova* was uneventful. As well as the Remounts, she carried some members of the Artillery and Army Service Corps as well as a large number of female nurses. The NCOs and men underwent training every day and the officers attended lectures. The *Orsova* made a brief stop at Aden to stock up on coal, and then, with smoke belching from her stacks, she continued her voyage to Egypt. She arrived on 7 December and the men disembarked the next day. They travelled by train to Zeitoun and a few days later they marched the 16 miles (26 kilometres) to Maadi in Cairo where they were to form a depot. Despite the advanced age of some of the men, the march was made in good time and only six dropped out.

When they reached Maadi, the men learned the evacuation of Gallipoli had begun and the unit's purpose—to supply horses to the soldiers in Turkey—was redundant. The roughriders dreaded being returned home, but any fears they held were groundless. The British army decided to merge the two Australian remount units into one and bring them under the command of a brigadier-general. The horses they trained would be sent not to Gallipoli but to the killing fields of the Western Front.

In March 1916, the Remounts formed a new base at Heliopolis. Captain Paterson was sent to Moascar near Ismalia on the western bank of the Suez Canal. There he oversaw the management of about 50,000 horses and 10,000 mules, which came through the depot in lots of about 2000 a time. The horses had to be subdued and conditioned for combat, as well as being fed and watered twice a day, seven days a week. The manure had to be carted away and burnt and the animals thoroughly groomed. The Methusaliers, said Paterson, were in a state of perpetual motion. In May, he wrote to his niece, Doris Kennedy (*née* Lumsdaine), who lived in Ireland. Paterson and Doris shared a love of horses and he wrote to her of the animals that were under his control: 'I think everybody who had an incorrigible [horse] . . . in his possession sold it to the army,' but, 'I only ride horses intended for generals and thus I get the pick of the mounts.'

At around this time, Paterson's wife Alice arrived in Ismalia to work as a volunteer aide at a British military hospital. It is likely that the children, Grace and Hugh, were left in the care of Barty's sister, Grace Taylor, at her home at Sydney's Darling Point. Alice worked for nine months at the hospital's Red Cross store and later operated a canteen at the Moascar camp. Barty and Alice were rarely apart during their long marriage and Alice's proximity meant they could spend time together. It was a blessing in a place where the reminders of war were rarely far away.

In May, Paterson noted in a letter to his niece that he had hoped to get to France, but had now accepted it would not happen. In Egypt, he said, the weather was 'deadly hot' and his time in camp was monotonous. In June, he wrote again to Doris, expressing concern about the condition of the horses under his charge. He was more impressed by the mules, which fattened up nicely and did not kick viciously unless mistreated. As for his own wellbeing, he was at that time 'messing in my own tent on the men's grub and doing very well out of it, my outback experiences have made me very easy to please in the food line'.

The depot was situated near a railway station. To the west lay the desert and, on the horizon, the great pyramids jutted into a hazy blue sky. These ancient monuments were intriguing to the Australians, whose oldest surviving buildings had stood for only a little over a century. The pyramids had seen the victories and defeats of some of history's great generals and now they stood as silent witness to the flying steel and burning oil of modern warfare.

Aircraft were becoming an increasingly useful weapon of war and the skies over the desert reverberated with the roar of engines, as young men from a nearby British flying school risked their lives in fragile contraptions of canvas and timber. All too often, as Barty recalled later, Alice Paterson and her compatriots had to sew funeral shrouds for these young pilots who 'perhaps make one little mistake in the first solo flight' and never saw their green and pleasant homeland again.

In *Happy Dispatches*, Paterson remembered the trainee pilots were encouraged to fly close to objects on the ground. One young pilot, who had a natural gift for flying, got things terribly wrong when he swooped on an Egyptian man who was fishing in the canal. The plane's undercarriage struck the fisherman and killed him:

> Then the young boy lost his head and after landing his plane by the side of the canal he set off to walk blindly across the desert. The flying people had a nice problem on their hands—an abandoned plane by the side of the canal, a fisherman with his head smashed to pieces in a boat and beyond that, nothing. Sherlock Holmes would have been puzzled.

The young pilot, still dazed, later walked into an army camp to face the music. The Royal Air Force conducted a quick court martial and came up with a practical punishment. The pilot was confined to camp but allowed to keep flying. Paterson noted: 'One life doesn't matter much in a war, and the army couldn't afford to lose the services of a pilot with the big move just ahead.'

There were also lighter moments. Paterson, who was promoted to major in October, had an Australian's slightly cynical view of senior officers. He remembered that some ninety generals had gathered at Shepheard's Hotel in Cairo where they 'just existed beautifully or they made themselves busy about such jobs as reporting on the waste of jam tins'. There was not much room at the hotel for junior officers and none at all for non-commissioned officers or enlisted men. The troops—aggrieved at being barred from breathing the same air as the generals—rioted one night outside the hotel in protest. The riot did not achieve much in the way of achieving equality, but it did provide a salutary lesson for two Australian officers that their troops expected a fair go.

The two officers had bought a car, which they planned to drive to the pyramids with 'some female youth and beauty on board'. Reluctant to abandon dinner with their lady companions, the officers opted not to go outside and quell the riot, and instead enjoyed their meal washed down with some fine cognac. Eventually, the well-fed foursome ventured outside to discover that of 300 cars in the vicinity, the rioters had chosen to burn only one. That, of course, was the car belonging to the amorous officers. It is not known what the now car-less officers did for the rest of the evening but it is unlikely that they enjoyed a romantic evening in the moon-shadows of the pyramids.

True to form, Paterson was heavily involved in unit sporting contests and naturally many of these events revolved around horses. It was his idea to stage rough-riding displays at the depot and these rodeos on the edge of the Egyptian desert attracted plenty of interest from military and social worthies. On 10 November 1916, Lady McMahon, wife of the High Commissioner of Egypt, attended one such competition and, according to the unit's war diary, 'she was very much interested' in the display of horsemanship.

Paterson helped his men to more victories in sporting events over the following year. In March 1917, he wrote to his publisher, George Robertson, describing the rough-and-ready nature of his men. The letter revealed that the unit's daily work was 'hard, monotonous and dangerous' but Major Paterson's pride in his men comes through, albeit with a little interstate one-upmanship:

> I don't think the world ever saw such a lot of horsemen got together as I have in my squadron—Queensland horsebreakers and buckjumping-show riders from New South Wales. It is queer to notice the difference in the various States—the other squadron are Victorian, Tasmanian and South Australian farmers and they are quite a different type from my lot . . . not having had the real rough horses to deal with they cannot touch my men at horse work.

At the time of writing, more than ten of Paterson's men were in hospital with serious injuries such as broken legs and crushed ankles. Despite the risks, none of the men ever had to be told twice to mount a hostile horse—'in fact they dearly like to do a bit of "grandstand" work even though they risk their necks by it'. In this small way, the horsemen of Paterson's Remount Squadron were doing their bit to win the war.

While Paterson was busy in Egypt, his publishers back home in Australia were capitalising on enduring public interest in his work. In March, Angus & Robertson released *Saltbush Bill J.P. and Other Verses*, a collection of Paterson's works that included 'Waltzing Matilda' and 'A Dream of the Melbourne Cup'. The newspapers lauded the works and noted that they would be well received by the men in the trenches. The Sydney-based sporting publication, *Referee*, hoped the verses would bring smiles to the faces of the soldiers.

No doubt many copies of it will help to swell future mails to the men at the front. Possibly for trench reading (difficult and dodgy work at best), nothing could be much better than short, cheerful scraps that breathe the atmosphere of home, and of those there are plenty in *Saltbush Bill, J.P.* The book is nicely printed, strongly bound, and of just the size to be tucked handily away in a tunic pocket.

In October, *Three Elephant Power*, a book of ten Paterson short stories, including the titular account inspired by the famous Sydney to Melbourne motoring endurance run of 1905, arrived in stores. It, too, was praised by the papers and hailed as a welcome distraction for the troops. By this time, however, things had changed rather dramatically for Paterson and his men, thanks to the arrival in June of a new commanding officer of the British forces in Egypt.

The impressive General Edmund Henry Hynman Allenby—later Lord Allenby—had fought in the Boer War where he became acquainted with Paterson. Early in 1900, Allenby—then a mere major—had been about to walk into an officers' mess in South Africa where the occupants were the worse for too much rum. Paterson had intercepted the burly Allenby and informed him that the officers in the mess were drinking his health. 'That's no excuse for keeping the whole camp awake,' said Allenby. 'You tell them to be in bed with all lights out, in five minutes, or I'll have to do something about it.' Allenby was not a man to be disobeyed and the party was over for the rum-soaked officers.

Paterson found Allenby to be just as forceful when he visited the depot at Moascar in 1917, but now he had bitter personal experience and a general's clout to back it up. He had led a cavalry division on the Western Front, overseeing the carnage of Mons, Ypres and the Somme. Just prior to his arrival in Egypt, he had learned that his artillery officer son Michael had been killed in the fighting. Allenby was a changed man when he arrived in Egypt—'a great lonely figure of a man, riding silently in front of an obviously terrified staff'. He was there to shake things up. There would be no more shenanigans such as the staging of riots and the burning of motor cars, and Paterson's roughriders knew immediately that this particular general was not to be defied.

The men christened Allenby 'The Bull'—a nickname that stuck for life. And like a bull, the general immediately let everyone know he was boss. He dispersed the generals at Shepheard's Hotel and, for good measure he moved the Remount headquarters from its comfortable surroundings to a camp 150 miles (2414 kilometres) closer to the front, where the British were fighting the Turks in Palestine. Moving an army closer to a war was an obvious choice for the general. 'We're a bit too far from our work here,' he said. 'I'd like to get up closer where I can get a look at the enemy occasionally.'

The Bull went about picking his key officers with ruthless precision. He gave them one chance to prove themselves and if they passed muster they were given a bigger job to do. There was much debate about which general should lead the Mounted Division for the Middle Eastern campaign. Henry Chauvel—an Australian and a veteran of the Boer War and Gallipoli—was a frontrunner, but some in British high command did not fancy giving such an important job to a mere colonial. Besides, said one crusty brigadier, the Australian was 'such a sticky old frog'.

Sticky or not, Chauvel got the job—although many of his peers expected him to fail. At this time, Barty Paterson travelled by train with an Australian general to the front at Beersheba. The general, whom Paterson did not identify, expected to be given command of the cavalry when Chauvel failed. 'This chap Chauvel,' the general said, 'he's too damned slow. I've just come along to see how things turn out.' Predictions of the demise of the sticky old frog proved premature. On 31 October, British forces overran the Turkish trenches in the ancient town of Beersheba and the men and horses of the Australian Light Horse Brigade charged their way into military history.

By then, the horses had not been watered for more than seventy hours. Success had depended on reaching deep wells in Beersheba and, after the Turks were overrun, Chauvel led his men into the town, where the enemy had left bombs buried in the sand. Paterson saw a man blown to pieces when he triggered one of these booby traps. But Chauvel raced on, pursuing the Turks after giving the horses a much-needed drink. Later that day, Paterson saw the general who had wanted Chauvel's job 'walking disconsolately through the streets of Beersheba. Marius among the ruins of Carthage was nothing to it'.

Later, Paterson was among a group that collected a battalion of Turkish prisoners in the Jordan Valley. These were the first Turks he had met. Until then, he had imagined a Turk as a paunchy person 'who lounged under a tree, while his wives fanned him and filled him with sherbet'. But, showing the same humanity towards the enemy as he had towards the Boers seventeen years earlier, Paterson in fact saw the Turkish soldiers as people in need of help.

In *Happy Dispatches*, he wrote that the prisoners were shabby and exhausted. They had not eaten in three days. Their colonel said nothing except to refuse food until his men were fed. This colonel, said Paterson, would have won respect in any officers' mess in the world. Despite their bitter fighting, neither the British nor the Australians had any grudge against the 'Jackos' and the prisoners were provided with food and tobacco. Men who had been trying to kill each other days earlier now ate and smoked together in a desert that had soaked up the bloodshed of war for millennia.

In September, Alice Paterson received terrible news from France. Her brother Douglas, who had been with the Patersons when they survived the flood in the Murrumbidgee River eight years earlier, was fighting as a machine gunner when a bomb exploded. His brother Harold, who was fighting nearby, rushed to be by his side but thirty-four-year-old Douglas was already dead. He was buried at Maricourt. The war had less than three months to run when he was killed.

Back in Egypt, Barty Paterson was kept busy managing the transport of horses, but he had found time to write a few 'jingles' which, characteristically, he felt were unsatisfactory. 'A Grain of Desert Sand', written in that year, reflected on the timelessness of ancient Egypt, 'The Army Mules', published in March, paid tribute to the 'rankless, thankless man who hustles the army mules', and the brief 'Moving On', published in May, was a soldier's lament at the restlessness of war.

The British won the campaign in the Middle East, but the killing continued in Europe, right up until the guns finally fell silent on 11 November, and a battered world celebrated the end of what everyone hoped would be the last global war. By early 1919, the work for Paterson and his men in Egypt had petered out and it was almost time to go home. In April, Barty and Alice sailed from Egypt for Sydney. Their war was over.

16
AFTER THE WAR

The Patersons arrived home in May 1919 to a joyful reunion with their children, now aged fifteen and thirteen. The family stayed for a short time at the home of Barty's sister at Darling Point before moving back into their own home at Woollahra. During the journey home, Barty had completed a short novel called *The Cook's Dog*. Apart from the adventures of the sheepdog of the title, the story told of an Australian girl who worked for a Lady Grizel Muckleston of the English aristocracy. The problem with the novel was that it was not very good, a fact which was not lost on the author. Later that year, he wrote to George Robertson saying he was 'very dissatisfied with the thing'. Robertson was nothing if not honest and he bluntly replied that 'you probably will do no better if you rewrite it till hell's blue'. Accordingly, *The Cook's Dog* was not published in Paterson's lifetime.

Barty and Alice, meanwhile, had picked up where they left off in Sydney. Barty was a frequent visitor to the races at Randwick and was a regular on the tennis courts at Double Bay. Although he was now fifty-five, he was as active as ever and the newspapers reported he was still a formidable foe with the racquet.

Paterson resumed freelance journalism and travelled to the Tamworth district in June to report for *Smith's Weekly* on the suitability of a proposed land subdivision to create soldier settlement blocks for returned servicemen. The post-war Australia on which he was now reporting was a very different place to the bushman days of his youth. Motor cars and trucks were steadily replacing the horse and many of the young men who had 'humped their bluey' across the wide brown land were now lying beneath the blasted earth of France and Belgium or the hard scrub of Gallipoli.

In September 1919, Australia lost one of its great newspapermen when J.F. Archibald died at the age of sixty-three. Three years later, when Paterson became editor of *The Sydney Sportsman*, he wrote a fine tribute to his mentor, remembering him as the first Australian to call the English bluff. Archibald had the unusual idea for his time that an Australian doctor or lawyer or singer or actor was every bit as good as his counterpart from overseas, Paterson wrote. He was a provocateur who supported the underdog. He was a cynic and a pessimist but he always thought that Australians should believe in themselves. In short, Paterson wrote, the man who founded *The Bulletin* 'made people think'. Almost a century after his death, Jules Francois Archibald still makes Australians think. One of his last acts was to bequeath money to a competition to find the best portrait painted of a distinguished Australian. The Archibald Prize is now Australia's best-known art prize.

At around the time of Archibald's death, Paterson sold the film rights for 'The Man From Snowy River' for £100—a hefty sum believed to have been the largest book-to-film deal in Australia. The buyer was filmmaker Beaumont Smith, who began shooting the movie in the Cooma area later that year. Starring Cyril Mackay as the hero Jim Conroy, it reprised some of Paterson's characters, including Kitty Carew, the love interest of the dastardly horse thief in the poem, 'Conroy's Gap'. The hero of the poem, the horse known as The Swagman, was the movie's four-legged star.

The silent black-and-white film—which has since been lost—starts with country boy Jim's rather aimless life in the city. When he returns to the bush to work for a corrupt squatter, Jim falls in love with Kitty, who is played by Stella Southern—a former Sydney milliner who was plucked from obscurity to appear in the film. The squatter, Stingey Smith, conspires to release The Swagman into the bush to run with the brumbies, denying Jim the chance of winning enough money in a race to save Kitty's family farm, thus delivering the farm to Smith. But Jim rescues the horse and rides him to victory while beating a false charge of theft. Ultimately, Jim and Kitty get married and live happily ever after.

The film screened around the country in 1920. Ticket prices were set at a minimum of one shilling for adults. The promotional posters announced: 'You've thrilled over the book—laughed, yes, and wept over it. Now see it magnificently visualised.' Plenty of people did see it, and the reviews were kind. Perhaps with a sense of nostalgia for times that had passed, the newspapers lauded the film's depiction of the bush and praised Cyril Mackay for playing an 'everyday Australian doing interesting, plucky things'. The film won praise from Darwin to Hobart. In South Australia, *The Register* was especially delighted by the 'Australian-ness' of the production:

Sheep in the paddocks, a season of drought, a mountain stream in a favoured district, a bushfire, a country race meeting, a mortgagee's sale—all were there, and those who played the various parts were Australians, and looked it. The photographic work was magnificent, for the most interesting features of the bush and the life there were delineated. As with all Australian life, a horse took one of the principal parts, and its presence enabled a delightful country steeple chase meeting to be witnessed.

Other newspapers expressed similar sentiments. In fact, almost everyone liked it, except for the man who inspired it. Soon after it was released, Paterson remarked: 'What a pity they murdered the picture as they did.'

Meanwhile, his family life was a source of contentment and he enjoyed watching the children grow into fine young people. In a letter to his niece in September, he revealed Hugh was taking a leadership role in the cadets at Sydney Grammar School and showed signs of being a good runner. Grace was also a fast runner and 'quite clever', while Alice was 'fit and working very hard to keep the home together'.

Paterson took over the editorship of *The Sydney Sportsman* in August 1922—a position he held for the next eight years. As its title suggests, it was a newspaper that focused entirely on Paterson's passion for sport, and was well-suited to him personally. There was a strong emphasis on racing—the editor's forte—but it also covered all of the major sports such as cricket, football and tennis as well as sailing and swimming. During this time, Paterson also covered weekend racing for the *Sportsman's* stable mate, the *Truth,* and won praise for his insightful knowledge of racehorses and the people that surrounded them.

That year, Australia lost another of its great figures when Henry Lawson's destructive lifestyle finally got the better of him. Henry's death on 2 September saddened the nation but it was not unexpected. He had lived his final years in predictable fashion, defying persistent efforts by his friends to save him.

It was not that his early death was unavoidable. As late as 1916, newspaper colleagues had tried to beat his alcohol problem by sending him to a place where he supposedly could not get any. The new town of Leeton in the New South Wales' Riverina had been declared a prohibition area because of the large number of men working on an irrigation scheme there. Henry, with Mrs Byers, was sent to Leeton in January. He would earn a small stipend in return for writing positive stories and poems about the new irrigation district, in hope of attracting settlers.

Lawson had stayed at Leeton for twenty months, and at first it seemed the move might have been his salvation. He made friends and wrote several works, including *A Letter From Leeton*, which was published as a book and sent to the soldiers in France. He and Mrs Byers made their home in a four-roomed weatherboard cottage, surrounded by fruit trees and grapevines. Mrs Byers—whom Henry called 'the Little Landlady'—fussed around, keeping the home spic and span, and doing her best to keep Henry out of trouble. Lawson's moustachioed, slouch-hatted figure was a regular sight as he walked along the dusty streets with his loyal little dog Charley following close behind. His mate and fellow poet Jim Gordon lived nearby and often accompanied Henry and Charley on their perambulations around town.

Eccentric as ever, Henry was frequently heard to burst into song as he strolled along the banks of the Murrumbidgee River. The locals soon became accustomed to this strange sight and sound, and when Isabelle Ramsay, a reporter from Sydney's *Sunday Times*, visited in June, she found a happy Henry Lawson who was greeted with nods and smiles from the town's grownups and squeals of delight from the children. Ramsay had first met Lawson during the dark days when he stalked Sydney's Angus & Robertson bookshop, pestering publishers and book buyers for a handout. The reporter remembered a ghostly and haggard figure from those days, but found the new Henry to be sun-bronzed and healthy:

> Living in such an earthly Paradise, and with his mind relieved of all financial worries, he is drinking in renewed vitality for his body and fresh inspiration for his mind with every breath. Jim Gordon says that he is better in health and writing better than ever he did in his life—and surely a man's mate ought to know! It is good to remember the tragic-eyed man of a few years ago and contrast him with the sun-tanned being who is living in the sunshine down there, surrounded by his old friend, his mate and his dog.

But while Henry may well have been 'drinking in vitality', he had not stopped drinking alcohol either. Although Leeton was supposed to be dry, sly grog was available and there was little to stop Lawson from travelling to the neighbouring 'wet' towns of Whitton and Narrandera. There he could drink as much as he liked. And sometimes he did. His stay in the Riverina was productive, but even prohibition could not keep him sober and when he and Mrs Byers returned to Sydney in 1917, he was no better than he had been when he left.

He struggled on over the next few years, partly thanks to a pension of £1 a week from the government. In June 1920, he was back in hospital being treated for alcoholism or depression, or both. Syndicated newspaper reports updated the nation on Lawson's steadily fading health. One reporter recalled that Henry had been sent to Leeton to recover but 'the bush either kills or cures a poet. Henry Lawson did not stay long enough to make certain the experiment'.

In August that year, Henry suffered another blow when his mother, Louisa, died after a long illness. Louisa would have been pleased that her brief obituaries in the papers mentioned that she had been a pioneer of women's rights and a publisher of merit. She might have been equally disappointed that the same reports introduced her 'as Henry Lawson's mother'.

Henry spent much of 1921 in hospital, where he received dozens of letters from dignitaries and fans. But it was the letters sent by schoolchildren that he most cherished and he was moved to write a short piece for the papers praising the teachers who guided the young letter writers:

> They are the bravest body of people in the world—as brave as any of the early pioneers in any land; for whereas the worst that could happen to these was death at the hands of savages, many of our teachers have to suffer temperamentally many years of the worst kind of mental and heart-torture, and keep their pens still and tongues silent about it. I have never been a very good or a very brave man, but I stand bare-headed to these people now.

In December, the federal government increased Lawson's pension to £3 a week. He returned to his room at Mrs Byers' home in Sydney early in 1922 and for a while he seemed to be recovering. He was seen at his usual haunts, and in June he celebrated his fifty-fifth, and final, birthday. On the evening of Friday 1 September he suffered a seizure and retired to bed. His condition worsened through the night and, at half-past ten the next morning, Henry Lawson died of a cerebral haemorrhage. His brilliant, tortured life had come to an end and people across Australia mourned his passing.

Leading the mourners was Prime Minister Billy Hughes, who announced a state funeral would be held on the following Monday. Henry Lawson, said Hughes, was Australia's greatest minstrel. 'He loved Australia and his verse sets out its charm, its vicissitudes,'

Hughes said. 'None was his master. He was the poet of Australia, the minstrel of the people.' Echoing these sentiments, New South Wales Premier Sir George Fuller announced Henry would be granted a state funeral.

On Monday morning 4 September, Lawson's body lay in state at the city morgue and mourners filed past his open casket to pay their respects. That afternoon, the casket was closed and taken to St Andrew's Cathedral, where it lay covered in native roses, gum leaves and a spray of wattle. Every seat in the cathedral was taken as people gathered for a short but stirring funeral service. The cathedral organist played Chopin's 'Funeral March' and 'The Rock of Ages'. As the last notes died away, the church fell silent except for the muffled sobs of those overcome by grief.

When the service was over, so many people crowded busy George Street that trams and cars had to be stopped. Thousands of people, many of them schoolchildren with their hats doffed, lined the streets of Paddington as the hearse made its way through the busy city towards Waverley cemetery. A police band marching to the beat of muffled drums followed the hearse to the cemetery, where Lawson was interred in a grave containing the body of Henry Kendall, another great Australian poet who, like Lawson, had been plagued by poverty, mental illness and heavy drinking.

Henry's estranged wife Bertha and their two children were among the mourners at the burial. Also there were politicians and gentlemen who rubbed shoulders with unionists and working men. Henry's literary colleagues and representatives of newspapers from Sydney and Melbourne paid their respects, as did dozens of schoolchildren and their teachers. Barty Paterson did not attend, but he was moved by the death of his fellow poet and later fondly remembered him as having 'the insight of a seer and the mind of a child'.

In a radio talk he gave about nine years after Henry's death, Paterson recalled Lawson's epic battles with publishers over money. Inevitably caused by Lawson's irresponsible attitude to his own financial affairs, these scraps often played out at Sydney's Angus & Robertson bookshop. Lawson would announce, 'I'm just going down to shake up those cows for a few quid,' and his gaunt, thread-bare apparition so upset the clientele at the shop that the manager decided Henry should be paid a fee to go away. Paterson finished his broadcast with a whimsical reflection on the childlike man who nevertheless made such an impression on his country that, in 1931, a statue was erected in his honour in Sydney's The Domain:

> Whenever I see the statue . . . I sometimes reflect on how little the public will do for a literary man in his lifetime, and what a lot they will do for him when he is dead. Henry's tactics may not have been without reproach, but he faced his troubles in the only way open to him, and, as he says in his verses:

> > You have to face 'em
> > when your pants begin to go.

*

When Lawson died, Paterson was fifty-eight, his formerly dark hair and moustache shot through with silver, but he remained fit and active. As always, racing was a passion and he was a regular sight at Randwick where his reserved and dignified demeanour made him stand out among the track's more colourful identities. Although he kept a low profile, his name continued to crop up in social jottings. In October 1922, papers in Sydney and Melbourne noted that Barty and Alice attended a luncheon hosted by Dame Margaret Davidson at Randwick, while four years later he was pictured discussing the races with golfer and racehorse owner Una Clift at Victoria Park. As always, Paterson was neatly dressed in coat, tie and hat.

Everyone knew him at the track, but he usually kept to himself. A racing reporter with the pen-name of 'Cestus' later remembered that Paterson could often be seen sitting close to the rails, watching the horses thunder around the track through a pair of field glasses. When the race finished, Paterson would put the glasses away, look around and leisurely depart. Although he seldom spoke, he could occasionally be seen chatting quietly with trainers or owners. In a sport that attracts its fair share of rogues, Paterson's undoubted integrity and vast knowledge made him a sought-after and trusted commentator on the racing game.

As a journalist, he was not afraid to tackle the sport's unsavoury side. He summed it up neatly in the *Sportsman* on 24 October 1924 when he asked whether big punters were a help or hindrance to honest racing, and observed a truism: 'Whenever it comes to a struggle between a man's honesty and gigantic financial induce-ments, the average race goer will always harbour a suspicion that the money may have influenced the result.' Although he had been to more race meetings than most, nobody ever doubted that he took the same sober honesty to his racing passion that he did to his everyday life.

In 1930, Paterson resigned from *The Sydney Sportsman* but continued to freelance as a sports journalist for the racy *Smith's Weekly*. His children, Grace and Hugh, were now aged twenty-six and twenty-four. In the coming years, Barty would become a proud and hands-on grandfather, but before that there would be more books, a career change to the new-fangled broadcasting industry and more travels. As his life entered its final stages he would experience yet more world-shaking events. Ahead lay the Great Depression and another world war—even more terrible than the first.

17
THE WRITER REFLECTS

Tuesday 29 October 1929 became infamous as 'Black Tuesday'. When Wall Street stocks collapsed in a few devastating hours, the world was set on a course of hardship that would only end after the deaths of more than 60 million people in World War II. Whether Black Tuesday was the cause of the hardship—to be known as the Great Depression—or a symptom of it meant little to the millions of people around the world who had a decade of grinding poverty forced upon them. Australia, with its high dependence on agricultural exports, was among the hardest hit. Unemployment rose to a massive 30 per cent, families went hungry and the big cities were depopulated as a new wave of swagmen—many of them former soldiers traumatised by the war—took to country roads, desperate for work or a handout.

It was a time of political unrest. The federal Labor government led by James Scullin had come to power just a week before Black Tuesday and inherited an economy in crisis. In October 1930, as unemployment soared, the fiery Jack Lang was elected to his second term as New South Wales premier and pursued his own plan to deal with the economy, in defiance of the prime minister's ideas. A year later, as a bitter dispute between the state and commonwealth worsened, Lang's supporters in the House of Representatives brought down the Scullin government. Labor was bitterly divided and the new prime minister, the United Australia Party's Joseph Lyons, led a government presiding over an economy in a tailspin.

At the same time, far right activists gained massive ground, especially in the big cities. The fascist New Guard movement was formed in Sydney in February 1931 and soon grew to have some 50,000 members in New South Wales, mostly in the capital. Fanatically anti-communist, the New Guard was led by war veteran Colonel Eric Campbell and its members were given quasi-military ranks. The New Guard was bitterly opposed to Lang's New South Wales Labor and its increasingly thuggish efforts to depose him led to street fighting in Sydney and even a wild plot to kidnap Lang and place New South Wales under martial law.

But the New Guard's most infamous moment came on Saturday 19 March 1932, when it dramatically upstaged Lang at the opening of the Sydney Harbour Bridge. New Guard member Colonel Francis de Groot, dressed in military uniform, gathered with mounted soldiers stationed on the bridge and, when Lang went to ceremonially cut the ribbon, De Groot charged forward and dramatically slashed the ribbon with a sword. De Groot announced the bridge was now open 'in the name of the decent and respectable people of New South Wales'. De Groot was pulled from his horse and taken to a lunatic asylum. He was later declared to be sane and fined £5 plus £4 costs on a charge of offensive behaviour in a public place.

Meanwhile, the ribbon was hastily retied and cut again by Lang who belatedly declared the bridge open. It was not the end of the conflict, however. On the night of 13 May, as Lang's government descended further into turmoil, New Guard officers gathered in the basement of a store in Sydney, ready to march on parliament and overthrow the government if Lang did not resign by seven o'clock. It was a potentially violent political flashpoint, but, when the Governor, Sir Philip Game, sacked Lang at six o'clock, the crisis was over. It was the beginning of the end for the New Guard, which although it survived for a few more years, never again reached the stage where it could threaten to overthrow an Australian government.

Nonetheless, the radical New Guard and its muscular rightist agenda had struck a deep chord with many, especially former military men and, supposedly, a significant number of police officers. Among those said to sympathise with the New Guard was Barty Paterson, who was perhaps unfairly tarred by association, thanks to a brief mention of him by the New Guard leader, Eric Campbell, in 1965. In his book recalling the New Guard's glory days, *The Rallying Point*, Campbell wrote that Paterson called to see him one morning:

> I was delighted to make his acquaintance and to listen to his shrewd summing up of the situation. His trim, well-dressed figure and his alert crisp manner was quite unlike what I imagined any poet would be . . .

Although he would have shared the New Guard's nationalism and abhorrence of communism, Paterson would have disapproved of its penchant for violence and, as an establishment man, it is hard to see him supporting the violent overthrow of elected governments, regardless of their incompetence or otherwise. It seems far more likely that if he did meet Eric Campbell their association went no further.

Besides, Paterson had enough to keep him busy in his personal and professional life without meddling in politics. In December 1931, he proudly 'gave away' his daughter Grace at her wedding to naval officer, Lieutenant Kenneth Harvie. The ceremony was held in the grounds of Yaralla. Noting that a garden wedding was unusual in Sydney, the gossip columnists reported that Grace wore a classical frock of ivory satin and that the 'aisle' was created by rails of twisted asparagus ferns lining a path that led to a floral altar. The wedding made the society pages from north Queensland to South Australia. In Adelaide, the *Mail* reported on 19 December that a garden was the perfect setting for the wedding of a poet's daughter:

> The initials of the bride and the groom were outlined in flowers over the door. Although the wedding was the simplest that could be imagined a lavish appearance was gained by the gold braid and gilt buttons of officers of the navy who were present. Rugs were thrown on the lawns, on which the guests sat, fanning themselves with a dignified air, for mosquitoes and flies are no respecters of even garden weddings! Dame Eadith Walker and the bride's mother received the guests. And when they assembled inside the house for the reception it was almost as full of flowers as was the garden itself!

Paterson, meanwhile, continued to write racing notes for the papers, but also remained willing to embrace new ways of communicating with the public. Showing the same open-mindedness with which he welcomed the arrival of the motor car, he had become increasingly interested in the new wireless technology which could beam voices into lounge rooms around the country. From October 1931, he gave a series of talks on ABC radio on Wednesday nights. The cover of the October edition of *Wireless Weekly* that year showed a Paterson well advanced in years but looking quite at home smoking a pipe and boiling a billy on a camp fire. Although his very Australian accent put him at odds with the plummy-voiced broadcasters of the time, it was a measure of the quality of his writing that his talks were broadcast into homes around the country.

His topics were many and varied, ranging from his experiences of war to his definitions of news and news gathering, but it was his love of the bush and of sport that created his best broadcasting. Not many people could get away with giving a radio talk entitled 'Sheep', but Banjo did—and he did it with customary humour and the insightfulness of a lifetime's knowledge of the animal on whose back the nation had been built.

The talks shifted from tales of enormous Northern Territory mosquitoes that would leave 'nothing but a skeleton' of their victims to his views of 'political giants' such as Sir Henry Parkes and Sir Edmund Barton. He told of a rush for gold in Western Australia and the striking of liquid riches—bore water—in Queensland. And, as always, he found the quirky side of life in the bush. His tale of a cockatoo in Queensland that had learned to say, 'It looks very dry, don't it?' undoubtedly raised chuckles in living rooms around the nation.

Sport was a recurring theme. In one talk, he remembered the feats of the great rowers he had admired as a boy; in another, he recalled being 'crammed with facts' about Australian cricketers in his school days and being delighted to meet some of them when he grew up. One evening, he told his listeners of meeting a 'wiry sunburnt young bush chap' in a Sydney sports store. With an athlete's eye, Paterson could tell the young man was something special.

'That's a hard-looking young fellow and he's very light on his feet,' Paterson said to the store salesman. 'I should say he had done some boxing or was accustomed to riding rough horses. They have to be pretty active for that game.'

Not quite, replied the salesman, but the young athlete was nonetheless someone quite remarkable. His name was Don Bradman, the 'new boy wonder cricketer'. This Bradman lad, said the salesman, would become the world's hardest wicket to get. The salesman was of course proved right and Barty Paterson could say he had met another great Australian.

He also spoke of the indigenous Australians in his wireless talks. In a broadcast entitled 'Our Earliest Inhabitants', he showed admiration for people whom he thought had been given 'a very rough spin by their chroniclers'. He spoke of meeting an Aboriginal tribe in the Northern Territory and only realising later that he had observed a people living under an ancient and effective social system. Perhaps with fond thoughts in mind of Fanny, his childhood nurse, he was pleased to offer a 'few kind words' on behalf of a maligned race and noted that while their traditional culture was unsuited to modern civilisation, the people he saw in the Territory that day were enterprising and successful, and 'there seemed to be a reason for everything they did, a reason not always apparent on the surface'.

The radio was a good way of reaching a far-flung audience, but his thoughts were rarely far from books and publishing. In May 1932, he spoke at a meeting of the Fellowship of Australian Writers in Sydney. He gave some good advice to his fellow writers; if they wanted financial success, they should stifle dreams of genius and consider only the psychology of their readers. 'The reading public has its fashions in books, just as the female population has its fashions in dress,' he said:

At the moment the fashion is for 'thrillers' or detective stories. The popularity of this type of book is attributable to an inherited instinct. In cave-man days the murder of a member of the tribe would get everybody wild with excitement, and if the cause of the murder was a mystery, no member of the tribe would sleep soundly at night till the mystery was cleared up.

For this reason, Paterson added, modern civilised men 'from judges downward' would sit up half the night reading a detective story.

There were some trends in literature of which he was less approving. Although stories with a well-managed love interest were acceptable, the same could not be said for 'risqué matter'. Never one to mine this particular vein, Paterson felt there were already too many of these saucy books on the market and the theme was growing threadbare. But he was on more solid ground when he urged the gathered authors to write about what they knew best. 'If,' he said, 'you think you know how to manage a milk-run better than anyone else, set it down: it will be of interest.'

Meanwhile, he was continuing to write about what *he* knew best. Even though he had now lived most of his adult life in Sydney, he had not lost touch with the bush. In 1933, he brought this love of the land to life with his first book for children, *The Animals Noah Forgot*. Illustrated by Norman Lindsay, the book was a series of charming verses about Australian animals, as told by a koala and a platypus to a visiting English swan.

All sorts of animals familiar to Australian children starred in the book. Among them was Weary Will the Wombat:

He digs his homestead underground
He's neither shrewd nor clever
For kangaroos can leap and bound
But wombats dig forever.

There was also Old Man Platypus, who drifted down the river 'where the reed beds sweep and shiver', and some emus who formed a football team that played against a team of kangaroos, wallabies and wallaroos. It was Paterson's first publication for several years and its arrival was widely welcomed. Many were as delighted with Lindsay's drawings as they were with Paterson's words, but most agreed the book was a good buy at half a crown. One critic, writing under the pen-name of 'Mulga' in Rockhampton's *Central Queensland Herald*, paid Paterson a backhanded compliment in a mixed review:

> One has to admit that some of the verse borders very close to doggerel, but Banjo always had a habit of writing good verse or bad doggerel, and these verses with their short lines and simple words will certainly appeal to children.

Paterson might not have disagreed with 'Mulga' on the first point but was surely pleased that the second point proved true. Children *did* enjoy the book and families across Australia cheerfully parted with their half-crowns, ensuring the book was a big seller at Christmas that year. Among the many children who enjoyed *The Animals Noah Forgot* were members of Paterson's own family. His daughter Grace had delivered Barty and Alice's first grandchild, Eadith Rosamund, that year and, while it would be several years until she would be old enough to enjoy her grandfather's work, Paterson's nephew Andrew Taylor was lucky enough to get an advance copy of the book in his Christmas stocking. Inscribed inside the cover were the words: 'With best wishes, uncle and aunt A.B. and Alice Paterson, Xmas 1932.'

In February 1934, Paterson quietly celebrated his seventieth birthday. Always reluctant to share his private life with the public, he might have preferred that the newspapers did not mention the milestone in their gossip snippets and he did not give any interviews. The papers had to be content with observing that 'Banjo' was now living quietly after a series of adventures. As for the man himself, perhaps he spared a quiet moment to reflect on the changes he had seen in seven decades. As cars and buses rumbled through the busy streets of Sydney, his thoughts might have turned to the days when brumbies roamed the hills and bullock drivers battered their way through flood and drought. And, although his days of camping in the bush were over, he may well have spared a fond memory or two for Clancy's 'sunlit plains extended' or the clear mountain air of the Snowy River, where 'the white stars fairly blaze'.

With some of those memories in mind, he was putting the final touches on a personal project—his autobiographical observations, *Happy Dispatches,* published in 1934. He had first floated the idea of using his diary entries to write 'a rather amusing book of travel' in 1901 and had further discussed the idea with Norman Lindsay in following years. Lindsay agreed the diary entries were 'too good to throw away in talk' but Paterson felt he had too much, rather than too little, information for a book. Lindsay advised him to 'write everything in and then sub it out if you must'. Paterson took the advice and a few days before his birthday in 1934—despite still being unsure what to title the book—he was sending chapters to Angus & Robertson.

Eventually, 'Happy Dispatches' was chosen as the title over alternatives such as the rather dreary 'Famous Folk at Close Range'; the ambiguous 'All Nurses Swear'; and the forbidding 'Strictly Private'. The title mattered little in the end as the book was not a great commercial success. Although the critics were generally kind to the work, it largely failed to connect with a Depression-era readership still nostalgic for Paterson's great works. Its true worth became obvious in later years, however, as an important personal account of Paterson's life as seen through the famous people he met and for that, Banjo fans are surely grateful.

Paterson continued to write through the thirties, albeit at the leisurely pace due to the elderly. He enjoyed spending time with his family and rarely missed a race meeting of significance. At other times, he could be seen relaxing at the Australian Club, smoking a pipe and enjoying a friendly game of bridge with other gentlemen of status and refinement.

In 1935, Paterson was immortalised on canvas when his portrait was painted by Sir John Longstaff. The poet and the painter had a lot in common. Both were raised in the bush at about the same time, were physically fit and moved easily in society's upper echelons. They also shared a link to the late Henry Lawson. In 1900, commissioned by none other than Archibald of *The Bulletin*, Longstaff had painted Lawson's portrait in oil. The work expertly captured the essence of the tortured poet. His face and right hand, holding a pipe, emerge from an inky backdrop that seems to sum up the pall of the gloom that sometimes enveloped him, while the shadows in his eyes hint at the demons that lurked there. Archibald was so pleased with his commission that he was moved to establish the great portrait prize in his name.

Paterson's heart gave him trouble as he aged and he spent some time in hospital shortly before his portrait was painted. Once recovered, however, he enjoyed his own experience with Longstaff. In an unpublished script for his ABC wireless program, Paterson later wrote that the 'wiry and energetic' Longstaff worked at a rapid pace in a large studio, never sitting down and constantly revising his work:

> Having posed his sitter, he goes back to the far corner of the room and studies his subject. Then he dashes at the easel and paints feverishly for a moment. Then he dashes back again to the end of the room, compares the sitter with the work on the easel, and then makes another dash at the picture. All told, he must walk miles while painting a portrait . . . At the end of a two hours' sitting, he suggested that I, as the sitter, must be tired, but I replied: 'Well, if you can stand running a footrace for two hours, I can stand here watching you.'

The completed painting of Paterson showed the poet looking every bit his seventy-one years but nonetheless erect and full of life. In an appropriate close of the circle between Paterson, Lawson and Archibald, Longstaff's portrait of 'Banjo' beat more than 120 entrants to win the 1935 Archibald Prize, netting the artist £430.

Despite his advancing years, Paterson continued to work. His racing stories were widely read in the newspapers but he also had his mind on his latest book, a novel about racing called *The Shearer's Colt*. Released in 1936, it told the story of Hilton Fitzroy, the son of an English gentleman who experiences a spot of bother and is packed off to Australia to make something of himself. The fictional Fitzroy, who seems to bear more than a passing resemblance to Paterson's one-time friend Harry Morant, has a series of adventures on Australian racetracks before returning to England in the company of some new friends and Sensation, the shearer's colt of the title.

The book met mixed reviews. Melbourne's *The Argus* said it was 'a fine Australian novel' but Adelaide's *The Advertiser* thought it was 'a rambling and rather improbable tale, peopled by puppets'. Country town newspapers were more lavish in their praise but, balanced against that, the book came in for stinging criticism from an unlikely source, the *Hebrew Standard of Australasia*. A writer for that publication, Catherine Lindsay, was appalled by the book's portrayal of Jews in London. Although she admitted her feelings were coloured after supposedly hearing Paterson refer to Jews as 'Yids' in a slighting tone at a Fellowship of Australian Writers' Luncheon, she was scathing in her opinion of *The Shearer's Colt*.

> Cheap sneers and badly drawn characters should be unworthy of one whose verse appears in our school readers and has to be learnt by all children—Jews and Gentiles alike. The 'Banjo's'

new strings are made of cheap gut and are not worthy of the instrument to which they are fitted.

She might have taken some satisfaction in learning that *The Shearer's Colt* was not a strong seller, despite its price of just six shillings. This relative failure must have come as a disappointment to Paterson, who had just published his final book. Now aged seventy-two, he was entering his twilight years and he could take comfort in knowing that his greatest works had already been established as the stuff of legend. Ahead lay more travel and personal rewards, but the land of which he had sung had changed forever.

*

In March 1938, Paterson and his wife Alice took a holiday in Tasmania. They stayed in Hobart, visiting the pretty Derwent-side town of New Norfolk to the city's north, and made a trip to the hamlet of Ouse on the edge of the rugged highlands to the north-west. As part of the visit, Paterson was a guest at a Hobart boys' school. During an address to the students, he spoke of the best book, the best man and the best woman he had known. His choice of best book went to Thomas Carlyle's *Past and Present* (a difficult book, Paterson said, but one that rewarded those who could master it); the best man honours were shared by Lord Roberts and Rudyard Kipling; and, showing he could still look to the future and not just the past, Paterson's choice of best woman was Marie Curie for her discovery of radium. As he left the school, the boys burst into a rendition of 'Waltzing Matilda' in his honour.

The year of 1939 was an eventful one for the Paterson family. On New Year's Day, Barty was presented with a CBE from the King in recognition of his services to literature. Similar awards went to the essayist Professor Walter Murdoch and Mrs Aeneas Gunn, author of *We of the Never Never*. Paterson's CBE surely pleased his establishment soul but, as ever, he was outwardly modest about it.

The Mercury in Hobart reported that a twinkle in Paterson's eye gave away his pride in his achievement but he was quoted as saying that he saw the award as recognition for all Australian writers, and not as a personal accolade. Brisbane's *Courier-Mail* was more effusive, saying the CBE was long overdue 'but at least it has been bestowed worthily'. In rather loftier terms, *The Sydney Morning Herald* agreed, saying the 'Commonwealth [had done] well to recommend Royal recognition of the writers who interpret the life and spirit of this land'.

The shadows were now growing long for A.B. Paterson, but he kept busy as his seventy-fifth birthday approached. He had been penning his series of memoirs for *The Sydney Morning Herald* and the first was published on 4 February. The stories, which ran weekly, are regarded as unreliable and contradictory with Paterson unwilling or unable to check some of his facts, but the series was nonetheless an entertaining insight into history seen through the prism of an old man's memories. At about the same time as the first article was published Barty and Alice arrived in Melbourne for a short stay en route to another holiday in Tasmania.

They sailed from Melbourne on the *Taroona*, arriving in Launceston on 11 February. There, Paterson chatted about Tasmanian racing with local journalists and said he intended to visit the city's racetrack and stables. A few days later, the couple took a leisurely trip to the state's south, celebrating Barty's birthday on the way to Hobart. After a couple of weeks in the southern capital, he returned to the highland town of Ouse where *The Mercury* photographed him getting a lesson in fly-casting for trout. In the autumn, they returned to Sydney. Barty Paterson had taken his last long journey.

There was more baby joy for the Patersons when their second granddaughter, Philippa, was born in December 1939. With her older sister, Rosamund, Philippa would compile the twin volumes of Paterson's complete works, *Singer of the Bush* and *Song of the Pen*, published in 1983. At the time of Philippa's birth, the Patersons lived next door to their daughter's family. The granddaughters wrote in their introduction to their 1983 works that Paterson was 'remembered as a splendid grandfather' who greatly enjoyed reading aloud to the girls.

The family had some luck in June. A wealthy relative of Alice's, Thomas Walker, had died, leaving an estate of £400,000. Advertisements calling for claimants to the estate were placed in newspapers around the world. A total of 650 people made claims and thirty-three were successful. Among them were 'titled people in England and Scotland' as well as members of the Walker family in New South Wales. Alice Paterson, *née* Walker, was among the thirty-three claimants who each received a sum of £12,000. It was a windfall that provided the family with a level of wealth that Paterson's artistic success could not deliver.

After a lifetime of hard work, Barty and Alice Paterson might have expected to enjoy their remaining years in comfort with their extended family—but the world was changing again, and this time the changes would be catastrophic. At a quarter past nine on the evening of 3 September, Australians huddled around their wirelesses to hear the scratchy tones of Prime Minister Robert Menzies confirming their worst fears. 'Fellow Australians, it is my melancholy duty to inform you officially that in consequence of a persistence by Germany in her invasion of Poland, Great Britain has declared war upon her and that, as a result, Australia is also at war.'

If the Patersons were among the millions of Australians listening to the radio that night, their thoughts undoubtedly turned to their son Hugh, now thirty-three and of fighting age, and to their naval reserve officer son-in-law Kenneth Harvie. Of all the family, only Barty had seen the horrors of war firsthand, but all must have been aware that their young men might well be called upon to fight. These fears were soon realised. Kenneth, the naval officer, served in Australian waters throughout the war while Hugh Paterson became one of the famous Rats of Tobruk.

*

The world watched and trembled in May 1940 when the German army thundered into Belgium and then France, crushing all oppos- ition and forcing the British into the humiliating evacuation of their troops at Dunkirk. For people of Paterson's generation, the German blitzkrieg brought back alarming memories of the Great War. Many men who had fought in the first war were now asked to fight again. Old men like Paterson could do little except pray for the safety of their sons.

It might have been some comfort to Paterson that 'Waltzing Matilda' had leapt into popularity as a patriotic war tune. A big London music studio was producing thousands of recordings of the song. The record's cover was illustrated with a photograph of the Second Australian Imperial Force marching through Sydney and the song was a hit at camp concerts. The 'old junk' that Paterson had sold a decade earlier was on its way to becoming the most famous Australian song of all.

That year, Paterson wrote 'The Dry Canteen', a verse put to sheet music, and it was published in March. Also in that year he wrote 'Song of Murray's Brigade', a whimsical if not very good reflection on the thoughts of soldiers serving far from home. These works were his swansongs. His heart had continued to cause problems and he had been told to take things quietly. In January 1941, he was admitted to a private hospital in Sydney. On 5 February, while sitting in a chair at the hospital waiting for Alice to take him home, he took his last breaths and died quietly, away from the gaze of the public. Australia had lost the man who had defined the essence of a nation in verse. Even though his work would live on, it had delivered little financial reward. Paterson left just £225 in his will.

The public reaction to the death of 'The Banjo' was heartfelt, if a little muted. He would perhaps have preferred it that way. But a friend and journalistic colleague, G.A. King, wrote in *The Sydney Morning Herald* that Paterson would be remembered as a great Australian who loved his country. It did not matter, wrote King, whether Paterson was in the shearing shed, fishing in the Snowy River or playing on the polo field, 'Barty was always a fine fellow'.

The Canberra Times said Paterson had bequeathed to Australians 'a legacy and cheerfulness that will be the prize of generations yet unborn' and *The Worker* in Brisbane said he would be remembered as a poet laureate of the outback. Even in far-away Perth, his passing was mourned. *The West Australian* said Banjo was not a great poet but his work would ensure the leather-skinned, hard-riding bushman would be remembered as the typical Australian, even in a nation that had traded the bush for the city in a time when the 'gramophone, wireless and imported jazz music [had] created a drought in Australian spontaneity'.

Paterson's death marked more than the passing of a beloved poet. He was among the last of the greats who had risen to fame in the tumult of the 1890s. The 'bards of *The Bulletin*' were almost gone. Henry Lawson was at peace at last and 'Breaker' Morant lay in his African grave. The memories of these men and their contemporaries would live on in a nation reluctant to break with the heritage that the poets had helped to create.

Many of the other players in the 'Banjo' story had also died. Some
perished in obscurity. Christina Macpherson, who had provided a
tune that would be known to all Australians, had died a spinster
in 1936. She was buried at St Kilda cemetery and her grave was
unmarked until 1994, when it was restored by members of the
Macpherson family. Sarah Riley had left Australia for Scotland and
England after the incident at Dagworth Station and did not return
to Australia until 1930. Never married, she shared a large home
at Panton Hill near Melbourne with her sister and a friend. The
three 'spinster ladies' volunteered for good works, helping the Red
Cross during the Great War and giving generously to philanthropic
causes. Sarah died in August 1935.

Barty Paterson was buried in a private family service in Sydney.
There was little or no press attention to the funeral—an appropriate farewell to a private man who was loved by many but was
truly close to only a few. To his family, he was not a celebrity,
but simply a much-loved husband, father and grandfather. It was
fitting that in September, his son Hugh penned a poem of his
own, 'This Place They Call Tobruk'. The verses would surely
have made his father proud. And, like his father's greatest works,
the son's poem nicely incorporated the essence of Australia, with
a twist of dry humour:

> There's places I've been in,
> I didn't like too well
> New England's far too blooming cold,
> And Winton's hot as hell
> The Walgett beer is always warm,
> In each there's something crook
> But each and all are perfect
> To this place they call Tobruk.

Soon after Banjo's death, the papers began to discuss a memorial to him. Writers suggested his childhood home at Illalong should be preserved in his honour. The idea was popular in the press, but the old house, although still standing, had been past its best when Rose Paterson had raised her family there and the years since had not been kind to it.

The house endured for another generation or so but eventually lost its battle with the elements, and its sagging remains had to be demolished. Not all was lost though; when her children were young, Rose Paterson had planted a tiny wisteria shrub next to the homestead's rear verandah. The shrub grew strong and wide and, when the house was torn down, the wisteria was left in place. It now forms a huge, climbing outdoor shade area for the property's current owners and remains a living link to the home that helped inspire some of Australia's best-loved verses.

EPILOGUE

In 1946, the council for the New South Wales town of Orange formed a committee to investigate the possibility of developing a Banjo Paterson memorial at his birthplace of Narrambla. The following year, Paterson's widow Alice, who had by then moved to Orange, unveiled an obelisk and plaque honouring her husband at the site. The homestead that had belonged to Paterson's aunt, Rose Templer, had been demolished, but the crumbling ruins of the Templer family's mill still dominated the shallow valley. The old kit home in which some believe Paterson was born had been moved to the top of a hill overlooking the homestead site. Several hundred people gathered by the roadside to see the unveiling of the monument, the first public structure erected in tribute to Australia's famous poet.

Other honours soon followed. In the same year, the town of Yass began to discuss its own monument to Paterson in recognition of his childhood at Illalong. A bust of the poet's head to be erected in the town's central park was the favoured option and a plaster cast to make the bust was created. The idea faltered for a while, but in 1949 the cast was found in a farmer's hayshed and a Sydney sculptor was commissioned to make the statue from bronze. By 1950, the park had been renamed the Banjo Paterson Memorial Park and, in November, Alice Paterson visited the town to witness the unveiling of the bust.

Paterson was given national recognition in 1968 when he was included in a select list of Australians to be featured on a postage stamp. Twenty-five years later, he was pictured in profile on the ten-dollar note. Also on the note is a horseman cracking a stockwhip and some lines from 'The Man From Snowy River'. Earlier editions of the ten-dollar note had depicted Henry Lawson, but it is Banjo who survives today on the currency. It is fitting that the duelling poets who had seen the bush through such different eyes shared the same honour.

But Paterson's real memorial lives on in the words that he wrote. Today, schoolchildren around the country are still taught about 'The Man From Snowy River' and Australians everywhere recognise the stirring opening words: 'There was movement at the station/ For the word had passed around . . .' Even those who cannot recite the words might appreciate Clancy's 'vision splendid of the sunlit plains extended', while city dwellers do not have to venture far from the bright lights to see 'the glory of the everlasting stars'. Drovers today may be few and far between, but hardy men and women, with their loyal dogs and horses, still drive their cattle along the 'long paddock' and enjoy pleasures that the townsfolk never know.

Ironically, however, it was the work that gave Paterson the least reward that still delights us most today. Only in Australia could a song about a suicidal swagman be officially considered as a national anthem but, in 1974, 'Waltzing Matilda' came second behind 'Advance Australia Fair' in a national poll to choose a replacement for 'God Save the Queen'. Regardless, 'Waltzing Matilda' remains the song that Australians choose when they want to express national pride.

In 1995, when Prime Minister Paul Keating addressed a crowd at Winton, Queensland, on the accepted hundred-year anniversary of the song's creation, he described 'Waltzing Matilda' as a tale of class struggle, born in a time of drought and conflict. It is unlikely its author saw it that way, but Paterson would surely have taken pride in Keating's statement that his simple little song had 'caused more smiles and tears, and more hairs to stand up on the back of more Australian necks than any other thing of three minutes' duration in Australia's history'.

At the 1952 Olympic Games in Helsinki, 'Waltzing Matilda' was played when Australian athletes stood on the dais. At the closing ceremony of the 1956 Melbourne Games, the song was performed with rewritten words, 'Farewell Olympians', prompting *The Argus* to declare it the perfect end to the best games ever. In the same year, a French band struck up 'Waltzing Matilda' when Prime Minister Robert Menzies laid a wreath to honour fallen soldiers in Paris. The French musicians thought the song of the swagman was Australia's real national anthem. It was Paterson's best-known legacy.

Three years before his death, Paterson wrote a short piece entitled 'Looking Backward' for *The Sydney Mail*. In it, he compared himself unfavourably to Rudyard Kipling and Adam Lindsay Gordon, and said he never aimed high; he just wrote about what he knew. Such was the inspiration for his work. As for how that work would be remembered, Paterson was as modest as ever. He wrongly predicted a short future for Australia's greatest bush poems but correctly observed that he and Henry Lawson were in the right place at the right time to create words that might live on while ever Australians stand under the Southern Cross.

Our 'ruined rhymes' are not likely to last long, but if there is any hope at all of survival it comes from the fact that such writers as Lawson and myself had the advantage of writing in a new country. In all museums throughout the world one may see plaster casts of the footprints of weird animals, footprints preserved for posterity, not because the animals were particularly good of their sort, but because they had the luck to walk on the lava while it was cooling. There is just a faint hope that something of the sort may happen to us.

—Andrew Barton Paterson, Sydney, 21 December 1938

SELECTED REFERENCES

BOOKS

Banjo & Christina, The True Story of Waltzing Matilda, Peter and Sheila Forrest, Shady Tree, Darwin, 2008

The Banjo of the Bush, Clement Semmler, University of Queensland Press, St Lucia, Qld, 1974

Banjo Paterson, Poet by Accident, Dr Colin Roderick, Allen & Unwin, Sydney, 1993

Bohemians at The Bulletin, Norman Lindsay, Angus & Robertson, Sydney, 1965

Breaker Morant, F.M. Cutlack, Ure Smith, Sydney, 1962

Bushman and Buccaneer: Harry Morant – His Ventures and Verse, Frank Renar, H.T. Dunn, Sydney, 1902

The Essential Henry Lawson, Brian Kiernan, Currey O'Neil, Melbourne, 1982

Happy Dispatches, A.B. Paterson, Angus & Robertson, Sydney, 1935

Henry Lawson, A Stranger on the Darling, Robyn Lee Burrows and Alan Barton, HarperCollins, Nerang, Qld, 1996

Illalong Children, A.B. Paterson (published in *Singer of the Bush*, 1983)

Radio Talks, A.B. Paterson (published in *Song of the Pen*, edited by Rosamund Campbell and Philippa Harvie, Lansdowne, Sydney, 1983)

The River: Sydney Cove to Parramatta, Gregory Blaxell, Halstead Press, Sydney, 2007

Rose Paterson's Illalong Letters, edited by Dr Colin Roderick, Kangaroo Press, Sydney, 2000

Scapegoats of the Empire, George Witton, D.W. Paterson and Co, Melbourne, 1907

Shoot Straight, You Bastards! Nick Bleszynski, Random House Australia, Sydney, 2002

Singer of the Bush, A.B. Paterson, edited by Rosamund Campbell and Philippa Harvie, Lansdowne Press, *1983*

Searching for the Man from Snowy River, W.F. Refshauge, Arcadia, 2012

Song of the Pen, A.B. Paterson, edited by Rosamund Campbell and Philippa Harvie, Lansdowne Press, 1983

Vision Splendid; A History of the Winton District, Peter and Sheila Forrest, Winton Shire Council and Winton District Historical Society and Museum inc., Winton, Qld, 2005

The Walkers of Yaralla, Patricia Skehan, P. Shehan Publishing, Sydney, 2000

Waltzing Matilda, The Secret History of Australia's Favourite Song, Dennis O'Keeffe, Allen & Unwin, Sydney, 2012

The World of Henry Lawson, edited by Walter Stone, Lansdowne Press, Sydney, 1974

NEWSPAPERS

The Advertiser

The Age

The Argus

The Australian Star

The Barrier Miner

The Bathurst Free Press

The Brisbane Courier

The Bulletin

The Burrowa News

The Canberra Times

The Catholic Press

The Clarence and Richmond Examiner

The Corryong Courier

The Daily Telegraph

The Evening News

The Goulburn Evening Penny Post

The Goulburn Herald and Chronicle

The Hawkesbury Herald

The Hebrew Standard of Australasia

SELECTED REFERENCES

The Mercury
The Northern Territory Times and Gazette
Referee
The Register
The Sunday Times
The Sydneian
The Sydney Mail
The Sydney Morning Herald
The Sydney Sportsman
Table Talk
The Town and Country Journal
The West Australian
The Western Mail
The Yass Courier

WEBSITES

adb.anu.edu.au
australia.gov.au
awm.gov.au
bwm.org.au
firstworldwar.com
foundingdocs.gov.au
navy.gov.au
sl.nsw.gov.au
trove.nla.gov.au
wikipedia.org

ACKNOWLEDGEMENTS

Thank you to Jen Lamond for her enthusiasm and passion for this project, and particularly for unearthing all the little details that helped to bring 'Banjo's' story to life. My thanks also to Gregory Blaxell, Alf Cantrell, Gordon Cooper, Elizabeth Griffin, Peter Forrest, Richard Hubbard, Foong Ling Kong and all those who gave up their time and knowledge to shed light on the Paterson story.